LIFE WITH RUSTY

LIFE WITH RUSTY

My Redheaded Furry Twin

JO ANN ROSEO

Printed in the United States of America.
First Edition.

ISBN: 0996821813
ISBN 13: 9780996821810
Library of Congress Control Number: 2015915324
Jo Ann Roseo, Boca Raton, FL

Dedication

*This book is dedicated to the memory of
my Irish setter, Rusty.
Until one has been lucky enough to have a dog
in their life, it's hard to fully understand
the true meaning of unconditional love.*

*I would also like to dedicate this book
with all my love to my family,
who I am very blessed to have in my life.*

Acknowledgments

There are many people who helped out along the way, and offered me tremendous support in keeping Rusty's legacy alive. I would like to thank you from bottom of my heart. Unfortunately, I can't name all of you, but you know who you are.

First and foremost, all my love to my wonderful husband, John, for his continuous support, suggestions and respecting my need to share Rusty's story. I would never have come so far without him by my side. Lastly, for being Rusty's daddy, every step of the way, sharing in all the fun and crazy moments until the very end.

My loving mom, Paula, "Ma" for always believing in me, and inspiring me to achieve my dream to write this book. I am thankful for her encouragement and her memories of Rusty that helped turn this book into a reality. Above all, for loving Rusty unconditionally and being the best grandma Rusty could ever have had.

I cannot express enough how grateful I am to my daughters, Kristine and Jennifer, and sons-in-law, Harry and Matthew, for all of their suggestions, guidance and input. I couldn't have written this book without them. I would also like to thank them for reminding me, that you can take the girl out of Brooklyn, but you can't take the Brooklyn out of the girl.

My amazing family and dear friends who were always there for me, offering advice, feedback and reassurance during this process: my sister, Bridget; my brother, Andrew; my sister-in-law, Stephanie; my brother-in-law, Tommy; my friends: Judy Cromer, Jim Tierney, Bob DiChristopher and Dr. Thomas Sessa, DVM.

Last, but certainly not least, I would like to express my sincere gratitude to Dr. Alan Baum, DVM, and Dr. Gary Baum, DVM, for their unconditional dedication, knowledge, kindness, and efforts as Rusty's doctors.

Contents

Chapter 1

The Newlyweds

Canarsie was where my husband, John, and I grew up. It's a neighborhood in Brooklyn, one of the five boroughs of New York, not too far from the famous Coney Island. Italian and Jewish immigrants settled in Canarsie in the early nineteen hundreds. In fact, our grandparents came to New York from Italy through Ellis Island, taking residence in Canarsie.

Spending our younger years in Canarsie, Johnny and I lived only four city blocks away from each other, but we didn't hang out together growing up. Actually, we met when we were both sixteen on the "LL" Canarsie Line train. We both had part-time summer jobs in New York City through our schools. One day on the train on my way home from work, I was standing because it was overcrowded and no seats were available. I saw this cute guy sitting down; he looked up and smiled at me with the most beautiful dimple. Then he got up and offered me his seat. Who would have guessed this cute and thoughtful guy would be my future husband, the love of my life, and the father of my children?

We only saw each other that summer when we rode the train and didn't start dating until four years later. We met again at the wedding of my cousin Mary, who was his neighbor, when I was a bridesmaid and he was a groomsman. That day sparked the beginning of our wonderful, fun life together.

Two years later we were married, and upon returning from our honeymoon, we rented an adorable three-room apartment. It was nestled in a two-story house located in Mill Basin, ten minutes south of Canarsie. Both of us loved dogs, and we really wanted to get one, but as renters we weren't allowed to. It was then we made a promise to each other that when we bought our first house, our number-one priority would be getting a dog.

Much to our surprise, our first pet wasn't a dog but rather two parakeets. Fuzz and Buzz were the parakeets belonging to my sister, Bridget, and my brother-in-law, Tommy. There was no question which parakeet was which. Fuzz was the female, a bright green and yellow parakeet, whereas Buzz was the male, a royal blue and light blue one. At the time, they bought a Chesapeake Bay retriever that they named Duke. The parakeets were afraid of Duke; maybe they sensed that he would display the bird-hunting behavior intrinsic to his breed. Bridget and Tommy didn't want to give the parakeets up, so they asked us if we would care for them until Duke was a little older and less energetic. Of course we were happy to since it was just the two of us.

When we went over to their house and met Duke, we could see that Duke formed an instant attachment to our nephews. Tommy Jr. was six, and we called him Little Tommy, and Danny was three. Just watching Duke with the boys solidified the idea that we really wanted to get a dog before we had children; we couldn't wait to have a dog of our own.

About six months later, Tommy thought it was time to return Fuzz and Buzz to their original home. For a few days, all was good, but then, all of a sudden, Duke's bird-hunting instinct kicked in. One day as Buzz was flying around the house like parakeets normally do, Duke jumped up and caught Buzz. According to the vet, Duke didn't harm Buzz; the parakeet got so frightened, he had a heart attack and died instantly. As one of a pair of love-birds, Fuzz was saddened without Buzz, and she passed away a few days later—probably of a broken heart. Poor Fuzz and Buzz.

As newlyweds, we found married life a blast, with the exception that I was the clumsiest new bride. For some reason, I was always breaking things. Even our landlord got pissed off because I broke his washing machine several times and flooded his basement. I guess it was a shell-shocker for Johnny that there was never a dull moment with me, as he was quickly finding out. But the truth is, I did keep my new husband laughing most of the time.

A year earlier, when we got engaged, my older brother, Andrew, had a conversation with my fiancé about me. "Johnny, I hope you know what you're getting yourself into, marrying my sister. You know Lucille Ball from the TV show *I Love Lucy?* Well, I named my sister 'Little Lucy' years ago. Jo Ann is just like her, without the red hair. Just so you know, my sister is the clumsiest, most destructive person I have ever met. She comes up with the craziest ideas; and she breaks everything she touches. You have been warned."

Johnny smiled at me. "She can't be that bad, Andrew," he said.

"Just wait. You'll see for yourself," my brother answered.

Little did Johnny know, my brother was telling him the absolute truth; and little did he know, our first dog would follow in my footsteps.

After a year and a half of married life, Johnny and I started looking for our first house. Since both of us grew up in Brooklyn, we decided to venture out to the suburbs of Long Island. Each town offered a variety of styles of homes. Best of all were the properties with large backyards for our future dog and kids to play in—as well as being away from all the traffic, noise, and hustle and bustle of Brooklyn. The problem was with mortgage rates being at 17 percent back in 1980, it wasn't easy to find a house that we really liked and could afford.

Searching for a house that fit our needs as a couple, we saw one we liked in Valley Stream, a small village in Nassau County, Long Island. We found it offered the best of both worlds—living in the suburbs and easy access to the city. The house was a Cape Cod model that sat on a corner lot. The previous owner had added a second story with a dormer, which is common in Cape Cod homes, and they had made the second story into an adorable three-room apartment. Downstairs, the two bedrooms, living room, dining room, and bathroom were in decent condition. The kitchen was very large, but was in dire need of being updated. It wasn't our dream house, but it was within our budget, so we decided to go ahead and put an offer on the house.

Later that day, the Realtor called us and said the owner accepted our offer. We were so excited. Giving our deposit, we signed the contract for our first house,—"the American dream," as my grandfather who was originally from Sicily called it.

That night, Johnny made a suggestion to me. "I know how close you and your mom are. Since she is alone, instead of renting the apartment to strangers, let's rent it to her," he said.

I was surprised and asked with delight, "Really?"

"Sure. I don't feel comfortable leaving her behind in Canarsie. Knowing you, you'll be driving there all the time to go see her anyway."

I threw my arms around my sweet husband. "What a great idea. You're the best!"

I was so happy. We were moving to Long Island, and my mom, whom we called "Ma," was coming too. Fortunately, we bought all new furniture when we moved into our apartment. The only furniture we needed was a formal dining room set, but that would come in time.

The banking institution I worked for had several branches throughout Brooklyn, Queens, and Long Island, including one in Valley Stream, which was only five minutes from our house; so transferring job locations for me was going to be seamless. Johnny worked for a major television network in New York City. To commute to the city, the best option for him was to take the Long Island Railroad to Penn Station and catch the local train heading uptown.

Moving into our first house was very exciting. Best of all, we were going to start looking for our first dog once we got settled in. To me, that was the best part about getting a house. Listening to the birds chirping, watching the squirrels running around, and having no neighbors attached to us was surely nice. Our future dog would love it.

When we were children, Johnny grew up with his dog, Rex, a male border collie. He was very attached to Rex, who lived a long, happy life. My family had a female Irish setter named Duchess. Unfortunately, when I was two and a half years old, one of our cousins came over and accidently left the front gate open in our yard, and, without our knowing, Duchess ran away. According to my brother, Duchess ran out of the yard several times to play with the kids and the other dogs on the block, but she always came home in time for dinner. Duchess didn't come home that night or the next. My family posted signs for our lost dog, but no one ever called. We all cried and were very sad for a long time. It is still a mystery what happened to our precious dog. We all hoped that a nice family found her and gave her a loving home.

Duchess with my sister Bridget

The time came for us to make our first house a home. Johnny and I wanted a large dog, but we didn't have a clue as to whether it was to be a purebred, mutt, or rescue dog. We went looking at the local animal shelter to see if there was a puppy or young dog that needed a home, but all it had available were small dogs. Times were different; it wasn't as easy to find a dog back in 1980 as it is today. Nowadays, you just go on the Internet, do a Google search, and there are hundreds, if not thousands, of dogs that need a home.

One Saturday morning, Johnny was reading *Newsday*, Long Island's newspaper. Searching for the perfect dog, he turned to the classified section. Ma happened to be sitting at the kitchen table with us and began telling Johnny all about Duchess. "She was the sweetest, most beautiful, loving, and docile dog. We were heartbroken when she ran away. She was also very intelligent and had a great disposition, especially with children."

After hearing my mom talking to Johnny about Duchess, I suddenly got a soft spot for Irish setters. Duchess's disposition with children was surely an important factor to consider since we were hoping to start a family in the next few years. Subconsciously, I guess I wanted to replace Duchess, our dog who loved me, but with whom I never had the chance to grow up with.

"Hey, Johnny, while you're looking through the classified section for puppies, could you see if there are any Irish setter puppies for sale?"

"Sure, I'll take a look."

A few minutes later, I heard the excitement in his voice. "Jo, you're in luck. I found an ad that says purebred Irish setter puppies for sale."

"Yes!" I shouted. "Johnny, can you call?"

"Absolutely."

While Johnny was on the phone with the breeder, he told Johnny that the litter consisted of eight puppies—four females and four males. The females were already sold. All he had left were three males at three hundred dollars each. Getting the directions from the breeder, I overheard Johnny saying "Lynbrook?" Smiling at me, with his thumbs up, he was giving the go-ahead. Lynbrook was the next town over, only a fifteen-minute ride from our house. The three of us were excited about seeing the Irish setter puppies.

When we arrived at the breeder's house, Johnny asked him where the parents of the puppies were. He called out, "Casey, come here." The proud mama, Casey, was three years old, very pretty, petite, and affectionate, and she displayed a sweet disposition. Her coat was a rich mahogany color. Casey happily accepted our affection, especially from my mom. Casey must've sensed that she absolutely loved Irish setters. The breeder said the stud lived at a friend's house, and he claimed that the stud was also a beautiful dog with a good disposition, but much larger than Casey. The puppies were fully weaned at eight weeks, ready to go to a good home. He escorted us to his backyard to see the remaining three male puppies as Casey followed us. Watching the puppies running around, we saw that two of them had an enormous amount of energy. Casey walked over to her pups as if she was guarding them. All of a sudden we got the attention of one puppy. Alert and inquisitive, this little red puppy caught my eye. He looked up at us while standing in his mother's shadow.

The same puppy walked over to me cautiously and let me pick him up. He certainly was a cuddler. The other two puppies didn't even notice us. As soon as he licked my face, that was it for me. Instantaneously, I fell in love with the sweetest, most beautiful little red puppy.

"Oh, Johnny, he is the one! This is the puppy that I will love and protect always."

"Are you sure, Jo? He's really cute, but look at the size of his paws. This little guy is going to be a really big dog."

I was hooked. "We wanted a big dog anyway; he'll be a good protector when we have kids."

The breeder could tell that Johnny wasn't sold yet on this puppy. "Listen, guys, a family with two kids is coming by later today to see the puppies. I can't guarantee that this one will still be available if you come back."

"Johnny, no more looking at puppies; he is perfect!"

My mom was also smiling in agreement. Then he gave me one of his sweet dimpled smiles and told the breeder, "My wife wants this one. I guess we'll take this little guy."

From the moment I laid eyes on him, I knew this little puppy was meant for me. He had beautiful hazel eyes, long red ears, a bright pink little tongue, and a solid black button nose. This puppy was really affectionate, giving me little wet kisses.

"See, Johnny, look how friendly he is, just like his mom. Casey is so sweet. I'm sure he has his mother's good calm genes, not like his two brothers who are acting crazy. He is more timid; he looks like a little angel. He'll be great!"

I went into my pocketbook and wrote the breeder a check for three hundred dollars. Johnny handed him the check, and he gave us the American Kennel Club registration papers to complete so that we could register our new puppy, along with a small bag of puppy food. He also gave us a list of the vaccinations the puppy had received. Johnny and I were so happy; we had just gotten our first dog as a married couple, which was truly a momentous occasion.

I carried our puppy to Johnny's Toyota Celica. At first he was scared and started shaking. I carefully placed him on my lap, cradling him like an infant baby so that he wouldn't feel frightened for the car ride. He then burrowed his little head on my shoulder, and my heart melted. After a few minutes, he calmed down, looking around in the car, taking it all in. I kept his little face close to mine, gladly accepting his kisses. He was a good boy on the car ride to his new home and bonded with me immediately; he was so sweet. Then he threw up all over me. Laughing, I said, "Welcome to puppy parenthood."

When we arrived home, it was such a good feeling bringing our new little family member inside. Carrying him from room to room, acquainting him with his new home, I desperately wanted for him to feel a sense of belonging. I put our little red puppy on the kitchen floor. Within a couple of minutes, he began to race around the house, exploring each room and inhaling every nook and cranny through his nose. Then our little angel peed all over the floor. Getting paper towels and disinfectant, Johnny cleaned it up right away and then covered our kitchen floor with newspapers to start paper-training him.

We started tossing names around for our puppy, but nothing really suited this little Irish fellow. Suddenly, my mom said, "What do you think about the name Rusty?"

"Wow, I love it!" I exclaimed.

"I like that name too," Johnny added. "He looks like a Rusty."

As I was thinking about it, I said, "Something is missing. When the sun is shining on him, he looks more red than rust. How about we name him Red Rusty?"

"It sounds good to me," Johnny agreed.

So there it was. Our little Irish puppy's name on paper for the American Kennel Club would be—Red Rusty Roseo, but we would call him Rusty.

Mommy with Rusty at eight weeks

Meanwhile, we thought we were only going to look at the puppies and hadn't planned on bringing one home, so we weren't prepared with the puppy necessities. Ma stayed home with Rusty while Johnny and I went to the pet store.

Pet shopping was fun. We bought an array of accessories, including his first leash and matching collar. The pet store carried the same puppy food that the breeder gave us, and we added a twenty-pound bag to our shopping cart. It had a large selection of toys. Each one I looked at was cuter than the next; I just had to throw them into the shopping cart. We couldn't forget the treats, shampoo, and brush. Looking at each other, we couldn't believe the amount of dog basics we were buying. I guess I overdid it with the toys. Luckily, there was no need for us to buy a crate. Tommy was giving us Duke's crate since they didn't use it any longer.

While Johnny was paying for the items in our shopping cart, I threw in one last item, a book about Irish setters. I really wanted to know what the breed was all about and what we needed to do as first-time dog parents to make him a good, healthy, kid-friendly dog. Little did I know this book would become our "doggy bible," a source we could rely on more often than I ever thought.

Upon returning home with our puppy goodies, Johnny put Rusty's collar on. At first Rusty seemed startled. Clearly, he'd never had anything around his neck before, so Johnny started petting and playing with him so that he would forget about the collar. A little later, Johnny tried to attach the leash to the collar. Sitting down, not budging, Rusty looked confused not knowing what was expected of him. "Jo, could you get me one of his treats?" Johnny asked. "I'll try to get him to come with me when he smells the treat."

I went inside, opened the box of dog biscuits, and handed him one. Holding the treat in his hand, Johnny tugged on Rusty's leash and started walking. "Come on, Rusty. Let's go."

Being patient with our puppy, Johnny showed him how walking on a leash is done. He was absolutely right. Rusty went straight for the treat, not even realizing he was walking on the leash. Actually, he picked up walking on the leash rather quickly. I stood there smiling, looking at them walking around the backyard. Rusty was sniffing everything in sight and rolling around in the grass; he truly was a sight for sore eyes. It seemed that we got our puppy's approval, and he liked our backyard.

Rusty running in our backyard

While I was playing in the yard with Rusty, Johnny went inside and called his friend, Gary on the phone. Johnny and Gary worked together, and Gary was also the owner and breeder of basset hound dogs. With Gary's knowledge when it came to training puppies, he would be the one to guide us. After Johnny hung up the phone, he came outside and told me about their conversation. "Jo, do we have an alarm clock that ticks and a hot water bottle?"

"Why?" I asked.

"Gary said that the crate is the best way to train Rusty; but I told him that we hadn't picked up Duke's crate yet, so he suggested we wrap an alarm clock in a towel and put it close to where Rusty will be sleeping. The ticking sound from the alarm clock will remind him of his mother's heartbeat, and when we are ready to go to bed, we'll fill up the hot water bottle with warm water and lay it next to him. He said he will feel as if he is lying against his mother."

"Wow, what a great idea. Leave it to Gary. I'm pretty sure we have an alarm clock that ticks. I'll go look for it, and I'll see if Ma has a hot water bottle."

My mom gave me a rubber hot water bottle that she had had for years. Giving it to Johnny, I said, "Here you go; this should work."

"Great! Thanks," Johnny replied.

It was time to puppy-proof the house, given that dogs are notorious for chewing electrical cords and licking the electrical outlets. Johnny took everything out of the puppy's reach that could possibly hurt him. In the meantime, we tried to make our precious pup feel comfortable in his new environment so he could gain a sense of security. We wanted to establish a routine for him—a meal schedule, potty training, and a sleeping pattern. And we wanted to bond as a family.

Rusty was rather entertaining on the first day in his new home. We watched him frolicking with his toys, chewing away with his tiny baby teeth. One toy was a plastic hotdog, which became his favorite toy and lasted throughout his lifetime. Staying occupied, wagging his skinny tail, he looked happy as can be. Resting my head on my husband's shoulder, I asked, "Isn't it nice having our own puppy? Look how cute he is."

"Yeah, he is pretty cute, and he does love his mommy."

I surely felt like the proud parent. It was so precious to me to watch my little boy running around with his big smile and red floppy ears. Rusty was a bright, affectionate little puppy. He seemed eager to engage with us and became accustomed to his new surroundings pretty quickly.

We planned for Rusty to sleep in the bathroom that was across from our bedroom. But bedtime for Rusty on his first night in his new home didn't go too well. I put down a soft blanket and a few of his toys on the bathroom floor for him. Johnny attached the baby gate and put a night light on for him. I gave Rusty a goodnight kiss and placed him on his blanket. Then Johnny and I went into the living room to watch TV. Rusty wouldn't stop whining for fifteen minutes, and then all was quiet.

"Wow, Johnny. Our puppy is amazing. He must've been so tired from his first outing today."

"I don't think so."

I stared at him for a second, puzzled. "What do you mean?"

"Look who's here."

"Well, hello Rusty." I was pleasantly surprised as I picked him up.

"Jo, apparently he is so small that he squeezed right through one of the accordion slats in the expandable baby gate."

"There is no way he can fit through that little space," I said.

"Watch this. I will put him back in the bathroom, and let's see what he does."

As logical as Johnny sounded, I thought there was no possible way Rusty could squeeze through that small opening. Picking him up,

Johnny put him back in the bathroom. We waited anxiously in the hall-way, and there he went, squeezing his tiny body through the gate, just as Johnny said. Smart as a whip, Rusty had figured out a way to escape. Each time we put him back in the bathroom, he squeezed through the gate and got out. Johnny ended up tying a towel on the outside of the gate to prevent him from squeezing through it.

It seemed like Rusty cried for the longest time. After a while, I just couldn't take his crying anymore. I went into the bathroom and picked him up, and immediately he stopped crying. All he wanted was to be held, just like a real baby. Technically, he was; he was only eight weeks old.

"Honey, you're making a mistake," Johnny said. "It's a normal part of the acclimating process. We need to ignore him, or he'll never get used to going to sleep. I'm going to bed and you should too."

"I will, but I feel so bad for him. I'm sure he's lonely and scared. Don't forget he's in a strange place and he must be missing his mother and his brothers."

"Gary said that he will eventually cry himself to sleep. It's typical for a new puppy."

"Fine!" I said with discontent. Reluctantly, I put Rusty back in the bathroom and went to bed. I lay there silently, waiting for Johnny to fall asleep. Once I saw him sleeping peacefully, I tiptoed out of our bedroom and walked across to the bathroom. Our little red puppy was standing in front of the gate, shaking. Right away I climbed over the baby gate and entered the bathroom to lie down on the floor beside him. About ten minutes later, I heard footsteps coming down the hall. *Rats! Johnny is coming.*

"What are you doing? You are going to get him into a terrible habit. He will never go to sleep alone."

I put on my sad face. "Look at him; he looks so unhappy."

Johnny didn't want to hear it. "No, we have to be stern. He has to learn."

"Okay, okay, okay," I said, even though I didn't agree with him. I put Rusty down on the bathroom floor. We closed our bedroom door to try to block out his pitiful cries, but it didn't help. Neither did the alarm clock, nor the hot water bottle. I knew it was going to be one sleepless night for us. It took Rusty over an hour to finally fall asleep, at about one o'clock in the morning, and then we were able to get some sleep.

The next morning, feeling sleep-deprived, we were awakened at the crack of dawn by Rusty's crying. After Johnny cleaned up his soiled newspapers, he brought him outside to potty. Rusty squirted drops of pee here and there, knowing he would get a reward each time he went. At such a young age, he already knew how to manipulate us.

Chapter 2

Our Irish Puppy

That Monday morning, it was difficult for me to leave Rusty when I had to go to work. Being a first-time mom of a puppy, I didn't want to be away from him for most of the day. Too bad I couldn't take "pet-ernity" leave from work to stay home and spend more time with our puppy.

After work we took Rusty for his checkup at a local veterinarian in Valley Stream. Upon arrival at the vet, the receptionist handed me paperwork to fill out while Johnny held him. As soon as the vet walked into the examining room, he smiled, introduced himself, and started petting Rusty, making him feel comfortable. While he was talking to us, he was also playing with our puppy. I could see he liked Rusty. I gave him the paper from the breeder that showed the list of shots Rusty had received so far. We discussed the food the breeder started him on, a meal schedule, parasite prevention, puppy training, and all the shots that were required within the next few months. Then he placed Rusty on the examining table as Rusty gazed up at me trustingly with his hazel eyes. A sense of protectiveness took over while I held him down to keep him still. "Rusty, it's okay; the doctor isn't going to hurt you," I said to him.

The vet gave Rusty a thorough examination. "You're puppy is very alert, responsive and has beautiful features. His paws are oversized compared to the rest of his body, but his body will fill in as he grows. Let me give you a heads-up of what to expect from this little guy. Irish setters are beautiful, fun-loving, intelligent, affectionate, and loyal dogs, but they can also be stubborn, mischievous, and high-spirited. Do you have a large yard?"

"Yes, we do," I responded.

"Good, because this is an active breed; they are known for their high energy level and enthusiasm. They love to run and need plenty of space so they can go full speed. This breed is slow to mature. You'll need patience and endurance to accept living with a grown-up puppy for at least four to five years. It all takes getting used to, but this is all a part of the irresistible Irish charm."

Johnny looked at me. "Just great; this is all we need."

"Oh, stop. He'll be a great dog, especially with me as his mother."

"That's what I'm worried about."

I smiled and rolled my eyes.

The vet laughed. "It looks like you have a good, healthy dog here. Apparently, he's going to be one very large beautiful canine."

I was beaming from ear to ear.

"One more thing, this breed is prone to ear infections. It is common with the breeds with floppy ears. I advise you to clean the ears at least once a week to prevent any infections. I'm going to administer his second series of vaccinations that are due."

"I don't know much about this breed. What is the life span?" Johnny asked.

"Normal life expectancy for the Irish setter tends to be twelve to fifteen years."

Those statistics were good enough for me, meaning we would have Rusty as part of our family for a long time, hopefully to the fifteen-year mark. Best of all, our children would get to grow up with him.

The vet handed Rusty back to me. "Bring him back in four weeks for his next series of shots and enjoy him. Irish setters are a lot of fun."

Earlier that day, Johnny was making fun of the little bump Rusty had on top of his head. I decided that before we left, it would be a good time to find out what the bump actually was.

"Doctor, my husband is concerned about the little bump that is on top of Rusty's head. Is it normal?"

"Yes, it's certainly normal. Quite a few Irish setters have this type of bump. It is nothing to worry about. Some Irish setter lovers call it a knot on their head, meaning it is a knot of knowledge, whereas others call it a kissable knot. I've even heard people say the bump is the size of a knuckle, leading them to call them knucklehead knots."

"See, Johnny, his bump is a knot of knowledge."

"I hope you're right, Jo, and that he's not a knucklehead."

Smiling, the vet said, "Only time will tell."

Straight from the vet, we headed to Brooklyn to have dinner at Bridget and Tommy's house and to pick up Duke's crate. Rusty was well behaved as he sat calmly on my lap for the entire drive. When we arrived at their house, Little Tommy and Danny were so excited to see our new puppy. Right away the boys started playing with him. Duke came over to check out who this little dog was, and then they started sniffing each other. Duke, another male dog, caught us by surprise when he took Rusty under his wing. Tommy let Rusty run loose in the house, as the boys chased after him. Rusty went exploring, with Duke not too far behind.

A little while later, Tommy brought Rusty over to Duke's crate. Rusty was apprehensive to go in, and I couldn't blame him. The crate was made out of a hard plastic with metal bars on the front. To me, it looked like a portable prison cell in Riker's Island Correction Facility, but I didn't say a word. Tommy trained Duke very well, so the crate must've been something that worked for them. Little Tommy crawled inside the crate with a treat and called Rusty to follow him in. Then Little Tommy kept going in and out of the crate getting more treats, repeating the process until Rusty felt comfortable going inside the crate.

"Tommy, do you really think Rusty will like the crate?" I asked.

"All dogs like their crates, Jo. It's their comfort zone. Let me give you guys some advice."

"Please do, Tommy," Johnny said.

"Okay, first you have to set some rules. Start training him early, like now. You want a dog that will have manners and follow your commands. Look at Duke, I was really strict with him, and he turned out to be a great dog. I don't even use a leash to walk him. I mostly use hand signals. You have to be stern and do not let him get his way. He will try to take advantage of you any way he possibly can. Do not feed him people food; only feed him puppy chow for his first year, then move on to adult dog food. Do not let him drink from the toilet, unless you like sitting on wet toilet seats. Hide your shoes; puppies love to chew them up. Beds and couches are off-limits. If you don't set these rules, he will control you, and your life will be a living hell."

"Thanks for the advice, Tommy. I guess we'll have our work cut out for us."

"I know you will do a good job with him Johnny, but I'm not so sure about your wife."

I was a little annoyed. "Why don't you have a little faith in me? I can do it."

Bridget stepped in. "Little sister, we know you. You have a big heart and you will give in to your puppy. Tommy is right. You will spoil him and he will walk all over you when he gets older."

"Well, he is cute and little. We will scare him if we yell at him."

Tommy shook his head. "See what I mean Johnny. Jo will be your worst enemy when it comes to training this dog."

"Johnny, don't listen to him. Rusty will be just as good as Duke. You'll see. I will be the perfect trainer. Rusty loves me, and he will listen to me." I replied as Tommy and my sister were laughing.

When we came back home, Johnny placed the crate in the kitchen. Putting a few dog biscuits in his crate, I tried to get Rusty to go inside, just as Little Tommy did. At first, he went in to get the treats but came right back out. Rusty wasn't happy, as I kept putting him back in the crate. Finally he lay passively inside, but he looked so sad. Of course I gave in and opened the crate door to let him out, but I waited until Johnny left the room. As the disciplinarian, Johnny was setting the rules for Rusty, whereas I was already breaking them.

That night at bedtime, I put a plush towel on the bottom of his crate with a few of his toys. Surprisingly, Rusty went inside, cuddled up in a ball, and fell asleep within minutes. I guess Tommy was right. Rusty did feel safe in his crate. He slept peacefully for the whole night, and that meant we slept too.

Quickly, we started to fall into a routine. When it came to Rusty's eating habits, at first he was a patient little puppy. He ate slowly, savoring every morsel. Sometimes he even left food in his bowl. Even when it came to his treats, he accepted them gently, but not for long.

Each morning I took Rusty for a leisurely walk, followed by play-time before I had to leave for work. When I tried to put Rusty in his crate, he fought me, refusing to go in. I ended up stocking the crate with his toys, chew bones, and snacks to keep him busy and happy. On the plus side, having my job only minutes from our house gave me the opportunity to go home for lunch and spend time with him.

When I arrived home, it was awesome walking into the house and see-ing how excited Rusty was to see me, especially while I opened his crate door. I've never experienced such an amazing greeting like that before. Rusty's tail would be wagging away, and he would give me soft, wet kisses. I would take him out to go potty and give him his midday meal. After he ate, we would run around in the yard so he could burn off some of his high energy.

Our attachment to our puppy grew rapidly. Playing with Rusty each day was so much fun. Johnny taught him how to fetch, play tug-of-war and the Frisbee toss. Every day we found something new to play with him. Our little redhead was really good at the doggie treat hunt; he loved finding the dog biscuits.

Whenever we went upstairs to Ma's apartment, I carried Rusty up the stairs as if he were my baby, with his little head and long ears rest-ing on my shoulder. As he was getting bigger, Johnny started teaching him how to climb the flight of stairs. Going on his hands and knees right alongside Rusty, Johnny showed him how to move his little legs up and over the steps. Rusty tried going up the steps, and he fell down a few times, but eventually he was able to climb the stairs on his own. Coming down the stairs took longer for him to master. I think he took after me and was afraid of heights. But once he got the hang of it, he ran up and down nonstop.

One evening, I was looking through the book on Irish setters and came across some interesting facts about the breed. The origin of these beautiful redheads dates back to the eighteenth century in Ireland. The Irish setter is believed to be the result of combining a variety of spaniels, setters, and pointers. They were bred as field hunting dogs. Back in the day, the name "setter" came from the word "set" or "stopped game," particularly partridges so the hunter could trap the birds in a net.

The general appearance of the Irish setter is an active, attractive, aristocratic bird dog. Most commonly seen, is their rich chestnut red or mahogany color coats; moderately fine and glossy; longer on the ears, chest, tail and back of the legs. Standing over two feet tall at the shoulder, they display their elongated neck and are elegant in build.

Regarding their beauty, they are incredible by all means. The general appearance of the Irish setter has been termed an artist's dream. In the world of dog art, this breed has been considered one of the most breathtaking dogs.

The first Irish setter imported to the United States came in 1875, and the first Irish setter registered in the American Kennel Club was documented in 1878. This breed belonged to the group known as sporting dogs, and they were used primarily for bird hunting. They quickly became a popular breed in America and a favorite in the show ring. Seven hundred and sixty Irish setters became champions between 1874 and 1948. Three United States presidents owned Irish setters: Harry Truman, Richard Nixon and Ronald Regan.

The author pointed out that they are great with children, and other pets. They are extremely smart, loving, friendly, devoted and willing to please, but they can become reckless and high-strung if they don't get enough physical activity. They are also known for their flamboyant personality to match their flame-colored coat; a lot of rocket-launcher energy; and certain traits: mischievous, inquisitive, mysterious, frustrated, destructive, thickheaded and independent. As far as I could see, Rusty did not fit any of the author's negative descriptions. According to my mom, Duchess didn't either.

Autumn arrived a few weeks later. Even though the multiple colors of the leaves on the trees were absolutely beautiful, the number of leaves on the ground was endless. Living on a large corner piece of property with many trees, it surely gave us an abundant amount of yard work to do, but it was fun. While Rusty was moseying around in the backyard, we started raking up the leaves—Johnny on one side of the yard and me on the opposite side, meeting in the middle. The idea was to combine our piles and make one mountain of leaves to put into the trash bags. But guess who showed up?

As we were raking, Rusty pulled the bottom of the rake, trying to drag it and making it difficult for us to pick up any leaves. Finally forming one big leaf pile, Johnny and I jumped into the pile of leaves holding hands and rolled around. Crazy in love, we began playing leaf fights. We threw the leaves at each other, burying each other and then making out like two teenagers. Waiting for the right moment, along came Rusty, joining in on the fun, landing in a belly flop into the mountain of leaves and rolling around with us. He was so adorable wagging his tail and giving me kisses too. Our frolicking puppy was a lot of fun; but between the three of us, we destroyed the pile of leaves we worked so hard to make. So we had to start over, raking up the leaves that were scattered all over the yard to form another large pile. As we tried to put the leaves in the trash bags, Rusty was trying just as hard to disrupt our work by messing up the pile, rolling around, and burying himself in the leaves. Our puppy didn't want playtime to end, and neither did I.

Between the sweet aroma of the dried leaves, and listening to the birds chirping, we were enjoying our new suburban life and, of course, our little Irish puppy too. Johnny and I weren't newlyweds anymore; we became our own little family—Daddy, Mommy, and puppy makes three. Our new home was complete.

Daddy and Rusty

As the months flew by, Rusty started going through the gawky stage. Our precious, cute little puppy grew into an awkward adolescent. He was growing at a rapid pace. Johnny started making fun of him. "Jo, Rusty is getting funny looking. He looks like an ugly duckling. Check out the size of his head and his paws. His paws were big to begin with, but now they are huge, and his head is getting just as big."

I snapped at him. "No one insults my Rusty! Don't make fun of him; he is still cute. The vet said that his body will grow into his head and his paws, just give him time."

As Rusty's body grew, so did his tail. Forget about putting anything on the coffee table or end tables; those days were over. No matter what was on the table, it flew off with one hit of his long feathery tail. *And to think, I was the clumsy one.* By the time Rusty was five months old, his razor sharp baby teeth were gone, replaced with a massive set of fangs that would destroy anything. He also became fast as lightning and ran full speed around the backyard like a racehorse. Our redhead's high energy level was undeniable. When he started running, we had to get out of his way and fast.

I enjoyed walking Rusty every day. He was fairly easy to control when he was smaller, but the bigger he became, the more difficult he was to control. I used to introduce Rusty to our neighbors and their dogs. At first Rusty loved the attention and sat there while they petted him, but not while he was getting stronger and more vocal. I could see that our neighbors didn't care for him when they saw what he was all about—jumping and barking at them. He wore out his welcome.

Rusty's gawky stage

While Rusty was in the yard, he would see the neighborhood kids playing in the street. On his own, he figured out how to lift the handle on the gate so he could run out of the yard toward them, which became a habit and drove me crazy. Chasing them on their bicycles and skateboards, Rusty thought he was one of the kids as he ran along with them. With boundless amounts of energy, he kept on going on and going. Being good neighborhood kids, they held him for me until I got there to take him back home. At times, when they were playing ball in the street, they threw the ball to Rusty, and he always caught it. I could see that the kids enjoyed playing with Rusty as much as Rusty enjoyed playing with them. I guess he took after Duchess in that respect.

While Johnny and I did yard work, I didn't want to leave Rusty cooped up in the house, so we let him outside with us. In the back of my mind, I was always afraid we would get busy, take our eyes off of him, and he would let himself out of the yard and run away. I told Johnny of my fear, and he said we couldn't put a lock on the type of gate we had. His solution was to build Rusty a dog run in the backyard so he would have the best of both worlds—protection, and the freedom to run in his own space.

So, that weekend, Johnny went out and bought the fencing materials he needed. With my help, as our weekend project, Rusty's superduper large chain-link dog run was completed.

Curious as our redhead was, Rusty checked out his new outside quarters. He got plenty of exercise running back and forth chasing cars and watching the kids playing in the street. When we were working in the yard, he was outside with us, but he stayed out of trouble and kept busy in his domain. Rusty's dog run was a necessity and a blessing on all counts.

Chapter 3

Potty Training

At first, Rusty impressed us and was potty trained within a month, but as he grew older and began experimenting, potty time didn't go as well as when he was younger. Johnny even tried rewarding him with treats to do his business, but Rusty wouldn't listen; he would rather play and ignored us.

One day after work, I took Rusty in the backyard to his designated area to go potty. As we headed back into the house, I smelled something funny. I looked at him closely and saw that he had poop all over his face. To make matters worse, he was licking away. *Did he really eat his poop?* I couldn't even fathom the idea of him eating his poop. I dragged him inside and put him in the bathtub. "Rusty, what did you do? You don't eat poop! That is disgusting! Don't you ever do that again!"

Trying to take poop out of a five-month-old dog's mouth was not an easy task. Our redhead was stubborn to the core. Holding him down in the bathtub, he refused to cooperate with me. I tried prying his mouth open, but he clamped it shut. When I finally was able to open it, I took wet paper towels with soap and wiped the soft poop off of his tongue and from in between his teeth. If that wasn't bad enough, I had to scrape the poop off of his teeth with my fingernail. Of course, my face had to be right up against his face to see it in order to get it off, making me gag the whole time! Then I took the baby shampoo, washed his face, and rinsed it off. Rusty didn't like it one bit.

A little later, while Rusty was playing in the house after his bath, I was looking through the Irish setter book. In one chapter it stated that eating feces could put the dog at risk for ingesting eggs of intestinal parasites and potentially harmful bacteria that could lead to severe illness. That was all I had to read. I grabbed his leash and attached it to his collar, and we ran to the car. I pushed him on the back seat and drove straight to the vet. I was so scared that Rusty was going to get really sick, or even die.

I burst into the animal clinic and told the receptionist, "I need to see the vet right away; my dog is sick!"

She escorted me straight back into the examining room; then the vet came in. "Doctor, my dog just ate his poop. All of it!"

The vet laughed as he petted Rusty. "Please calm down, Mrs. Roseo. Your dog is fine. This is nothing to worry about. It is normal for a puppy. Ten percent of puppies eat their poop and they eat other dogs' poop, too."

That surprised me. "Really?" I asked.

"Mrs. Roseo, there is a medical term that describes what your dog is doing. It is called coprophagia, which means the consumption of feces. This is a common problem in puppies up to a year old; most of the time they stop as they mature. Apparently, puppies like to experiment, and they simply think it tastes good. Sometimes they are bored and inquisitive. It is a self-rewarding behavior, eating while or directly after defecating. Some dogs are highly motivated, and the behavior seems to become compulsive."

"What do we do to make him stop?" I asked.

"Perhaps the food you are feeding him may be lacking something in his diet. I suggest you change his food. If you are feeding him beef, try chicken, lamb, or turkey. I'm going to run blood work on him just as a precaution."

Wait till Johnny hears this one. Not knowing that it was just the beginning of the crazy things Rusty would do. I thanked the vet, and we left.

When Johnny came home from work, after a sweet kiss hello, I mentioned, "I took Rusty to the vet today."

"What happened? Is he sick? Did he get hurt? Why didn't you call me?"

His concern was a good thing, but I knew he wouldn't think this was normal.

"No, he's fine, but he ate his poop."

"He what!"

"According to the vet, it's common for puppies up to a year old. Sometimes dogs get bored, and they experiment. He said Rusty is normal and it's nothing to worry about. He recommended changing his food."

"I don't believe this." *I knew that was coming.*

After dinner, we walked Rusty outside, and within a few minutes, there he went, as if he wasn't doing anything wrong or anything out of the ordinary. Trying to stop him, Johnny started yelling, "Rusty, what are you doing? Stop that now!"

Rusty began to move with obvious reluctance, sensing he was in trouble.

"You said the vet thinks he's normal? No way! Our dog is abnormal."

"Well, let's try changing his food like the vet recommended," I suggested.

"Fine, I'll go to the pet store tomorrow and buy a different food. But I'm telling you, this dog is a psychopath. He needs a shrink. Now I guess I have to clean the poop out of his mouth."

"I guess so," I answered.

Looking disgusted, Johnny turned away from me and pulled Rusty by his collar and dragged him into the bathroom. "Jo, I don't even want to pick him up to put him in the bathtub; he stinks of shit."

"Hey, I went through it earlier. Now it's your turn; you'll get used to it."
Boy, did he glare at me as I giggled.

While Johnny was bathing Rusty, I was peaking in as Rusty was licking off the shitty soap suds while Johnny was scrubbing his tongue. Johnny even poured mouthwash in Rusty's mouth, something I didn't think to do earlier. That was a good idea. It was hilarious watching them, but I'm sure when I washed Rusty's mouth out earlier, I looked just as funny and had the same frustrated expression that was on Johnny's face.

Rusty and Daddy after Rusty's bath

Later that night, we were trying to figure out a way to stop Rusty from eating his poop. We came up with the idea of pouring Tabasco sauce on it. Assuming that the sauce was hot and spicy, he would spit it out. Wrong. Apparently, it had the opposite effect. He still enjoyed the smell and taste of his poop with the new seasoning on it; who knows? *Go figure.* We fed him enough food, changed food brands, and he still ate his poop. It was pretty evident that he wasn't going to stop any time soon.

Day by day, we closely monitored Rusty, trying to put an end to this disgusting behavior, but Rusty became quite a contortionist. He actually twisted his body around so his head came closer to his rear end, giving him the opportunity to eat his poop as it was coming out—soft and hot, right out of the oven. To make matters worse, he would lick his upper lip, just in case he missed some. I couldn't help thinking that maybe Johnny was right calling Rusty a knucklehead in reference to the bump on his head.

After two weeks of applying the Tabasco sauce, Rusty was still eating his poop. At that point, Johnny had had enough and called Tommy for advice.

"Jo, Tommy said that he used baby suppositories to potty train Duke and it worked. I think we should try using them. When we notice that Rusty is ready to poop, one of us will hold a bag to catch it as soon as it starts coming out; this way, his poop will fall right into the bag."

"Sounds good to me, but who is going to put the suppositories up his butt?" I asked.

"I guess I will," Johnny responded.

It was obvious to me that my husband had a point, and Tommy's suggestion was worth trying. As soon as Johnny put the suppository in Rusty's butt, Rusty turned his head around to see what Johnny was doing to him. Fortunately, he just went along with it, which was a good thing.

Finally, after one week of using the suppositories, Rusty stopped eating his poop. *Thank God!*

Chapter 4

Bored and Destructive

Just as I read in my dog bible, most Irish setters, especially the males, are quite energetic and usually act like puppies until they reach about five years old. At the rate our redhead was going, he would never calm down and outgrow the "puppy" phase. Another interesting fact I learned was that it was common that this breed couldn't be left alone for long periods of time. Lack of activity can lead to a bored, destructive, and hyperactive dog.

Rusty was a robust little fellow who was alert, inquisitive, and stubborn as can be. At one year old, he was not too thrilled about his crate anymore, and it was pretty apparent why. I could see that his body was getting too large for it. Rusty already towered over Duke. Every time I put him in the crate, it was a struggle because of his rebellious demeanor and endless barking. Once I got him in the crate, he shook it nonstop, rocking it in eagerness to get out. It surely looked as if the crate was going to tip over.

At that point we decided Rusty was no longer a puppy, but a full-size adult dog, and it was time to put the crate away. Johnny and I discussed it and felt it wasn't a good idea to let him have the run of the house. We knew we couldn't trust him, not yet. Anytime he saw a newspaper or magazine, he shredded it to pieces. Rusty got into the habit of raiding the kitchen garbage pail and constantly tore things apart. We couldn't even leave our shoes on the floor, he destroyed them within minutes. When Rusty hung out with us while we were watching TV, we had to keep an eye on him. If we didn't, he would sneak off somewhere and cause some kind of minor destruction. So, Johnny attached the baby gate at the entrance of the spare bedroom, which would then become Rusty's room.

During the week, I bought Rusty a bed and put some of his toys in his new room, along with his water bowl. This was going to be Rusty's test to see how he did without sleeping in his crate. Rusty was excited and looked pretty comfortable lying on his bed and playing with his toys. Shockingly, he did extremely well—no fussing and no barking. I could tell he liked his new sleeping quarters, which were right across the hall from our bedroom. As long as Rusty could see us, he was one happy dog.

That Saturday, I drove to Canarsie to meet up with my friends, Sara, and Michelle, and then we went to Riis Park beach. Johnny had work to do around the house, so he and Rusty were going to hang out at home.

After a fun day in the sun, we strolled backed to the parking lot, only to see that my car, a red and black Plymouth Duster, was no longer there. We frantically searched row after row of cars, realizing that my car was stolen. With no cell phones back then, we had to walk back to the concession stand and find a pay phone to call Johnny.

About an hour later, Johnny and Rusty arrived at the beach. My friends and I squeezed into Johnny's car which wasn't easy to do. Rusty jumped from the hatchback area to the backseat, and hogged the whole seat in the small Celica as we rode around the parking lot searching for my car, with no success.

Break-ins and car thefts weren't anything unusual back in the seventies and eighties. Sometimes people would go into their cars and see that their eight-track tape player and radio and speakers were missing. Other times, they would walk out of their house and see that their tires were missing. If the thieves were considerate, they usually left the car on cinderblocks. More often, the car was just gone. Some people actually wanted their car to disappear to collect the insurance money, and their car would wind up in the chop shop, leaving no evidence behind.

About a week later, a police officer from the 69th Precinct in Canarsie called and informed me that they had found my car. I was excited, only to hear that they had pulled my car out of the swamps located off of the Belt Parkway—swamps known as "the cemetery for stolen cars." We really weren't surprised, because in some areas of the Belt Parkway in Brooklyn and Queens, it was like driving through a dump site of demolished cars. My poor car was going to get crushed. We decided that instead of buying another car, I would drive Johnny to the train station and pick him up. His car was just sitting in the parking lot all day while he was at work anyway, so I would get another car down the road when we really needed two cars.

Monday morning as we were leaving for the train station, I thought it would be a good idea to start taking Rusty with us. Rusty enjoyed the car ride, and when we came home, I let him out again, and he ran around the yard. Before I left for work, I put a bowl of fresh water, some dog biscuits and a few of his toys in the spare bedroom, gave him a kiss good-bye, and closed the baby gate. I assumed that he would be content since he enjoyed his new room for the past few days. Boy, was I wrong.

While at work a few of the big bosses came into the branch, and I had to attend a mandatory lunch meeting. That meant I was stuck at the office unable to go home for lunch and spend time with Rusty. Racing from work at four o'clock to get home, I walked in the house to see a snowstorm—not outside, but inside our house. Silently and slowly, I walked through the chaos seeking to find the culprit. Rusty appeared like a sneak, carefully creeping down the hall with the evidence in this mouth.

"Rusty, what did you do?" Rusty gave me one big kiss with a mouth full of purple fur. I grabbed his snout and looked deep into his hazel eyes. "Gee-whiz, Rusty! Did you have to destroy all of my stuffed animals?" Rusty and I had some kind of mental connection. Most of the time, I could read his mind. *Mommy, I had so much fun today. A whole bunch of soft fuzzy animals came into my room, and I swung them around, and we played together.*

"I don't think so, Rusty. You took my stuffed animals and destroyed them."

Our rascally redhead tore up every stuffed animal that Johnny had won for me at carnivals when we were dating, including a five-foot purple teddy bear that sat in the corner of the spare bedroom. He managed to have a feast on my precious keepsakes. Now that Rusty had adult teeth, my stuffed animals didn't stand a chance. There were feathers, fluffy material, and tiny pieces of popcorn stuffing all over the house—from the front door to the back door and everywhere in between! Apparently, he jumped on the twin-size bed, knocked the stuffed animals off the shelf and went chomping away. Not thinking ahead, I should've put them away in the closet for safekeeping.

By the time I had to leave to pick Johnny up at the train station, I cleaned up the mess that Rusty had made. When Johnny got in the car, I told him what Rusty had done to my stuffed animals. He felt bad for me and yelled at Rusty, but the damage was already done.

A few weeks later, we were invited to attend the wedding of our dear friends, Anna Marie and Frank, in Brooklyn. Unfortunately, Ma wasn't going to be home that weekend. She was going to Saratoga with Cousin John—my older cousin, and his wife, Delores (who also lived in Valley Stream), to watch their horse compete in a race, so she couldn't watch Rusty. I felt guilty leaving Rusty all alone, but we couldn't miss our friends' wedding. Besides, Rusty was improving each day being left alone in his room, so I thought we could trust him, but Johnny wasn't so sure.

Before we left, Johnny let him run around the backyard to release some of his energy and do his business. Since we were going to be gone for quite a few hours, we thought it was a good idea to put some news-papers down on the floor just in case Rusty had an accident. Johnny filled up Rusty's food and water bowl, put some snacks and his toys in his room, and secured the baby gate. We left the light on in the spare bedroom and the TV on in our bedroom so he wouldn't feel alone.

We had a great time that night. It was a typical Italian wedding with tons of food and lots of dancing. More importantly, we shared in our good friends' happiness. Meanwhile, we had over an hour drive and couldn't wait to get home and go to sleep.

By the time we arrived home, it was just past midnight, and all was quiet. When Johnny turned the lights on in the foyer, we saw news-papers and magazines shredded everywhere. Walking toward the bed-rooms, I shouted, "Oh no, the baby gate is down! Where is he?"

Johnny and I ran through the house looking for our mischievous dog. We were shouting in a panic. "He's not in the spare bedroom! He's not in the kitchen! He's not in the living room! He's not in the dining room! And he's not in the bathroom! Where could he be?" Letting out a gasp, Johnny shouted, "Found him! There he is, in our bedroom! Look what this crazy dog did! He destroyed our bedroom! And he made a gigantic hole in our mattress!"

Walking into our bedroom, I was speechless. Johnny started yelling at him, "You wild animal, you really are a psychopath! You belong in the zoo behind bars! What the hell is wrong with you?"

It appeared that our bedroom was hit by a tornado. Our pillows were exploded and our down comforter was torn to pieces. But worst of all, a big chunk of our queen size mattress was missing. The guilty redhead was sitting up tall in the hole, as if he were a king on his throne, watching TV. He had pieces of feathers and foam hanging from his tongue. Rusty looked happy like a pig in shit, with a big smile and wagging tail.

"Rusty!" I yelled, "What did you do?"

He sat there thinking for a minute and then he looked at me, like an excuse would benefit him. *Mommy, you should've left me the whole box of Milk-Bone cookies, instead of just a handful. And a few more toys would've been nice. I couldn't sleep all day, so I needed to do something that was fun.*

"Rusty, don't you dare try to make an excuse for what you did! You were a very bad boy."

Johnny was fuming. "You'd better say your good-byes to him. I'm getting rid of him tomorrow. I've had it with this mutt! This dog is mentally unstable!"

First, Johnny took a water bottle and sprayed water on his snout, which confused Rusty since he hadn't experienced that before. Then the little monster tried to run for cover. Johnny caught him and dragged him outside, screaming at him in the middle of the night as he put him in his dog run.

Sternly, I said, "Stop screaming; you're gonna wake the neighbors!"

"I don't care. I've had it with this dog!"

Between Johnny yelling and Rusty barking so loud while he was outside in his dog run, I was afraid our neighbors would come over and start banging on our door. Thankfully they didn't.

Even though it was the middle of the night and Johnny and I were exhausted, we had no choice but to clean up the disaster Rusty made because we had nowhere to sleep. Johnny started cleaning up our bedroom and basically put all the destroyed contents into trash bags. "Now what are we supposed to do with this mattress?" he asked.

"I'll sleep on the side with the hole in it. I'm lighter than you anyway," I suggested.

"Are you sure?"

"Yes, I'll be fine."

"Okay, but before I flip it over, I'll stuff some towels in the hole to make it more comfortable for you."

"Thanks."

As I was cleaning up the shredded newspapers and magazines, a thought came to my mind. *We didn't have to buy a paper shredder since our dog became a professional at it. And forget about cutting coupons; those days are over.*

We didn't finish the cleanup until two o'clock in the morning, and we were utterly frustrated and exhausted. Since we couldn't afford to buy a new mattress at the time, we had no choice but to live with the fact that the missing piece of our mattress would be a constant reminder of our first dog's destructive actions.

Finally, my husband fell into a sound sleep, but sleep wasn't happening for me. It wasn't because the mattress was uncomfortable, but because Rusty wouldn't let me leave him. He was barking nonstop for my attention. I guess he really missed me. Even though I was so upset with him for what he had done, I knew he was sensitive and had feelings, so I went into his room and lay down with him on his bed. We cuddled until we both fell asleep.

The following morning I jumped off of Rusty's bed to the sound of Johnny yelling, "Are you out of your mind? What are you doing on that crazy dog's bed?"

I got up, totally ignoring him, and went into our bed. It was pretty evident that Johnny's frustration with Rusty's disobedience and destruction when he was home alone was boiling over.

"I'm telling you, Jo, we need to get rid of this dog and find him another home. He is too destructive and untrainable. No matter what I try to teach him, he doesn't listen. This dog is thick-as-a-brick. Look at Duke. He is a normal dog. There is something wrong with this pooch. My grandparents had many dogs when I was growing up. Every single one of them was trained and they even understood Italian. This dog doesn't even understand English!"

"Let's give him one more chance. Technically, he's still a puppy."

How many more times was I going to repeat that sentence in the following months and years to come? What can I say? I had a soft spot for our nutty redhead. I did vow to be a good dog parent, to love and protect him always. I refused to go back on my promise to him. In his poem "If," Rudyard Kipling referred to the virtue of patience. I kept reminding myself of that virtue each time I cleaned poop out of Rusty's mouth, picked up hundreds of tiny pieces of paper, and, after the last episode, slept with a hole in our mattress with no pillows.

After three months of displaying good behavior in his room, Rusty led us to think we could trust him, and we gave him full rein of the house with the exception of our bedroom; but our mysterious redhead calculated a plan that seemed to work for a little while until he got busted.

One day, I couldn't find any of his toys. I looked all over, inside and outside in the yard, and they were nowhere to be found. Usually, his toys were scattered all over the house, as if it were a child's playroom. Toys were a real necessity in our house; they definitely kept him busy. Since Rusty was "BC" (before children), he was one spoiled little boy. Every holiday, or for no reason, I swung by the pet store and picked up a new toy for him. Some toys I had to throw away within a few days, as his sharp teeth chewed them into pieces.

"Johnny, did you put Rusty's toys away because he was bad?"

"No. What are you talking about?"

"Most of his toys are missing," I said.

"I have no clue. Maybe he buried them in the yard." Johnny's response was short and to the point. Obviously he was still frustrated with Rusty.

The next step was to ask my mom. I rushed upstairs. "Ma, did Rusty leave his toys up here?"

She was just as baffled about the missing toys as I was. "I'll look around, but all I can see is that he left one of his rawhide bones in my living room."

Left with no answers, I knew I had to replace the missing toys before our rascally redhead destroyed something else in the house when he was home alone.

Not more than two days later, his new toys were gone. The only explanation I could come up with was either I was going crazy, or Johnny was playing a trick on me. *Could it be that Rusty was chewing them up and swallowing them?* So, I began being on poop watch—looking for remnants of toys. It was weird because I didn't see any evidence of pieces of toys. A week had passed and still no sign of the missing toys.

I came home from work early one day, and I thought I'd take Rusty for a walk around the neighborhood, but that didn't happen. When Rusty wasn't at the door to greet me, I knew he had to be up to no good. As I went into the house, something didn't seem quite right—it was utterly silent. As I quietly walked down the hall looking for him, I saw him in the living room. Doing a double take, I thought I was seeing things. He had his head inside the couch, and the seat cushion was on the floor. Our mysterious redhead was so focused on what he was doing that he didn't even hear me enter the room. Instead of yelling at him, I decided to watch him in action. Determined to hide his toys, our rascally redhead was going through them, taking each one out of the couch and putting it in a pile on the floor. I think he was deciding which toy he wanted to play with. After he made his selection, he started putting them back inside the couch, one by one. Then he grabbed the seat cushion with his mouth, and with his paws he pushed it back in place. After seeing enough, with a sense of disbelief I announced I was there. "Aha! You little toy thief! What are you doing?"

Rusty turned toward me and gave me one of his sweet, innocent Irish setter smiles. *Look Mommy, I found a place to keep all my toys so the house wouldn't be messy anymore. Aren't you proud of me?*

I removed the seat cushion and was horrified when I looked into the couch. "Oh my God! Rusty, are you kidding me? I'd rather have your toys scattered all over the house, than a hole in our couch!" *When Johnny sees this, he's really going to kill him this time.*

Our rascally redhead had actually dug a huge hole in the couch all the way down to the wooden supports that held it up. There had to be at least twenty of his toys and bones inside the couch—nothing of ours, just his. It took me a minute to assess the situation and conclude that our dog was a toy hoarder. I called up to my mom to show her Rusty's latest destruction. "Ma, come downstairs. You are never going to believe what Rusty did this time."

As she walked into the living room, I removed the seat cushion so she could see it for herself. She looked inside the couch. "Oh my goodness! Rusty, what did you do?" He sat there smiling, looking proud of himself.

"Ma, Johnny is going to have a conniption when he sees this—first he ripped apart all of my stuffed animals; then he demolished our bedroom and left us with a hole in our mattress; and now the couch. Can you keep Rusty upstairs with you when I leave to pick Johnny up?"

Ma, being the protective grandmother, said, "Of course I can. I think he's better off staying at home."

Rusty was definitely a possessive, mischievous little boy, but after I was thinking about it, I thought it was brilliant on his part. In my opinion, for a dog to execute such a well-thought-out plan just to protect his toys was definitely clever. My question was this: How did he come up with the crazy things he did? I must say, he was pretty smart to know that each time he went into the hole in the couch, he had to put the seat cushion back in place to cover up what he did. Later, when I thought about it, every day when I came home from work, the seat cushion was always in a different position than it was when I left in the morning. Not giving it a second thought during those times, I assumed the cushion was out of place due to Rusty's need to jump up on the couch and look out our front window.

At eight o'clock that night, I went to pick Johnny up at the train station by myself. After a kiss hello, Johnny asked, "Where's Rusty?"

I didn't want to tell him yet. "He wanted to stay home with his grandma, but guess what?"

"What?"

"I found his toys."

Johnny seemed pleased. "Finally. Now you can stop spending money on all those toys for the little brat."

Keeping my mouth shut, I didn't say anything else about the toys. I knew my husband wouldn't agree with me about Rusty's brilliance.

When we arrived home, I needed to break Rusty's latest destruction to him gently. "Before you wash up, can we sit down for a minute? I have to tell you something."

"I don't see Rusty. What did he do now?"

"Well, something in the living room. But he did have a good reason to do it."

Hurriedly, Johnny ran out of the kitchen, and as soon as he stepped into the living room he stopped dead in his tracks. And boy did he start yelling. "Holy shit! Did you see the couch? There is a freaking hole in our couch. Look at the size of it. There are all his toys. This is the second hole that he has made in our furniture. That's it! He's outta here! I am so done with him! This dog is certifiably nuts!"

"Certifiably nuts? Are you a dog psychiatrist? All he wanted to do was protect his toys and he did."

"Protect his toys? Are you as crazy as he is? Where is he? I'm gonna kill him."

"I have no idea where he is!" I snapped back at him.

Of course I knew where Rusty was, but I would never rat him out. At that moment Johnny gave me a dirty look, knowing I was covering up for my little boy. He ran through the house to find our mischievous pup. Searching the downstairs with no dog in sight, he headed upstairs to Ma's apartment. Rusty probably sensed that Johnny was angry and hid from him. Johnny went looking under the bed, behind the furniture, and under the couch, and then he found Rusty hiding behind his grandma's closet door.

"There you are, you psycho! What did you do to the couch? Bad boy!" Johnny dragged him downstairs and started chasing him around the house like a crazy person. I stood in the background, laughing, watching the two of them—crazy dog and crazy dog parent. It was a funny sight. Johnny pulled Rusty outside in the yard, put him in his dog run, and started yelling at him, "What is wrong with you? You are one sick pup!"

While I was washing the dishes after dinner, Johnny ended up going to Pergament Home Center, similar to Home Depot and Lowe's to buy the materials he needed to fix the couch—the first of countless repairs Johnny would be making on Rusty's behalf. When Johnny came home, he took the sheet of plywood and a two-by-four, cut them in pieces, and nailed them to the wooden supports inside the couch to cover up the hole; and boy was he pissed.

From that day on, we realized it was inevitable that more destruction by our crazy dog would occur, proving once again that Rusty could not be trusted. We never knew what to expect from his irrational, bizarre behavior and couldn't guess what destructiveness he would create next. As long as someone was home with our destructive redhead, and gave him the time and attention he demanded, he was perfectly fine. But if we left him alone, he went into boredom, panic, resentment, and destruction mode. So, we ended up attaching the baby gate again, putting him back in the spare bedroom when we left the house.

One Saturday night, Johnny and I went out to dinner to a really nice restaurant that just opened on the bay. After an enjoyable time, when we arrived home we saw that everything was ransacked. I screamed. "Oh no! Johnny, we've been robbed, and where is Rusty?"

I shouted in a panic, "Rusty, where are you? Come to Mommy!"

Rusty didn't come to me, and I got really nervous. "Johnny, do you think the robber tied Rusty up?"

"Jo, let's get out of the house and go in the shed so I can get my baseball bat; then I'll go back inside and check out the house, while you wait outside."

"Should I drive to a pay phone and call the police?"

"No, not yet."

"Well, what about Rusty? You have to find him."

"Will you let me get my baseball bat already?"

"Okay, but when you go back inside the house, please be careful."

"I will."

I was so scared that whoever broke into our house took Rusty, or hurt him, since he didn't come to me when I called him. While Johnny walked into the house, I waited outside by the front door. All of a sudden, I heard Johnny shouting, "Holy shit! What do you think you're doing, you crazy dog?"

I felt relieved Rusty wasn't hurt, but I sensed he was in some kind of trouble. I went inside and yelled out, "So I guess we weren't robbed?"

"No, we weren't robbed, but someone is going to get killed tonight! I've had it with this dog!"

Johnny grabbed Rusty by his collar and pulled him to where I was waiting at the front door. "Here take this psycho."

"Wasn't he inside the baby gate?" I asked.

"He knocked the baby gate down. Do you want to see what you little angel did to our house?"

Our dog was a little firecracker, which suited him perfectly because of his bright red coat. Walking into the living room, I couldn't believe what I was seeing. The ceramic lamps were on the floor, broken in pieces. The lamp shades were on the floor, ripped apart. All of the seat cushions on the couch and the love seat were on the floor. The curtain rod was pulled out of the wall, and the curtains were shredded all over the floor.

As if he didn't destroy enough of the house, when I went into our bedroom, I shouted, "Oh my God! Look at our closet!"

Johnny ran into our bedroom. "What closet? Our closet is gone! The psychopath must've slid the closet doors open and he pulled everything out."

The wooden pole holding our clothes was on the floor with teeth marks all over it. Our clothes were scattered all over the room, including our shoes and sneakers and our wedding album.

"Wait till I get him!" Johnny snapped.

I got to Rusty before Johnny did. I grabbed Rusty's face and looked right into his eyes. "Rusty, what did you do?"

Mommy, don't blame me. Things just started falling on the floor from everywhere. I couldn't leave it all on the floor, so I played with everything.

"No, Rusty. Things don't just fall on the floor. Why would you destroy our house? You were a bad boy!"

All of a sudden, Johnny screamed. "No!" I ran toward him while Rusty tagged along.

"Jo, look! My JBL speakers are destroyed!" Johnny grabbed Rusty by his collar and started yelling at him, "Rusty! You lunatic! What did you do to my speakers? What the hell is wrong with you?"

Johnny's speakers were like diamonds to a woman. Now Rusty is really in big trouble.

Johnny bent down to see that his four-foot speakers were knocked over and turned on their sides. All of the black open-weave fabric was shredded. The round speakers inside the wooden cabinets had holes in them, and the wires were dangling.

"Jo, these are really expensive speakers. Do you realize how many hours I had to work overtime to save enough money to buy these speakers?"

I didn't know much about speakers, so I just kept quiet.

"Jo, I'm telling you. This dog is crazy. Just look at this house!"

"Well, at least someone didn't break into our house and steal everything," I said.

"Jo, you'd better get him outta here. I am so done with this dog! We need to get rid of him. Something is wrong with him."

"I'll take Rusty for a car ride."

"Come on Rusty, let's go." Putting his leash on, we ran straight toward the car.

When we came back home, Johnny was sitting on the floor trying to connect the wires to his speakers. I don't think he cared much about the rest of the house.

"Since you're busy with your speakers, I'm going to start cleaning the house. Where should I put Rusty?" I asked.

"Just open the door and let him go."

"I know Rusty messed up, but there has to be another solution," I said.

"Then put him outside in his dog run in time-out."

"In time-out? He's not a child. Punishing him won't work. I read in my dog bible that dogs are known to have a short attention span. If we didn't catch him in the act, he wouldn't remember what he did and why he is being punished."

"I don't care what your book said. Either you put him outside in his dog run, or I am opening the door and letting him go, with the hope that he doesn't come home."

"Fine!" *Men could be so cranky.*

While Johnny was trying to fix his speakers, I was cleaning up the mess throughout the house while Rusty stayed quietly in his dog run.

Trying to figure our crazy dog out, Johnny felt we should've insisted on seeing the stud. Surely, Rusty's dad could've been nuts too; it may have been something in the male genes that he inherited—the "abnormal gene." However, for Rusty's sake, we had to keep trying to understand him and be patient with him, because dogs do have personalities of their own. Rusty was part of our family, for better or worse. Even though our dog was a problem child, he was still a Roseo, and we had to accept him. I only hoped that, in time, he would calm down and act as a normal, civilized dog. I did have high hopes for him, but Johnny thought I was delusional.

Chapter 5

Ruler of the Backyard

Rusty enjoyed being outside with us; it was to our benefit that we had a huge backyard for him. On any given day, Rusty would take off in the yard at record speeds, covering every inch of the yard while his paws pounded the ground, ripped up the grass, and made a muddy track just like a racehorse. He displayed his athleticism and endless high energy as if he were running in the Triple Crown.

His intuition as a hunting dog, from which his breed was descended, caused him to have a fixation with squirrels and birds. As the ruler of our backyard, he targeted them and bolted right after them. Time and time again, he jumped up on one of the tree trunks as if he were a large cat attempting to catch them. The birds were smart and took off, but not the squirrels. Trying to get to the squirrels, his growl deepened, and then he erupted into a frenzy of barking at them. The fierceness of it stunned me. Rusty could act pretty mean when he was after something, but the squirrels just sat there staring at him, which antagonized Rusty even more. Good thing Rusty couldn't climb all the way to the top of the tree, or the squirrels would've been history.

When summer arrived, we bought an above-ground, four-foot swimming pool to enjoy. At first, Rusty looked at the pool cautiously, sniffing every corner of it; but every time I went in the pool, I splashed water on him, and he enjoyed getting wet. He loved seeing how much water he could actually catch.

One Friday after work, my sister brought Little Tommy and Danny over to spend the weekend with us. When they arrived, Rusty was in the yard focused on pulling branches off of the bushes. We went outside, and Little Tommy called Rusty. "Hi, Rusty, do you want to play?" he asked.

Standing on the opposite side of the yard from where the boys were, Rusty was mesmerized. Everything Rusty approached in life was with a rollicking attitude that was full of excitement. I guess he knew that when the boys came over, it was playtime for them. Suddenly leaping in the air, Rusty went charging full speed, high-spirited, across the backyard toward them, portraying a thoroughbred. Danny froze, paralyzed by fear, whereas Little Tommy was quick and jumped out of Rusty's way. Within seconds, Rusty jumped on Danny and knocked him down to the ground while his tail was wagging. Danny was bowled over by our rascally redhead, as Rusty was licking Danny's face in pure excitement. It was happiness for Rusty, but not for Danny and he shouted at him in his squeaky little voice, "Stop, Rusty! Get off of me!"

Johnny ran over and pulled Rusty off of him. "Rusty, I know you love the boys, but you could've hurt Danny. You need to play nice with them. You know better."

I held Danny as he started crying. Little Tommy, fulfilling his role as the big brother, couldn't stop laughing and called his younger brother a wimp. He loved to tease Danny, a common trait of older siblings.

I went over to Rusty as he was just sitting there, looking so sad. I could tell that he understood that he had made a mistake being overly excited. I told him, "Rusty, Little Tommy and Danny love you and want to play with you, but they are small. You need to play nice and easy with them."

I truly felt that he understood what I said, because he slowly walked over to Danny, and gently kissed him. Then they all started playing again, but carefully this time.

Bright and early on Saturday morning, the boys were eager to go outside and play. Boys being boys, they loved helping their Uncle Johnny do handy things around the house.

"Boys, I have a project to do, and I need your help. The plan is to build Rusty a doghouse."

Our nephews were excited and shouted, "Yaaay! We're going to help Uncle Johnny build Rusty a doghouse!"

The boys were busy with their uncle building Rusty the cutest red and white wooden doghouse with gray roofing shingles, while Rusty and I were on the other side of the yard playing. When it was completed, Johnny put it right next to Rusty's dog run and gave the boys the honor of showing Rusty his new doghouse.

"Rusty, come look at your doghouse. It's really cool," Little Tommy said.

At first Rusty was apprehensive to go in, just as he was with Duke's crate. Then Little Tommy crawled into the doghouse. All of a sudden we saw the happy expression on Rusty's face. *Wow, this doghouse is for me? Now I have my own place to hang out.* Smiling and wagging his tail, Rusty ran right into the doghouse, and Danny tagged along.

Rusty's doghouse

The following day, we took the boys to Adventureland Amusement Park. When it started getting crowded, we left and stopped for a fast-food lunch. Driving home, I noticed that there was a new community being built, and they had model homes. I thought it would be fun to go see them and get decorating ideas. Going up the walkway into one of the models, my stomach didn't feel quite right, but I brushed it off. While we were walking through the model, Little Tommy and Danny went exploring in the living room. Little Tommy was so excited. "Wow, Aunt Jo Ann, this house is cool. Look at the big fireplace. We can play inside it," he said.

I was about to tell them to be careful, and all of a sudden I got really bad stomach cramps. "Johnny, I have to go to the bathroom."

"Okay, let's go to the office. I'm sure they have a bathroom you can use."

"No, that won't work. I'll never make it. I have to use this bathroom."

"You can't use this bathroom. There are signs all over that say the toilets are out of order, and there is no water in the toilet bowls."

"Sorry. When you gotta go, you gotta go."

He shook his head and gave me one of his snide looks. He gathered up the boys. "Tommy, you stand guard by the front door and don't let anyone in. Danny, you stay put in the living room."

Both boys nodded and said, "Okay, Uncle Johnny."

Waiting outside the bathroom, Johnny stood guard for me. Something inside me exploded. I puked my guts up and then I shit my brains out. It must've been food poisoning from the food I ate for lunch. The next problem was there was no toilet paper. To make matters worse, there was no lid to put down on top of the toilet bowl. Truthfully, I couldn't leave the bathroom in such a mess, so the only solution I could come up with was to take off the shower curtain, which was made from a very pretty fabric. I wiped myself and cleaned the surrounding area with the shower curtain and stuffed it in the toilet bowl. I guess Johnny heard me. "What is that racket in there? What are you doing?"

When I opened the door Johnny looked astounded. "You gotta be kidding me. Why would you take down the shower curtain and stuff it in the toilet?"

"Why do you think? I had no other choice."

"Your brother was so right about you."

"You had your chance. Now you're stuck with me for better or worse," I said with a laugh.

"Boys, let's go. We're outta here."

Johnny grabbed the boys' hands, and we hightailed it out of there.

By the time we came home, I was feeling much better. The boys and I went in our pool. They were riding Shamu, the whale float, while I was pushing them around. Johnny was busy filling in a hole in the yard that Rusty had dug earlier. All of a sudden, Johnny looked up. "Jo, don't make such big waves. There is too much movement on the pool."

"Okay." *I thought it was odd that the pool was moving, but whatever.*

After we got out of the pool, we were hanging out with the boys in the patio while Rusty was chasing the squirrels. Ma was upstairs looking out her kitchen window when something caught her eye. She opened the window and called down to us. "Look at Rusty! He's next to the pool, and something is wrong."

At that point, we ran from the patio to see that Rusty's body had tensed up as he stared at the pool. His red hair was electrified. It stood straight up, resembling Albert Einstein's wild hair. His nostrils were flaring, drool was hanging from his jowls, and his upper teeth looked like a set of dentures ready to fall out. His tail was fully pointed, as if he were hunting and had found prey. Running over to the pool, Johnny looked around and thought it could be the pool float Rusty was afraid of. He brought Shamu to the edge of the pool. "Rusty, is this what you're afraid of?"

Rusty was beside himself with fear from the moving whale. He started barking like a lunatic while his body was trembling. I hugged my little boy to calm him down, but it was useless. There was no getting through to him. I guess all Rusty could see was the black and white face of Shamu moving on its own. Rusty was too low to the ground to see the water moving it. Johnny took Shamu out of the pool and started deflating it. He tried to show it to Rusty, but Rusty ran behind me for cover. Johnny came over and spoke to Rusty as if he were a small child. "Rusty, look, this is only a plastic blowup float; it won't hurt you."

Johnny tried his best to reassure and calm Rusty, but it didn't work. Instead of listening to Johnny, Rusty looked at the float and took off. Moving as fast as lightning, he ran around the yard; there was no stopping him. As we were standing on the sidelines, all of a sudden Rusty made a dash straight toward the pool. He hit the pool wall head on. We grabbed the boys and stood there astonished, unable to say anything as the pool came tumbling down, dumping over three thousand gallons of water on the lawn. Rusty looked horrified. Johnny and I were speculating about what was going through Rusty's big red head. The expression on his face clearly said, *Oh boy, I'm in big trouble now.* Then he ran into his brand new doghouse, his safe haven, with his tail tucked between his legs.

I thought for sure Johnny would flip out, but instead he amazed me. "Honey, I had my doubts earlier about the pool when I saw it moving when you were making waves. If a dog can knock a pool down, it surely isn't sturdy enough for people. I'm going to call the store and tell them that the pool caved in, and to pick it up and refund our money."

"I guess it was good that Rusty hit the pool in the exact spot he did, or it could've collapsed while the boys were in it," I said.

"That's for sure," Johnny answered.

For the first time, Rusty didn't get punished for the destruction that he caused. This time, it was a good thing. That was one weekend we would never forget, thanks to Rusty and me.

Little Tommy and Danny next to Rusty

Chapter 6

The Charming Granddog

Strangely enough, Rusty's alter ego would come out, and he was on his best behavior for his grandparents. Maybe he relished being a spoiled granddog.

My mother-in-law, Kay and my father-in-law, Joe enjoyed taking a ride out to Long Island every Sunday and having dinner with us. Following family tradition, "Sunday sauce" is a ritual in our home, just like it was in our parents and grandparents homes. When Johnny and I were dating, I always enjoyed his mom's sauce. Kay made the best meatballs, along with bracioles, sausages, and spareribs. When we got engaged, she gave me her recipe and I have been making it for our families ever since. Some people call it Sunday gravy, but our families call it Sunday sauce. To me, gravy is brown, and sauce is red, but there is some controversy on that. I guess everyone is entitled to their own opinion, but I'll stick with the sauce version.

Rusty was always excited to see his Grandma Kay and his Grandpa Joe, especially when they picked up marrow bones for him from the butcher in Brooklyn, which made a nice treat. Thriving on human companionship, Rusty loved all the attention he received when they visited us. Every time they came over, Joe took Rusty for a walk through the neighborhood, and then they would play a long game of fetch in the backyard, which Rusty enjoyed.

I would call it dog's intuition, because Rusty acted differently with my mother-in-law. Kay was battling cancer, and Rusty was always well behaved, overly affectionate and charming with her—as I knew he could be. Displaying a sweet and gentle side, he was constantly putting his head on her lap so she could pet him, and he gave her much-needed kisses. As soon as Kay would get up to walk to another room, concern was written on Rusty's face as he followed her. He would even wait outside the bathroom for her to come out. Our caring redhead was always at her side. Even when we were eating dinner, or hung out in the living room, he sat right next to her, as if he was protecting her.

According to my mom, anytime Rusty was upstairs with her, he was always good and never caused any trouble. They enjoyed each other's company. Rusty was always comforted by his grandma's presence. He knew she was there for him and that she would protect him. There was no debating that Rusty had a big heart filled with love for his grandma, and she had the same soft spot for her granddog.

After one of Rusty's crazy episodes, I went upstairs to talk to her. "Ma, Johnny's frustration with Rusty is running thin. He is always yelling at Rusty when he destroys something, and then Rusty gets even more crazy and he starts barking at Johnny, which doesn't help the situation."

"Jo Ann, I have an idea. When you and Johnny leave for work, I'm home most of the time, so send Rusty upstairs and he could stay with me. He listens to me and he is always a good boy. This way he won't cause any destruction downstairs and he'll stay out of trouble."

"That would be great! I can't wait to tell Johnny. Thanks, Ma."

My mom was a seamstress by trade and made the most beautiful clothes, back in the day. Her factory sewing machine also led to Rusty's sewing machine hideout. To cover up the motor and the wiring which was pretty extensive and noticeable, she made a skirt out of a thick brown fabric and draped it around the sewing machine.

While Rusty was staying upstairs with his grandma, he found that it was the perfect hiding place for him. Even when he knew he had done wrong and he would probably be in trouble, he would run up to her apartment and hide underneath the sewing machine.

For the longest time, I had no idea where he was hiding, until one day I saw him poking his head through the skirt looking to see if the coast was clear. Ma just smiled. She knew what he was doing, but she covered up for him, just as I did once I found out. I thought it was a good idea on his part, so I let him keep his hiding place.

For Rusty, being with his grandma outside was quite different from being inside with her. One day after work, I pulled into the driveway, and the first thing I noticed was that our backyard was in disarray. *What did he do now?* I got the distinct impression that Rusty had something to do with the condition of our backyard. I went upstairs to Ma's place, and Rusty was happy to see me and acted as if nothing was wrong. He greeted me with his enthusiastic full-body wiggle, a jump on me bear hug, and a wagging tail that meant happiness. I responded happily to see him, but he didn't fool me for a minute. I had to find out what transpired outside.

"Ma, I'm sure I don't even have to ask, but what happened in the backyard?"

My mom frowned. "Rusty was what happened. He dug holes and got into the mulch. Earlier he was pulling branches in the yard while I was gardening. I turned my back for a few minutes, and that was it. I didn't even hear a sound. When I looked up, the yard was full of holes, and Rusty was dragging the bags of mulch around the yard, ripping them apart. I tried to go after him, but I couldn't catch him."

"Ma, I don't think you could ever catch him. He's just too fast. I'm really worried because Johnny is going to flip out. He keeps saying that he wants to get rid of Rusty, claiming that Rusty's destruction just doesn't stop."

"Don't worry. Johnny knows how much you love Rusty. He won't get rid of him. Yes, he will definitely be upset, but he'll get over it. He always does."

Rusty and Ma

After our conversation, I rushed outside and tried to clean up the backyard as best as I could while Rusty stayed upstairs with his grandma. Glancing at my wristwatch, I knew I had to pick up Johnny soon, and all hell would break loose. I dreaded to tell Johnny about Rusty's latest destruction, but I needed to tell him before he saw it himself, so I left Rusty home with Ma (again).

After a kiss hello, Johnny looked in the backseat. "Where's Rusty?"

"He's hanging out with Ma." *Now was the moment I had to tell him.*

Softly and calmly, I said, "Well, remember we were going to put the mulch down this coming weekend?"

"Yeah?" He looked at me inquisitively.

"Well, I have a feeling we picked it up too early."

"Why, what do you mean?"

"Well, I don't think we can put it down."

"Why not, is there rain in the forecast?"

"No, the weather is supposed to be nice."

"So why aren't we putting the mulch down this weekend?"

"Well," I said in a squeaky voice.

"Okay Lucy, every time you start a sentence with 'well' it means either you or Rusty did something. Let's hear it."

"Well, Rusty was in the yard with my mom, and she was busy in the garden. She turned her back for a few minutes."

"And?"

"Well, he got into the mulch."

"How bad?"

"Well."

"There you go again with 'well'.

I guess I had to spit it out. "Okay, here it is. Rusty ripped apart all thirty-five bags of mulch and spread it around backyard; and he also dug holes all over the backyard."

"You gotta be kidding me. I don't get it. Usually he is really good when he is with your mom. Wait till I get him. I'm gonna put his sorry ass in his dog run and keep him in there."

"Chill out. What are you going to do? Rusty did the damage hours ago. He will never remember what he did. You can't punish him now."

"Oh, yes I can. He will remember what he did when I'm through with him."

"Yeah, right! I don't think so," I said.

Once we came home, Johnny went upstairs by Ma, snatched Rusty and brought him downstairs and took him outside. He was pushing his nose in the mulch while yelling at him, "What did you do? Don't you ever do that again! Bad boy!" Confusion was written all over Rusty's face. He didn't have a clue as to why he was getting yelled at. This happened quite often. It appeared that Rusty was in trouble over and over again, but he never knew why.

After dinner, Johnny and I filled in the holes that Rusty had dug earlier. Instead of putting down the mulch over the weekend, it was raking time. We managed to rake up as much mulch as we could, but it was difficult because it was embedded deep within the grass. Getting on our hands and knees, we had to handpick the mulch that was impacted in the grass, and there was a lot. Our mischievous redhead surely knew how to keep us on our toes. Johnny still went on ranting, "What a waste of time and money. This dog is always giving me work to do."

Here we go again. It seemed that Johnny was constantly complaining about Rusty, over and over again, day after day. To be funny, I straighten my left arm out, and with my right arm I pretended I was playing a violin.

Johnny looked at me curiously. "What are you doing?"

"This is my imaginary violin. Every time you complain about Rusty, I'm going to play it."

"I guess you'll be playing it all the time, because your dog is crazy."

I got defensive, "My dog? I thought he is our dog?"

"Well, not when he does stuff like this. He is your dog."

I started laughing. "Who said 'well' this time, huh?"

"Okay, you got me," he said with a laugh.

I won that round, but, actually, he was right. I couldn't disagree. We never argued, or had a heated discussion, about anything except our rascally redhead. Johnny was always easygoing, even with all the crazy stunts I pulled, but when it came to Rusty, he had no patience.

I vowed to always protect my little boy no matter what, and my husband knew I always would. To me, the warm, loving greetings and the affection I received from my crazy redhead every single day outweighed all the wrong he did.

Chapter 7

Obedience School

There comes a time when enough is enough. Clearly some attempt at serious training and guidance was called for. At a year and a half old, Rusty had no manners, he didn't listen, he was stubborn, and he was thickheaded to the core. It was time for obedience school.

Glancing through the neighborhood pennysaver, I came across an advertisement for dog obedience school. The training class was a six-week program offered on Monday nights at the local high school. After I showed Johnny the article, we both said, "Let's do it!" Considering the fact that Johnny worked overtime practically every night, I was the one who was going to take Rusty to school.

The first day of obedience school, I was eager to get our crazy dog some training. "Rusty, come with Mommy. You are going to learn manners and be taught to behave like a normal dog." Rusty was energized when I put his leash on and we proceeded into the car.

Rusty and I arrived at the high school twenty minutes early so I could meet the trainer before class started. I wanted to introduce myself and, most importantly, Rusty. I needed for the trainer to know all about my dog before anyone else arrived in the classroom, given that Rusty was so unique, but not in a good way. As I entered the training room, which was in the school cafeteria, I saw that it was spacious. I also noticed this guy setting up the chairs, and I assumed he was the dog trainer.

Making the grand entrance, my enthusiastic dog and I walked in. Well, rather, Rusty pulled me in, trying to break away as if he was going after a squirrel. Startled, the guy turned and looked at us. Walking over to me, he introduced himself as James, the dog trainer. I introduced myself to him while Rusty was jumping all over the place. James commented, "You have a dog here that certainly has a lot of stamina. I see he is quite on the rambunctious side. It looks like he needs some training."

"That's for sure. His energy level is through the roof. His behavior is so irrational and even bizarre at times. He doesn't listen to me. He can be destructive, and I can't control him. I desperately need your help."

"Don't worry; I've dealt with strong, problematic dogs before. I am well aware that the Irish setters are an energetic breed. They have an independent spirit, and are impulsive with a mind of their own, but they are also affectionate, intelligent, willing to learn, and sensitive to the tone of our voice."

I was curious. "How will you start training him? He isn't like most dogs."

"Dog training 101 is normally a black-and-white exercise starting with manners. It also includes basic commands of obedience, repetitions, walking on a leash, and learning to behave in a civilized manner. One thing you need to keep in mind is to remain calm, yet possess authority. The Irish setter can be stubborn and calculating, especially the males. You need to outwit him at his own game."

Stubborn, you got that right. I guess James noticed the uneasiness on my face. "You can do it. Every dog is trainable. Just remember, the key is firmness and consistency. One step at a time; you'll be fine."

James wasn't aware that my dog was thick-as-a-brick, but I knew he would find out quickly enough. However, I was receptive to James's guidance, needing all the help I could get.

"I see that your dog is wearing a choker collar."

"Yes, my brother-in-law suggested it. He used it to train his dog."

"Good call. Based on his size and strength, it will definitely help."

At first, when Tommy showed me Duke's choker collar, it looked torturous to me with the spikes going into his neck, but he was right. It was the only device I could use to walk him somehow, and it was better than just a collar.

During the time James and I were chatting, Rusty started lunging at the other dogs walking into the cafeteria with their owners. I should've known it was just the start to a crazy six weeks of obedience training. James excused himself to greet the other parents. I saw just by the way he interacted with the dogs that he loved his profession, and training dogs was his passion.

Just as I expected, Rusty wouldn't sit still for a minute. The other dogs sat patiently beside their masters, listening to James and awaiting instructions, but not Rusty. The first class already wasn't going too well. Rusty aggressively made the rounds to greet the other dogs. His logic must've been that it was playtime, not learning time. Every now and then, for no apparent reason, Rusty started with his incessant barking. No matter what I tried to do, he just wouldn't shut up. It echoed throughout the cafeteria. He also had no manners. Anytime he would get close to another dog, he would sniff the dog's private parts and try to hump it. Although it was only the first day of obedience school, it was becoming increasingly clear that Rusty was having a hard time staying focused. Looking back, he probably would have been diagnosed with doggy "ADD", *attention deficit disorder.*

At the time, I was talking to one of the other parents and lost my grip on Rusty's leash, and he broke away from me. He took off as if he was running full speed in the backyard. When the large dogs saw Rusty running around, some of them broke away from their owners to join my dog. As the ringleader, Rusty got the other dogs in the class to participate in playing and have a grand old time. The dogs chased each other, stood on their hind legs play fighting, humped each other, barked and growled at one another, and wagged their tails the whole time. Thanks to my dog, the classroom appeared to be a circus instead of a training room. I could see that James was getting frustrated, ordering all the dogs to sit. They all sat except mine.

James directed us, "Everyone please line up and form a single line. Hold your dog's leash close to you at your side."

As we formed the line, Rusty started humping the black Labrador retriever in front of us. I smacked him on his behind. "Rusty, you stop that!"

Our first task was to have our dogs heel while we walked in the large circle around the cafeteria. "Rusty, let's go." All of a sudden, one of the smaller male dogs lifted his leg and peed. My dog saw that and had to show that he was bigger and more territorial. Pulling me to the same spot, he lifted his leg and peed right on top of the little dog's pee. Rusty definitely had a knack for dominating any area he occupied. Then the other male dogs followed Rusty's lead, each one claiming its territory. Puddles of dog pee were everywhere. There always had to be one clown in the class, and, unfortunately, it was my dog that started this chain reaction.

James abruptly stopped the class and brought over rolls of paper towels so "we," the dog parents, could wipe up all the dog pee.

"Folks, next week class should go more smoothly. The first class is always a challenge. The dogs were excited tonight, and they needed to adjust and get used to each other."

Handing out an instruction sheet with the exercises, James explained some simple commands we should practice at home with our dogs. "Remember, be consistent with your daily training and please, do me a favor, do not give your dogs any water one-hour prior to coming to obedience class."

Training was over for the night. As soon as I met Johnny at the train station, he was eager to hear how Rusty did in school. "How did our student do tonight? Did he make any friends?"

"He sure did. He made friends with the big dogs; he socialized pretty well and had fun, but the learning part went a little slow. The trainer said they needed to get acquainted." *If only my husband knew that our dog was the class clown, but I thought I would just keep it to myself for now.*

During the week, we practiced the exercises with Rusty that the trainer had handed out. Sometimes Rusty listened and he got a treat, but most of the time he didn't. All he wanted to do was play and act kooky.

The following week, I told my nutty Irishman that we were going back to obedience school for week two. Going to the car, he jumped right in, wagging his tail, not sitting still for a minute. As soon as our car approached the school, excitement kicked in for him. I couldn't get the car door opened fast enough. Pulling me through the parking lot, he couldn't wait to get inside. Once again, he made his grand entrance—jumping, barking, and lunging (his formal greeting to the other dogs) with a bountiful amount of energy. It was next to impossible to control him.

The first exercise that night was to form a line and trot around in a circle. "Rusty, let's go." That first time went pretty well. However, the second time around did not. I saw a glimmer of mischief out of the corner of Rusty's eye and that his brain was working overtime. James had placed a large folder on his chair toward the beginning of the class. Within minutes, Rusty pulled away from me, ran over to the chair, and just had to get ahold of it. *Why does my dog have to keep misbehaving?*

Doesn't he have any respect for anyone or anything? My dog is a menace to society. I ran after him. "Rusty, drop it!" His determination prevailed. Rusty started shredding the folder and everything in it. James called out from behind me. I turned around, and he did not look happy. "Jo Ann, your dog is out of control. You are his owner, and you are responsible for his behavior."

I was so embarrassed and apologized to James. I pulled Rusty to the side while James grabbed a broom and started sweeping all the torn papers to put them in the trash can. After he cleaned it up, James took Rusty's leash from me and brought him into the center of the circle trying to teach him how to walk nicely, but Rusty was jumping all over the place. I stood there and cringed. *My dog is really nuts.* I'm sure Rusty knew what was expected from him, but he chose otherwise. School was pointless. It was all about Rusty having fun.

When the class was over, James said, "I apologize folks; I don't have any handouts to distribute to you tonight. As you know, one of my notorious students with the red hair decided to chew them up. Just practice the exercises we did tonight."

I couldn't wait to get out of there. As soon as we got into the car, I went off on him. "Rusty, what did you do? You need to listen and behave like a normal dog. Can't you give in a little here? I'm trying to help you!"

It was frustrating to me as it was only the second week of obedience school, and he was already a nuisance. It was just like at home, we never knew what to expect from him and what commotion he would cause next.

Later that night when Johnny asked me how Rusty did in obedience school, there was no way I could tell him what really happened, so I just said, "Well, let me say, he is the most popular dog in the class." And I left it as that.

At night and on the weekend, Johnny and I practiced the exercises with him and got nowhere. "Jo, this dog is just not getting it. What is wrong with him?"

"Give him time; he'll eventually understand. He still likes to play."
"Okay, I hope you're right."

Maybe week three would be a turnaround for our dog. I could only hope. "Come on, Rusty. Let's go, it's time for obedience school." He grabbed his leash with his mouth and ran down the stairs waiting for me to open the door.

Arriving at the school, he dragged me through the parking lot and down the hallway, eager to enter the classroom. There he went again, making his grand entrance trying to get everyone's attention. I overheard from a few of the parents grumble with sarcasm, "Here comes the crazy red dog."

Just as he had done the first and second week, he pulled me in every direction in the classroom except where we needed to go. Walking in the circle, trying to keep my dog next to me wasn't easy as he kept humping the female dogs. Rusty tended to get distracted easily; walking in one direction wasn't his strong suit.

The other dogs seemed to be doing much better during week three. I had to stay hopeful that the training would sink in and my dog would get it, but no, trouble struck again. As the saying goes, dogs live in the moment. At least for my redhead, that seemed to be the case. While we were walking in line, Rusty spotted the cafeteria trash can on the other side of the room. I assumed that the school custodian hadn't come into the cafeteria yet to collect the day's trash. I tried to hold Rusty's leash, but because of his overpowering strength, the leash just slid out of my hand. "Rusty, stop!" I shouted. My dog's nose was working overtime for the greater good of his stomach, meaning food to feed it. We all watched in astonishment as he knocked over the trash can and all the contents came tumbling out. Scattered all over the floor were pieces of pizza, french fries, hotdogs, apples, and torn-up paper items. Attacking the food with enthusiasm, he helped himself to the remains from the students' lunches earlier that day. James got control of Rusty's leash, a little too late though.

"I am so sorry, James. Let me help you clean this up."

"Jo Ann, please take your dog outside and wait in the hallway. I'll let you know when to bring him back in."

As James turned away from me with a disgusted look, he turned to the other dog parents. "Would any of you like to help me clean all this trash up?"

Appalled would best describe how I felt at that moment. Nevertheless, it seemed like a good idea to get out of the classroom—and fast. I really felt bad leaving the mess Rusty made all over the floor. I felt sorry for James having to put up with Rusty, but in a way, I felt sorrier for myself because I knew trying to train Rusty was hopeless and a waste of my time. It was idiotic to think that our dog would succeed in obedience school.

Dragging my crazy redhead out into the hallway, I wanted to kill him. Watching James and the other parents picking up the scattered trash was very upsetting to me. Of all the dogs in the class, it had to be my dog that knocked over the trash can, causing all its contents to fall out in the first place. And the fact that I couldn't control him didn't help.

Shortly after, James called us back in the room. I apologized to everyone for my dog's behavior, but there was something unkind that some of the parents were whispering about me and my dog. I should have just left and gone home with my nutty dog and called it a day. Certainly I was not the role model of a disciplinarian.

Shockingly, James wanted Rusty to participate. Everyone lined up again. There were twelve dogs in the class and we were the first in line; no other dogs were in front of us. *Okay, this might work.* "Rusty, let's go."

We made it around the cafeteria three times. *Rusty is doing really well.* Who was I kidding? All of a sudden, as if the garbage wasn't enough, Rusty misbehaved again. He just had to make another scene. What do dogs do after they eat? Poop. In this case, it was one humungous pile of smelly dog shit. He took a few more steps and pooped again. The piles of Rusty's poop were bigger than some of the smaller dogs' heads. The other dog parents froze in silence and glared at Rusty with disgust, as if he were one low-class dog. If I ever wanted to curl up in a ball and die, it was at that moment. James became more and more agitated thanks to my dog. He walked over to me and handed me the roll of paper towels and a plastic bag, "Here Jo Ann, clean up your dog's poop."

"I don't know what to say, James. Again, I am so sorry. I guess my dog really needs help."

With the dirty looks the other parents gave to me, you would have thought it was me who shit on the floor. After I cleaned it up, James handed out the homework assignment. The class was finished for week three.

After having a frustrating night, I was so happy to get out of the classroom. I pulled my crazy dog into the car. I grabbed his face forcing him to look at me. "Listen, you," I said sternly. "What is wrong with you? Can't you be good like the other dogs? You can't behave like this; you are so bad! Don't you understand that I am trying to help you?" And, off we went on our way to pick up Johnny at the train station.

On the way home from the train station, Johnny wanted to hear all about our student. "So how did the psychopath do tonight?"

"Okay, I guess."

"Honey, you don't sound too reassuring. I just don't understand why we aren't seeing any improvement in him. It seems like school is a waste of time. He hasn't learned a thing. I bet he disobeys every command."

Some things are best to keep quiet about. "No, it's not a waste. Sometimes he does listen to my commands."

"You tell me where."

"Practice makes perfect. He's trying; he just needs more time."

"Yeah, right."

I knew he still wanted to get rid of Rusty. So week after week, I told him that Rusty was improving in school. *Imagine if I told him the truth, forget about it.* Good dog or bad dog, smart dog or dumb dog—there was no way I was letting Johnny get rid of him. That would never happen, not in this lifetime. Plus, my nutty redhead was my source of continuous entertainment.

We practiced the exercises with our crazy redhead each night and on the weekend. When Rusty did get it right, Johnny gave him many treats.

"Jo, maybe he's finally getting it."

"Yeah, maybe?" *Let's hope.*

If I thought the earlier weeks of obedience school were bad, they were nothing compared to week four. During that class, my dog was on a roll. The redheaded comedian, with his keen powers of observation, was at it again. *We should've stayed home.*

As instructed, we started off by walking in line. "Rusty, let's go." All the dogs trotted around the circle with their owners at a slow pace and were told to stop. Actually, Rusty received my commands pretty well. I was impressed. *Maybe he is finally getting it.* It was wishful thinking on my part; it was too good to be true.

Some of the women in the training class put their pocketbooks on the seats of their chairs, while others placed them under their chairs. In the flash of a second, Rusty got away from me. "Rusty, stop!" I yelled. He stuck his nose right into one woman's pocketbook. I assumed he was looking for treats that we were required to bring; but instead he found her spare sanitary napkin, grabbed it, and shredded it into pieces. There was an awkward silence for a brief moment as everyone in the training room stopped and looked at my dog in total disbelief. A few of the women stared with open mouths. I apologized to the woman whose sanitary napkin my nutcase dog stole. At that moment, I just wanted to disappear, but instead, I needed to pick up all the shredded pieces while trying to hold my crazy dog on the leash, which was not an easy task. James gave me a stern look and said, "Jo Ann, who is training who? Get control of your dog!"

Oops. Well, I guess he was right. My bossy dog thought he ruled me and the world. God only knew what made him tick. Of all the crazy, knuckle-brain things to do! Nonetheless, with Rusty there was always stress, caused by not knowing what he would do next. My nutty redhead and I sat the next exercise out, paying close attention to James as he interacted with the other dogs. James had the human-dog communication skills down pat. He took the time to give each dog a one-on-one exercise with him.

After James completed that exercise, he came over to me and took Rusty's leash and brought him into the center of the circle. "Come on Rusty, let's go," James said. Rusty seemed to respond to James that time. *Okay, this is good. Maybe there is hope for him.* Who was I kidding; there wasn't any hope for him. When James returned Rusty to me, he was already calculating his next move.

All twelve dogs were instructed by James to sit against the back wall. "Folks, drop your leash, take a few steps back, and tell your dog to stay. Also, give the 'stay' command with your hand."

Whether deaf or using selective hearing, Rusty acted as if I was giving my commands to a brick wall. Everyone was able to take steps back, going farther and farther back. Most of the dog owners made it all the way across the room. I just couldn't understand why my dog's eyes weren't fixated on me, as the other dogs' eyes were focused on their masters. I took four steps back, and that was it. Tireless and enthusiastic, there went my crazy redhead again. I chased after him as he went running to the chairs sniffing the pocketbooks again. "Rusty, get over here!" I yelled. This time he grabbed a lipstick from one and took off with it! Don't ask me how he smelled the scent of the lipstick, but with his hunting instinct, he found it and ran around the room with it. Without a doubt, he would've made a good dog for the Drug Enforcement Agency with his impeccable sense of smell. James too ran after Rusty to catch him. We all watched in disbelief as Rusty ate the lipstick, even swallowing the plastic cover. Again, I received more dirty looks from James and the other parents. Of course, I had to apologize to the woman whose lipstick had been eaten, and she wasn't too happy either. The only good thing was that Rusty pulled this stunt at the end of the class. Training was over for the night—time to go to the train station. *Thank God.*

I guess it was easy for me to say, but at the time I was thinking of alternative scenarios. Why couldn't all the women put their pocketbooks on the seat of their chairs, instead of on the floor? Wouldn't that have made more sense? That is what I would've done if I had known there was a crazy dog in the class. But that was me. People baby-proofed their houses; I guess I should've spoken to James about "Rusty-proofing" the training room.

Just thinking about what he did and how he did it, was pretty comical. I had to laugh on my way to the train station, knowing I was also immature like my dog. I too liked to have fun. Rusty did make me laugh, and, silly me, I thought some, well most, of the crazy things he did were pretty funny. I often wondered how my pooch came up with the things he did. I'd like to think he inherited that trait from me.

As soon as Johnny got into the car at the train station, he pushed Rusty toward the backseat and asked, "How did the nutcase do in school tonight? Please tell me he is getting it."

"Not quite. But he still has a few more weeks of training. Give him time."

"Why would I expect anything different? I told you he's nuts."

"Whatever."

The following morning, chunks of lipstick and pieces of the plastic case appeared in his poop.

Although my dog had a devious little mind, bizarre behavior, and was stubborn to the core, I still dutifully took him back to training every week. Trying to train my dog to follow my commands required much patience and consistency. In any event, I sucked at training him. I came to the realization that with me laughing at my crazy redhead's wild antics didn't help me earn his respect either. I was not firm enough with him, and I shouldn't have been the one to provide leadership. Regardless, I would never complain about Rusty's behavior issues in school to Johnny.

Off to obedience school for week five. After Rusty made his rounds lunging at the other dogs, getting it out of his system, he became a little calmer. Me trying to control my seventy-five pound, stronger-than-life, energetic dog was a joke. The truth is that I was pretty lax when it came to consistency. My dog had unbound enthusiasm and the strength of a bull that would destroy anything he came in contact with. Yes, sorry to say, the prankster was at it again—another one of his out-of-control episodes. I swear you can't make this stuff up.

Halfway through the class, as everyone was walking in line with their dogs, in the blink of an eye my overexcited dog yanked the leash out of my hand and took off. "Rusty, stop!" I shouted. Chasing after him, I tried to catch him, but as he ran faster and faster, grabbing his leash was impossible. Then, my luck, I tripped over another dog and fell on my ass. By that point, I had had enough.

I looked up, and in a matter of seconds the redheaded class clown was at it again. This time, he pulled off the avocado green seat cushion from the folding chair and ran around the room with it in his mouth. All of a sudden there was utter silence in the classroom. I awkwardly stood there, staring in disbelief at the nutty dog that just happened to be mine. James ran after him as I followed, but we couldn't catch him. Rusty had more speed and stamina than both of us together and it looked like he enjoyed showing off. There was absolutely nothing we could do to stop him. I stood there shaking my head in a gesture of disgust as he tore the cushion into pieces, shredding it all over the training room. *Who says blondes have more fun?* As in weeks past, I apologized to James.

During moments like that, I couldn't help but wonder if our dog would ever be normal. All the while the other dog parents looked on with disapproval again. James walked over to me. The agitation I heard in his voice clearly said that his patience with Rusty had run out. "Jo Ann, I need to speak to you after class." *I knew that was coming.*

At the end of the class, despite James's best efforts, in a firm tone he said to me, "I cannot indulge in Rusty's unacceptable behavior anymore. I was never wrong about a dog, but this time I may be. I must tell you, you are part of his problem."

Nervously, I cleared my throat. "Me?"

"Yes, you. You aren't strong enough to control him."

"I know, James. You're right."

"You aren't stern enough with him."

"I know, but I do try."

"He doesn't listen to you at all."

"I know. I guess I've spoiled him."

I agreed without hesitation. I knew it was just a matter of time before Rusty was going to get kicked out of obedience school. It didn't take a genius to see that he wasn't going to graduate.

"All things considered Jo Ann, it is best if you don't bring Rusty back to obedience school." *How disappointing for a dog parent.*

"James, can you please give Rusty one more chance? My husband can come here and train him. He will be a much better trainer than me."

"I understand, but your dog needs serious training. More than any other dog I have ever had in any of my classes. In all the years I've been teaching obedience training, I have never encountered a dog so destructive and so undisciplined. I will tell you, your dog is the most annoying student I have ever had. He is constantly disrupting the class week after week. It isn't fair to the other dogs, their owners, and me."

It was upsetting to admit, but I knew James was 100 percent right. *My dog is unstable. Maybe he has a chemical imbalance or something?*

Sadly, I answered, "I'm sorry James. I completely understand. I really needed for Rusty to succeed in school because my husband has had it with Rusty. He said he wants to get rid of him and find him another home if he doesn't change. I guess after this, there is nothing more I can do to keep him."

During our conversation, our eyes met. The disappointment on my face must've been pretty obvious, and I hit his soft spot.

"Irish setters are great dogs and exceptionally smart. I don't want to see Rusty go to another home. I can see how attached you are to him. I'll give him one more chance, but your husband must bring Rusty to all the classes for the next session. Also, I've seen a few dogs behave this way—well maybe not as bad as Rusty—but the secret is simply to outsmart him."

I felt relieved. The idea of Rusty staying in obedience school with Johnny training him meant there was hope for our crazy dog.

"Thank you, thank you, thank you. We won't let you down. Rusty will do better with my husband taking control. He is more consistent with him, and he does listen to him."

Okay, maybe I told a little white lie. Sometimes Rusty did listen to Johnny, but not too often. A small percentage is better than none. When

James started cleaning up the torn pieces of the seat cushion, I offered to help him, but he thought it was best if I just took Rusty home.

School was not a simple process for Rusty, by all means. In fact, one might say just by his actions in class, my nutty dog had a few loose screws. Maybe it was a blessing that James wanted to kick him out of obedience school. Each week I took him to school, Rusty was showing minimal, if any, signs of improvement. The bottom line was I needed to work my magic on Johnny since I already told James that Johnny would be taking Rusty to obedience school for a repeat of session one.

Later that night, while Johnny and I were watching TV, I filled him in on Rusty's behavior in obedience school and the conversation I had had with James.

He rolled his eyes disgustedly. "Are you kidding me? There's no two ways about it. I am not taking that nutcase to school and putting up with his nonsense. Don't you see another round of school will not help him? He is thick-as-a-brick. It's time to get rid of him. I told you, this dog is a lost cause."

Here we go again. I knew we had a difference of opinion, and he would strongly object, but I didn't appreciate his sarcasm. "Come on, he'll behave with you. You're his master; he looks up to you."

"You must be dreaming. No way. Forget about it."

"Dogs are highly adaptable; you just have to give him a chance. Rusty did pay attention to James a little bit. James said that I am the problem because I am not stern with him. He feels with a man training him, meaning you, Rusty will be more receptive."

"Your sister and Tommy were so right about you. You always give in to him, and he walks all over you."

"What can I say; guilty as charged."

As far as Johnny was concerned, there were countless reasons to say no, and to argue that a second round of obedience school wouldn't help him. My eyes started to tear up, and Johnny's stubbornness began to crumble as he looked into my eyes. He sounded unsure, but finally said, "Okay, I'll do it."

"Yes!" I shouted. I was so happy. Maybe there was hope for Rusty. Seeing the sweet expression on Johnny's face, I jumped right into his arms. Planting one big kiss on my husband's lips, I started jumping up and down. It was like I was a contestant on a game show and just won a million dollars. I couldn't stop hugging him while he stood there laughing, totally unsure if he was making the right decision. But reluctantly he agreed to leave work early, losing overtime pay to take our kooky redhead to obedience school. Undoubtedly, he agreed to take Rusty more to appease me and keep me happy. The things we do for our dog, or loved ones.

Chapter 8

Round Two

The following day, James called me on the phone after I came home from work. "Jo Ann, I've been thinking about this. Maybe you should speak to your veterinarian about getting Rusty neutered. His energy level is extremely high, and neutering will definitely calm him down."

Listening to James, I was certainly intrigued. "Do you really think it will help him?"

"From my experience with dogs, I've seen a big difference in their behavior once they are neutered. Rusty is a beautiful dog, and he does have potential. Irish setters are very intelligent dogs. He just needs the right trainer. No offense."

"None taken. That would be great. I'll talk to my husband and check it out. Thanks, James."

What mattered most was that Rusty needed to de-energize. The possibility that a little snip could actually do it was something to seriously consider. I called our vet and asked him about neutering. He explained to me that the surgery would lower the testosterone levels in his system, which would make him a much calmer dog. He also explained that another one of the benefits of neutering was that it would reduce the risk of prostate and testicular cancer. He claimed it was the way to go if we weren't going to breed him. *Hmm, I never thought of breeding him.* When it came to his appearance, he really was stunning. His athletic build was very attractive for a stud, and he did have that beautiful red coloring. I didn't think Johnny would go for it, but it was worth a try.

After Rusty went to sleep, I thought it was a good time to tell Johnny about the conversation I had had with James about Rusty. "James called me earlier and suggested we get Rusty neutered. He said it would calm him down significantly, and he would stop humping everything in sight."

Johnny was excited. "Let's call the vet and see what he thinks."

"I already did. The vet thinks it's a good idea if we aren't going to breed him. Do you think we should breed him? Owning a stud, we could have the pick of the litter."

"No, we're not going to breed him."

"Maybe we could pick one of the females. I'm sure she'd be calmer, and Rusty would have a playmate."

"No. Are you out of your mind? Forget about it."

"Fine! Just asking."

"Honey, I think we have no other choice but to go ahead with it."

"I agree. It's the only thing we can do because you know I will never give him up. Now who is going to bring him to the vet to take away his manhood? I can't. I will cry saying goodbye to my crazy little boy. Plus, I'm scared of what he'll look like. Do you think he will look deformed?"

"I'm sure he won't look deformed. Vets do this surgery all the time. I'll drop him off and pick him up."

His answer impressed me. I looked at my husband with admiration.

That Saturday morning, Johnny dropped Rusty off at the vet. Later that afternoon when he brought Rusty home from his surgery, he was groggy from the anesthesia. When he saw me, he wagged his tail slightly, but his eyes were droopy. Giving him a hug, I petted him for a minute, but

I could tell that he wanted to go to sleep. I tried to look, but I couldn't see where he was cut.

"Johnny, did they cut them totally off?"

"No, they just look deflated. Do you want to see?"

"Not now, let him go to sleep."

Rusty went on his bed, but he couldn't get into a good position. The large plastic cone that the vet put around his neck was in his way. He tried to take it off, but it was tied, so he couldn't. A few minutes later, Rusty slowly walked into the kitchen to drink water, but he found it difficult because of the cone. I followed him, nervous to see if he looked deformed. Instinctively, I glanced down at his private parts. They were swollen and a little red, but they weren't cut off, just like Johnny said. Thankfully, he had two big pieces of skin flaps—not too bad. Easy for me to say, but at least something was still there. Hopefully, he wouldn't even notice.

"Honey, by the way, the vet told me he may have some discharge from the surgical area, but that is normal. He said also no baths; we need to keep that area dry. When he needs to go out, we'll have to put him on a leash, and limit his activities."

"I think keeping him on the leash will be tough since he always wants to run, but I'll try my best," I said.

Every time Rusty moved, he was banging into everything due to the cone that was wrapped around his neck. I could see that Johnny felt bad for him.

"Jo, I'm going to take the cone off since it is bothering him. He is still groggy from the anesthesia. Just keep an eye on him so he doesn't try to lick where he was cut. Once he wakes up, I will put the cone back on him."

"Good idea. It must be so uncomfortable for him."

As soon as Johnny took the cone off, Rusty went into the living room, climbed up on the couch, and fell asleep. Surprisingly, Johnny let him sleep on the couch and did not disturb him. If only Rusty, our sleeping angel, would stay that calm. We did have high hopes.

At Rusty's follow-up appointment the following week, the vet told us that we should notice less hyperactive behavior in about four to six weeks. Sometimes it does take a little longer, but we will definitely see a difference. At that point, all we could do was wait.

Rusty recuperating from neutering surgery

Here we went again—round two of obedience school. Taking a deep breath before the class started, I hoped Rusty wouldn't act as irrationally as he had during the first session. Truth be known, Johnny had no patience with him. If Rusty pulled any stunts, Johnny would walk him right out of the class and never take him back.

Repeating the obedience classes this session with Johnny as Rusty's trainer, went much more smoothly than with me. I was passive at training him, whereas Johnny was stern and in command, as a trainer should be. However, Rusty was still excited and made his rounds each week, greeting the other dogs, but no more lunging at them. Johnny had that under control. Thanks to the neutering surgery, Rusty's humping days in school were over. I could see that James was impressed.

Anytime Rusty got distracted, Johnny yanked Rusty's leash and Rusty had no choice but to stop. Week after week, Rusty was a little thickheaded now and then, but he was making progress. From time to time, I saw Johnny was getting frustrated when Rusty didn't listen, but at least Rusty wasn't the class clown like he was when I was training him. At times, Johnny gave me an agitated look when Rusty acted up. Other times, when Rusty obeyed I would see a sly smile on his face. Sometimes, it looked as if Johnny was enjoying training him, but I'm sure he would've denied it. Being much stronger than I was, Johnny had the upper hand. Finally, after week four, there was a major improvement. Rusty obeyed the command 'stay' for an extended period of time when Johnny walked across the room. My little boy did great! Walking him on the leash required some more training, but toward the end of the session, Johnny had him walking obediently next to him. Occasionally, Rusty even responded to Johnny's hand signals, when he was in the mood to pay attention. The best part was that Rusty was listening to Johnny, and that was all that counted.

Graduation day finally arrived. Maybe our dog was not as disciplined or as well trained as the other dogs, but James did allow Rusty to graduate for the progress he did make with Johnny as his trainer, and he did receive his certificate of completion from dog obedience school. I was very proud of Rusty. I shouted, "Yes! He did it! Our dog is an obedience school graduate."

However, I was a little annoyed that James didn't have graduation caps for the dogs to wear. I felt Rusty deserved one after going to school for eleven weeks. I wanted to remember this proud day for my little boy, so I put a birthday hat on him when we got home. Rusty and I ran upstairs to his grandma to show her his diploma. Daddy and I gave him a new rawhide bone as a graduation present.

Rusty was very photogenic and loved posing for the camera. That night, he looked right at the camera, wearing his graduation hat, holding his new bone, and smiling as I was snapping his picture. He was too cute. Deep down, I'm sure he knew he had accomplished something very important, and he felt good about it. Mommy and Grandma were so proud of him, but Daddy still had reservations. "He graduated by the skin of his teeth," he said.

No one was going to take this night away from Rusty. "Give my little boy some slack. He tried his best, and he graduated. So there!"

Obedience school graduate

Chapter 9

Like Mother, Like Son

"Rusty, where are you? I'm gonna kill you! Do you have to destroy everything? Isn't there anything sacred in this house?"

I took out my imaginary violin. *Here we go again.* "What happened now?" I asked.

"I'll tell you what happened. Your crazy dog got into my grandfather's Enrico Caruso records. He scratched and chewed almost every single one of them!"

"Who's Enrico Caruso?" I asked.

"He was one of the most famous Italian opera singers from the early nineteen hundreds. I used to sit with my grandfather and keep him company while he listened to these records on his old wind-up Victrola all the time. These records are a classic and a family heirloom, and now they are ruined thanks to your dog. I can't take him anymore. I'm done with him!"

"I'm really sorry he destroyed your grandfather's records. I feel terrible. I'll put Rusty outside so we can go through them. Hopefully, he didn't ruin all of them."

While we were looking through the records to see what was savable, the doorbell rang.

"I hope someone is here to take that crazy dog away," Johnny said.

I just ignored him. I felt really bad, but if the records were that important to him, he should've put them on the top shelf in our closet instead of on the floor.

"It's probably my brother. He's coming over today to help you with the flood lights."

"Oh, yeah."

Opening the door, I let my brother in. "Hey, where's your nutty dog?"

"Don't ask," I said.

"I'll tell you where he is. He's in the backyard, and I'm gonna bury him," Johnny said.

Andrew looked at me curiously. "What did he do now?"

Johnny handed him one of the records. "Here, look at these records. These were my grandfather's, and now they are either chewed up, or scratched."

Andrew just burst out laughing.

"I don't think this is funny, Andrew. Why are you laughing?"

"Your wife did the same thing with my records, but without the chewing part."

"Are you kidding me? What did she do?"

"Little sister. Why don't you tell your husband this one?"

"Okay, fine. At the time, I was about eight years old. Andrew worked part-time for a record studio, and he would get the top record albums before they were released to the public. His sacred records were like gold to him, meaning his record player was off limits to Bridget and me. One day I was bored, so I went in his room. Finding his newest Beatles album, I was listening to it, and a few minutes later, I heard Ma coming up the stairs. Rushing to take the record off, I pulled it off too fast, before I removed the arm holding the needle out of the way."

Johnny was curious. "And what happened?"

"I heard a weird sound, and I saw a few deep scratches on the record."

"Guess what she did next," Andrew said.

"I have no idea, but I can't wait to find out."

She took a Brillo Pad and was trying to scrub the scratches out."

"Really, Jo?"

"What do you expect? I was only a little kid."

"I'm not surprised. Now I get it Andrew."

"Johnny, I hate to tell you this, but your dog and my sister are very much alike."

"Yeah, no shit."

"Very funny," I said.

Andrew and Johnny went to do the flood lighting, and I finished going through the records while Rusty was playing in the yard.

The truth is, Rusty and I were always getting into trouble—never meaning to, it just happened. Maybe that was why I was constantly covering up his destruction and bailing him out. Consequently, we really understood each other, even though it was clear that he took advantage of me every opportunity he could. Every time someone called Rusty crazy, my inner soul would be laughing, because when I was young, I pulled some crazy stunts myself. I always wanted to have fun, just like my Irish setter. In a weird sort of way, I was happy and proud that Rusty followed in my footsteps. Now I didn't look that bad because I was no longer the only destructive, clumsy one in the family. Rusty had me beat by a long shot.

One Saturday night, we were having a few friends over for dinner. The night before, I was in the bathroom, removing mascara from my eyes with Pond's Cold Cream. Somehow, the jar slipped out of my hand and slammed into the bathroom sink. *Oh, shoot!* As soon as I touched the crack, just my luck, a big chunk of the porcelain sink broke through. I couldn't believe that by simply putting my finger on the crack, it made a hole the size of a tennis ball. I picked up the broken glass, put it in a washcloth, and hid it in the hamper. Then I joined Johnny and Rusty in the living room without saying a word about it.

After watching a rerun episode of *The Honeymooners*, Johnny went into the bathroom. As he walked out of the bathroom, he came over to me and put his arm around me. "Honey, what happened to the sink?"

Defensively, I asked, "What's wrong with the sink?"

He curled his finger. "Come over here, and let me show you."

Following him, I acted surprised. "Wow, I wonder how that happened, I said."

"You wonder how that happened. You are what happened."

"What makes you think I had something to do with this? Something probably fell out of the medicine cabinet and accidently fell in the sink."

Not giving it up, Johnny asked me. "Then tell me why does the sink smell of your cold cream, and where is the missing jar? It was too big to fit in the medicine cabinet. And why is there a piece of glass with the letter 'P" under the sink? I know for a fact that Rusty doesn't use cold cream."

Rats! I thought I cleaned up all the broken glass. I'm not getting out of this one. It was time for me to throw in the towel. "Okay, it was me. It wasn't my fault. The jar just slipped out of my hand."

"Aha, I knew it! You just had to break the sink tonight? Our friends are coming over tomorrow night. We have only one bathroom with one sink, which now has a hole in it. Who is going to replace the sink before tomorrow night?"

Batting my eyelashes, I said, "You, I guess."

If it isn't Rusty destroying things, it is you breaking things. Do I ever get a break from the two of you?"

He sounded like a broken record, so I just ignored him.

The following morning, I was making my sauce for the lasagna, while Johnny went to the plumbing supply store to buy a new sink. When he came home, he showed me the new sink, and the color matched. He said the salesman at the store was extremely helpful and gave him step-by-step instructions on how to install it. When the salesman asked him why he had to replace the sink, he told him, "I have to thank my clumsy wife for this."

The salesman laughed and said, "Take it from me. I've been married for a long time. The key to a happy marriage is to say, 'Yes, dear', and simply ignore the minor mishaps."

I giggled, responding, "I guess that guy knows what he's talking about. I told you, being married to me will never be boring."

Johnny smiled. "I guess your brother was right about you after all."

"Hey, you can't say you weren't warned," I said with another giggle.

After Johnny installed the new sink, it looked great. He did an awesome job.

Later that evening, our friends came over. We were hanging out in the living room munching on the appetizers I had made earlier. Of course, my husband had to tell them the story of the broken sink. They all laughed and weren't at all surprised, as they knew me all too well. After chatting with our friends for a while, I looked at the clock and said, "Time to eat."

We all got up and were walking toward the kitchen; I was the first one who entered the kitchen. "Oh my God!" I screamed. "What are you doing to my lasagna?"

Everyone ran into the kitchen to see that the lasagna pan was on the floor while Rusty was devouring it. There was also broken glass all over the floor from my CorningWare that had the sauce meat in it.

"Rusty, what are you doing?" Johnny yelled. He grabbed him by his collar and pushed him down in a sitting position. "No! No! No! You little food thief! You ate our food! Get out of here!"

Rusty lowered his head knowing that he got caught in action, and ran into his room while Johnny continued yelling, "No dinner for you tonight! Bad boy!"

"Jo, how did he get to the lasagna and the meat?" Johnny asked.

"I put the tray of lasagna and the bowl with the sauce meat on the counter to cool off while the garlic bread was cooking. It was only out for a few minutes."

"It sure didn't take Rusty long to make a pig of himself; no wonder why he was nowhere in sight," Johnny replied.

I shrugged my shoulders and said to our friends, "I'm sorry guys; I don't know what to say. I guess our dog was really hungry."

"Jo Ann, isn't Rusty Irish? Shouldn't he be eating something like corn beef and cabbage?" Anna Marie asked.

"I don't think so Anna Marie. At eight weeks old, Rusty became a Roseo. He is all Italian, even though he may look Irish."

"Well, I hope he enjoyed all the food. It looked delicious," Anna Marie said with a laugh.

All my hard work was for nothing, what a waste. Whatever lasagna and meat were left went right into the garbage. We ended up ordering pizza as we laughed at Rusty's latest episode.

That Sunday, I was out running errands. I didn't feel like making Sunday sauce two days in a row, so I picked up fresh lobsters that were on sale. Johnny enjoyed making stuffed lobsters, and they always came out delicious. Later on that day, after he steamed them, he was stuffing them while I was washing the large pot in the kitchen sink. Rusty came over to me and was pushing his head against my leg, nudging me to go out.

I turned around to talk to him. "Rusty, wait a minute. Mommy has to clean the pot first. I will take you out in a few minutes."

All of a sudden, the pot slipped out of my hands and hit the kitchen window, creating a large crack in the glass.

"Jo, you gotta be kidding me. You just broke the bathroom sink, and now the kitchen window. If it's not Rusty, it's you. It seems like the two of you are constantly competing with each other."

"Chill out. It's not my fault. What was the builder thinking when he installed the window so close to the sink anyway?"

"I gotta tell you; you and Rusty were sure made for each other."

"Thanks, I take that as a compliment."

"Not in a good way."

"Ha ha."

"Honey, I am really curious who makes the most destruction, you, or Rusty. I'm going to make a chart and write both of your names on it, and hang it on the wall. I want to see who the winner will be; I bet it will be pretty close."

"Very funny."

Things do break and get destroyed all the time—at least for me and Rusty they do. I don't know why, but with our unfortunate luck, these things always happen to us. All right, I admit that I am a little rough around the edges, but I always have been, and I've never denied it. As for Rusty, who knows? Maybe it's in the genes.

Chapter 10

Rusty to the Rescue

Rusty's loyalty to his family and his heroic qualities would rise if he felt someone was in danger or felt threatened. Our redhead was exceptionally smart when he wanted to be, having the common sense to call for help when someone, meaning me, needed it.

With Johnny working so much overtime, we had finally saved up enough money to renovate our kitchen. We ordered new appliances and new kitchen cabinets, along with butcher block countertops and backsplashes. Butcher block? What can I say, that was the style back in the early eighties. When the salesman gave us the high price for the installation of the cabinets, my husband decided to try installing them himself. Doing a great job, he completed the installation of the cabinets in a couple of days—with my help, of course. I was elated with the way my new kitchen cabinets were looking so far, but Johnny needed help from my brother, an electrician, to run the electrical wiring and help him install the countertops, since they were fairly large and heavy.

Over the weekend, I was busy lining our new kitchen cabinets with contact paper, and one of the bottom cabinets was approximately eight inches wide, but we needed it as filler. I reached into the cabinet to put the liner down, and when I tried to back out of the tiny cabinet, I couldn't; my head was wedged in. Trying my hardest to get my head out wasn't working; my ears were in the way of the cabinet opening. I called out to Johnny for help, but he couldn't hear me. He was upstairs in Ma's apartment fixing her closet door, and since my head was inside the cabinet, my voice was muffled.

Wiggling my butt to get out, I felt Rusty's presence behind me. I called out to him, "Rusty, help Mommy get out. I'm stuck."

Being so smart, Rusty grabbed hold of my jeans by my waist with his strong teeth and started pulling forcibly. I felt my butt moving, but my head wouldn't budge. Again I called out to him, "Rusty, go upstairs and get Daddy."

There went Rusty to the rescue. I heard the sound of his paws thumping on the floor.

As my mom later told me, Rusty understood exactly what I asked of him. He ran up the stairs to her apartment in a barking frenzy to get help for me. Rusty tried to get Johnny's attention by his persistent behavior—barking and nudging at Johnny as he kept turning to face the doorway. He wouldn't stop barking until Johnny finally figured out that Rusty was trying to tell him something. Putting his tools down, he went over to him. "What's up Rusty? What are you trying to tell Daddy?"

Running toward the stairs, Rusty lead the way down as Johnny and my mom followed him. Entering the kitchen, Rusty stopped short outside the kitchen cabinet where I was stuck and wiggling my butt from side to side to get out. Instead of having concern for me, Johnny and my mom were just laughing. However, I didn't think it was so funny.

"Ma, will you look at my wife?" said my husband. "She is as kooky as our dog. She outdid herself this time. This one is a classic."

I started yelling at them through the cabinet. "Hellooo, I'm in here. Is anyone going to get me out?"

"No, Lucy, we'll keep you in there for a little while," he said laughing.

All I wanted was to be out of that cabinet; it was awfully hot in there. I started screaming, "Get me out of here!"

To my advantage, my brother hadn't come over yet to install the electrical outlets, allowing Johnny the space he needed to remove the countertop on the section where my head was stuck. Ma went to get petroleum jelly, came back, and rubbed it on the back of my ears so Johnny could slide my head out. As he was pushing my head down, I shouted, "Whoa! Could you not press so hard? That hurts!"

Finally, he was able to push my head out. Once I stood up, I saw the tears of laughter running down their faces at the sight of me.

"Now I know where Rusty gets it from—you, his mother. You and your dog could be twins. Maybe you should dye your hair red to match your redheaded furry twin."

"You think you're so funny, Johnny; but know what? I like that. My redheaded furry twin. Rusty and I are soul mates. He is my hero and my protector. I would still be stuck in that stupid cabinet if it wasn't for my little boy."

Grateful to my Rusty, I gave him many hugs when I got out of the cabinet. In return, I received lots of wet kisses from him. I made sure to give him well-deserved treats that day. It was pure eagerness on Rusty's part to help me, demonstrating to us that he really did have a useful brain. The bump on his big red head proved that it was the "knot of knowledge," like I always thought.

Kitchens and I didn't mix too well. Once our kitchen was fully installed, it looked beautiful. I wanted to share it with our families, and since Thanksgiving was only a few weeks away, we decided it was going to be at our house that year. Bridget always made Thanksgiving dinner, and her turkey came out great every single year. This was going to be my first time making a turkey. I hoped my turkey was going to come out as good as hers. I stuffed the inside of the turkey with our Sicilian recipe that was passed down from generations. Then I seasoned the outside of our eighteen-pound turkey and put it in the oven.

While the turkey was cooking, our nephews were performing a show for us in the living room, and I was preoccupied enjoying them. Suddenly, Rusty started barking his head off. Hearing the sound of his bark coming from the kitchen, my mother-in-law, Kay, ran into the kitchen first and shouted, "Oh my goodness! There's a fire in the oven!"

We all followed her into the kitchen and saw flames shooting out of the oven. I cried out, "Oh no! My brand new oven; I hope it's not ruined."

Johnny gave me one of his frustrated looks. My father-in-law, Joe, opened the oven door quickly and we saw that the turkey was totally burnt. He turned the oven off. "It looks like the turkey was too heavy for the aluminum pan and it cracked. The grease splattered everywhere. Keep the oven door closed; the fire will go out on its own. Meanwhile, I'll open the windows. Once the fire goes out, I'll remove the pan with the turkey."

Thankfully, Rusty alerted us, or it could've been worse. Rusty became our fire marshal and saved the day. He was always on target when it came to protecting us. There went my first turkey dinner, into the garbage. We ended up getting Chinese takeout. After the oven cooled down several hours later, my father-in-law took the burnt turkey and the aluminum pan out of the oven, put them in a trash bag, and threw it outside in the garbage pail.

The next day it was time to clean our dirty oven. When we purchased the oven, the cost was a considerable amount less than the self-cleaning oven. Since we were on a tight budget, we opted for the less expensive one, but now I wish we had purchased the self-cleaning one.

"Jo, I'm going to clean the oven."

I appreciated his help, but I was capable of cleaning the oven. "Thanks, but I'll do it. I thought you were going to clean out the gutters? All I have to do is spray the cleaner in the oven and wait. I'll be fine."

"Are you sure you can handle it?"

"Of course I can." *Why would he think I couldn't?*

Following the directions on the aerosol can, I sprayed the oven cleaner inside the oven. I noticed that the light bulb in the oven was also full of grease, so I sprayed it, too. Then I let the cleaner do its job for the hour. I was playing with Rusty in the house while Johnny was outside cleaning out the gutters. A little while later, he came in and asked, "How's the oven looking?"

"Good, I'm going to wipe the cleaner off in a few minutes."

"Okay. I'll go back outside."

Taking the role as the good little housewife, I started wiping the oven cleaner off with a wet sponge and soapy water. Suddenly my arm started feeling funny; there was a tingling, then painful sensation, and then my arm started to shake. At that point the light bulb inside the oven burst in my hand. I let out a scream. "Ouch!" Rusty raced to the window and started barking nonstop. Johnny ran into the house to see what was wrong. I showed him my hand. Immediately, he cleaned the pieces of glass out of my hand, drenching in it peroxide and then he bandaged it. Looking puzzled and concerned, he asked, "How did the light bulb blow up in your hand?"

"Well, the light bulb was full of grease, so I sprayed it with the oven cleaner and then I was washing it off."

"Honey, do you realize that you were just electrocuted? You never put anything wet on electric. Wait till your brother, the electrician, hears this one."

"Oops, first time for everything," I said with a laugh.

Surely I wasn't thinking when I washed the light bulb while it was still screwed in. From that day on, I learned my lesson. I will never do that again.

Thanks to my Rusty, he knew when I needed help—again—and he was always there for me; we had each other's backs.

Me and my hero

Chapter 11

North Massapequa, Here We Come

Our Valley Stream home looked great, but we decided we needed a larger house for our future family. We listed our house with a Realtor, who put our two-bedroom home for sale. Since Johnny and I were at work during the day, Ma offered to show the house when the Realtors brought potential buyers over. As far as Johnny and I were concerned, there was no possible way Rusty could stay in the house if strangers came to look at it. Without a doubt, he would go into protective mode and scare them away. We knew it wasn't going to be a simple task for her, considering Rusty's overall strength and stamina. It would also be difficult when he was asleep, since he didn't want to be disturbed. Our beautiful redhead loved getting his beauty sleep. When we told her about our concerns, she said Rusty was a good boy when he was upstairs with her, and he shouldn't be a problem.

Practically every day, as soon as she received a phone call from one of the Realtors, the chaos would begin. First, Ma attached Rusty's leash. She walked him down the flight of stairs, through our house, and out of the house, and into the yard. She then opened the gate brought him into his dog run, squeezed out of it, and made sure she locked the gate. Then she went back upstairs to join the Realtor and potential buyers to answer any questions. After they left, she went back downstairs, to get Rusty. She unlocked the gate, squeezed into the dog run, attached Rusty's leash, and brought him back upstairs. Thirty minutes later, another phone call came from a different Realtor. There she went again—she attached Rusty's leash, walked him down the stairs, through our house, out of the house, into the yard, opened the gate, brought him into his dog run, squeezed out of it, and made sure she locked the gate. Then she went back upstairs to join the Realtor and potential buyers. After they left, she went back downstairs to get Rusty, but he wouldn't budge. Our rascally redhead was too busy running back and forth chasing birds, refusing to go inside with her. He looked at my mom with a puzzled expression on his face, as if to voice his opinion. *Not again Grandma, I'm having fun. Leave me alone.* By this time, she had had enough for the day.

While our house was on the market, we went looking at resale houses. Many houses we saw had layouts that fitted our needs, but the backyards weren't large enough to offer what our athletic redhead was accustomed to. Luckily, we found a three-bedroom, high-ranch house in North Massapequa that we really liked. It was on another corner lot, in a pretty suburban town on the South Shore of Long Island. The backyard was fully fenced in for our rambunctious dog, which was a plus. It also had an apartment for my mother downstairs. Our house in Valley Stream went under contract in a matter of weeks. We signed the contracts for both houses and were to take possession in thirty days.

I wanted to get decorating ideas for our new house, so I thought it would be a good idea to take a ride to see the new community being built again. "Hey, Johnny, let's check out the model homes tomorrow and get some decorating ideas."

"Are you kidding me? Remember the last fiasco when we went to look at model homes?"

"That was because I probably had food poisoning. I'm fine now. It will be fun."

"Okay, sure. Let's go."

"Listen, I feel bad leaving Rusty home. We've been going out a lot lately house-hunting on the weekends. Let's take him with us. He likes going for car rides. On a Sunday morning, there shouldn't be too many people looking at the models. If there are, we'll just leave him in the car with the windows partially open since the weather is supposed to be beautiful tomorrow."

"No way, we can't trust him."

"Don't worry, he'll be fine. And it's early, he won't bother anyone."

"Okay, but he better be good, or I'll pretend I don't know that crazy dog."

When we pulled into the parking lot, our car was the only one there. Perfect! There was no one in the model homes, meaning we could take Rusty inside with us. We were having a good time going through the different models. The decor was very stylish, and they were all beautifully decorated. In one of the models, Johnny went into the garage to look at the hot water heater while Rusty and I were walking through the model home. All of a sudden, he saw a bird outside the window; he yanked the leash out of my hand, and took off. As I ran after him, I bumped into one of the coffee tables and heard a crash. Johnny ran out from the garage when he heard the loud noise. Returning to the living room, he saw me standing over a pile of glass on the floor, and Rusty was standing on top of the couch barking at the window. Shaking his head, he said, "Was it you, or Rusty?"

I giggled as I explained, "I guess it was both of us. Rusty saw a bird and took off. I ran after him, and I bumped into the coffee table. I don't know how, but my pocketbook hit the display of glass vases on the table. It was like a domino effect. One vase fell, and then they all started tumbling down, hitting the tile floor."

"Weren't you holding him?"

"Of course I was; but when he saw the bird, he pulled the leash right out of my hand."

Johnny just stood there and laughed, something he was getting accustomed to. "Wait until I tell your brother this one, Lucy. I don't know who is worse, you or your furry twin. Let's get outta here before anyone sees us, or we may have to pay for the damage."

"Sounds good to me; let's go."

So we ran out of that model home in a heartbeat.

Moving farther out east to North Massapequa, Johnny would have an extra half-hour commute to New York City, but he was fine with it. For me, I was going to transfer from the branch in Valley Stream to a branch in Freeport, about a twenty-minute drive away. The new branch wasn't close to our house like it was in Valley Stream. In other words, I wouldn't be able to go home for lunch to spend time with Rusty anymore. I was not happy about the situation, and I bet neither was my little boy, but I had a good position at that banking institution, so I did what I had to do.

My mother-in-law, Kay, was also excited for us. She loved the fact that we were purchasing a larger house and was hoping we would be starting a family soon. Johnny being the only child, Kay couldn't wait to become a grandmother. Even though she was attached to Rusty, she wanted to be a grandma to a real baby. One of the main topics of our conversations was that she wanted to be blessed with a granddaughter. For some reason, she said she knew it would be a girl when I got pregnant.

Unfortunately, two weeks before we were supposed to close on both houses, Kay was admitted into Sloan Kettering Hospital in New York City because her cancer had spread. Johnny visited her twice daily—once on his lunch hour and once when he went with me later after I got out of work. Ma stayed with Rusty, fed him, and let him out—a big help considering we usually came home after ten o'clock every night. It surely was an advantage having her living upstairs from us.

Two days before the closings, Johnny, my mom, and I went to the North Massapequa house to do our inspection. As we were leaving the house, Rusty seemed confused and looked sad, as if something was bothering him. He didn't like change and started to notice. Assuming we could trust him and leave him home alone since he was getting older, wasn't a good idea, as we later found out.

During the inspection, Johnny noticed that all the phone jacks and phone wiring had been removed in the house. That was really odd, but it meant we needed to call the phone company as soon as we took possession to have new phone service installed.

By the time we came home only two hours later, we were flabbergasted when we walked into our house. Disaster had struck. *News break: Earthquake of 8.0 on the Richter scale hits lovely home in Valley Stream.* Normally when we arrived home, Rusty greeted us with the utmost enthusiasm that made us smile, but not that time. When it came to our rascally redhead, we could always expect the unexpected, but we never imagined anything like this. We stared in dismay; it looked as if someone had come into our kitchen with a sledgehammer and demolished it. Catching him in action, we were outraged at the sight of him destroying our kitchen. Making holes in the kitchen walls,

Rusty tore off full sheets of wallpaper from basically every part of the kitchen. He had proceeded to rip off the sheetrock exposing the metal studs and electrical wiring. Bent nails, torn-up wallpaper, and pieces of sheetrock were scattered all over the floor. Every wooden baseboard had been ripped off the walls and broken in pieces. Besides destroying our kitchen, he had gotten into at least ten of the boxes we had packed. They were all broken up, and the contents inside them were spread all over the house.

As expected, Johnny flipped out. He took a piece of the baseboard molding that was lying on the floor and ran after Rusty, shouting at the top of his lungs. "Rusty, what the hell are you doing? Are you that crazy? You're not a dog, you're a bulldozing machine! You belong on a farm!"

Rusty looked deeply wounded and looked straight into my eyes. *Mommy, I have no idea what happened. The kitchen just went berserk and things started falling off of the walls.*

"Again, Rusty? I don't think so," I said.

Then Rusty dropped the large piece of wallpaper that was hanging from his mouth, lowered his head in shame, and ran out of the kitchen, knowing he was in deep trouble.

I was nervous to even ask, but I had to. "Johnny, is this fixable?"

He shot me one of his not-so-happy looks. "Fixable by who? Calling in a contractor who will have to work through the middle of the night costing us thousands of dollars, or me, working my ass off through the middle of the night and getting no sleep to fix up his latest destruction?"

I should've kept my mouth shut. Just as we had gone to inspect the house in North Massapequa before the closing, the buyers were coming over to inspect our house the following day. Of all the times to pull that crazy stunt, this was one when Rusty's timing was terrible. It meant that the three of us had to work hard and fast.

For Rusty's sake, I was always his advocate. After Johnny calmed down, I told him that maybe Rusty heard something in the walls. Who knows? It could've been a mouse or a rat, it was an older house. But Johnny didn't want to hear it.

Within minutes, we drove to Pergament Home Center to purchase the materials (again) that he needed to fix Rusty's latest disaster. Without a doubt, I surely thought Johnny was going to kill Rusty this time, but instead he put him in his dog run in time-out while we went to the store.

Once we came home, Johnny put Rusty in his room and put the baby gate up so he wouldn't get in our way. The three of us worked as a team repairing the kitchen so the buyers wouldn't notice anything out of the ordinary. It was to our advantage that Johnny had become handy and was able to replace the sheetrock and match the wallpaper and the color of the paint as closely as possible. Ma was pretty good at measuring, cutting, and hanging up the wallpaper with my help, and I was doing the bending, climbing, and pasting. Once we replaced the wallpaper, Johnny cut and stained the wood and put up the new baseboard moldings. It took us several long, hard hours, but when we finished, the kitchen looked good as new. After we repaired the kitchen, we started picking up all the contents that were scattered all over the house from the ripped up boxes, and repacked them.

When the buyers came over the following day, they never noticed the difference. *Now that was a close call.* Late Friday afternoon, both closings were completed and went off without a hitch.

On Saturday morning, Johnny's friends came over to help load the U-Haul truck in Valley Stream and then unload it when we got to North Massapequa. Tied down on the back of it was Rusty's doghouse. The red and white wooden doghouse with his name on the front of it stopped traffic as drivers honked their horns and waved, pointing to the doghouse in approval. *North Massapequa, here we come—and Rusty too!*

Our first day in North Massapequa

Chapter 12

Compassion Kicked In

Moving into our new house, we were so excited, but we didn't know our happiness would only last forty-eight hours.

Johnny and I took a week off of work to get settled in. The Long Island Lighting Company (LILCO) came out to the house right away and turned on the electricity, but not the phone company. We had to wait until Monday for a technician to come out and install the new phone lines. We never found out why the previous owner removed all the phone wiring.

Our section of the house was up a short flight of steps, with the exception of the family room, which was downstairs leading out to the backyard. My mom's apartment was also downstairs, but on the other side of the house. We had access to her apartment from a small hallway leading to our family room, or through her own private side entrance that faced Broadway, which was a fairly busy street.

The first thing Johnny did when we moved into the house was install the baby gate in one of the bedrooms for Rusty. Knowing we would be leaving the front door open, going in and out bringing all the furniture and boxes inside, we couldn't take the chance of our nutty dog running out. One of the two extra bedrooms was already painted blue and faced the back of the house. Considering Rusty was a boy, I thought we would give him the blue bedroom. The front bedroom was bright and airy, getting the southern exposure, perfect for our future baby's nursery.

Immediately, Rusty went on a tour of the house as he ran around with joy. Scouting out his new home, he explored each room. Next he proceeded downstairs to Ma's place, then out to his big yard. Thoroughly inspecting it, he went for a fast dash around—running back and forth, checking out each tree and bush, peeing on each to claim his new territory. I wondered just how much pee our dog could have in him. Pee just kept squirting out—the continuous fountain of pee. Then he moved on to digging his first hole, smiling wholeheartedly with his tail wagging. Adjustment to the new house went well for our rascally redhead; we got his approval.

The following Sunday morning, we went to visit Kay in the hospital. We arrived in Kay's private room, and her spirits weren't as good as the day before. As I sat on the bed with her, she told me that she was in excruciating pain. Her nurse came into the room a few minutes later and Johnny asked her, "Why isn't my mom doing as well as yesterday? She's in a lot of pain?"

"There is no change in her condition. Some patients have good days and some patients have bad days; however, her doctor did increase her pain medication," she said.

We stayed with Kay for several hours and then gave her a kiss goodbye. "We'll see you tomorrow. Feel better. We love you."

Something made me stop for a minute. Call it premonition. I don't know why, but as we were walking down the corridor to leave the hospital, I told Johnny, "Wait a minute. I'll be right back."

"Where are you going?" he asked curiously.

"I want to give the nurse Roe's phone number since we don't have a phone yet."

We didn't know any of our neighbors, and Roe was a good friend of mine who had moved to Long Island from Canarsie two years before we did. Living only ten minutes away from us, she was the only one I could think of whose phone number I could leave with the hospital in case they needed to reach us. I knew in my heart that we would see Kay the following day; it was highly unlikely that the hospital would call Roe. Knowing Kay, she would fight the cancer again; she was young and a strong woman. She was truly looking forward to my getting pregnant.

Johnny and I decided earlier that when Kay was released from the hospital, she'd come and live with us to recuperate for a month or two, or however long it took for her to fully recover. My father-in-law, Joe, couldn't take any more time off of work, and she needed care. Now that we had three bedrooms in our new house, we had plenty of space to take good care of her. Also, since my mom was living downstairs, she said she would love to help Kay and spend time with her while Johnny and I were at work. Plus, Kay loved Rusty, and Rusty adored his grandma. He would be great medicine for her. The change of atmosphere was going to be good for her, and Joe would stay over on the weekends.

On Monday morning we were getting ready to go to the hospital. We figured when we came home later in the afternoon, we'd start unpacking the boxes while the phone lines were being installed. All of a sudden the doorbell rang. *Who could that be?* Someone showing up unexpectedly was cause for surprise, or alarm. I thought maybe a neighbor was coming over to make an introduction with a *"welcome to the neighborhood"* cake, which was very sweet and common in Long Island. Answering the door, we saw it was Roe standing there crying. Walking into our house, she found it difficult to get the words out, but finally she told us that the hospital had called her a few minutes earlier and informed her that Johnny's mom had passed away. Neither Johnny nor I said a word; we were in total shock. Then the three of us just hugged.

Putting the burden on Roe to tell us this dreadful news, I felt awful. I never really imagined the hospital would call her. Before Roe left to go home, she offered to help us in any way we needed, which was very sweet of her. I thanked her and told her I would let her know.

The unexpected news was devastating. Knowing that Kay died all alone left us heartbroken. If only the doctors had told us that she didn't have much time, we never would've left her bedside. Kay fought the cancer so hard, going for treatments day after day for over a year. Even though the treatments made her feel terribly sick, she still remained hopeful. Kay's passing was so unfortunate. She had so much to live for; she wanted to be a grandmother more than anything in the world. I made a promise to her right then and there, that when we have children, I would tell them all about their Grandma Kay.

After the shock set in, I was hysterical crying and I saw the emptiness and the devastation on my husband's face. All of a sudden, Johnny stormed out of the house, grief-stricken, without saying a word as tears flooded his eyes. I ran out the door after him. "Where are you going?" I asked. He just kept on walking and ignored me.

Sensing that something was wrong, Rusty ran downstairs to get his grandma. When they came upstairs, I told her that Kay had passed away. She was also shocked and devastated. Besides being family, Ma and Kay had become very good friends.

"Honey, where's Johnny?" she asked.

"I don't know. I'm really worried about him. He stormed out of the house. I think he wants to be left alone."

"He shouldn't be alone. I'll see if I could find him," she said.

"Thanks. I'll finish getting ready so we can leave as soon as he comes home."

When Johnny came back in the house, he said that we needed to leave to go to Canarsie to pick up his dad, and make the funeral arrangements. Ma decided to stay at the house and wait for the phone technician to come. We couldn't be without phones. The plan was that after the phone installation was completed, she would feed Rusty, let him out, and then drive to Canarsie to meet us at my in-laws' house.

When we arrived, we saw that my father-in-law was in bad shape. Of course he was heartbroken, but Joe was also a heavy drinker. He couldn't deal with stress like most people. Hitting the bottle was his answer. Plus, his blood pressure spiked. Johnny was so upset. "Look at him, it figures," he said.

My heart was breaking for my husband during that difficult time. Losing his mom and seeing his dad in that condition, he now only had me. In the meantime, Johnny and I had to make major decisions and arrangements at the funeral home. We wanted everything to be perfect for his mom.

Ma met us in Canarsie a few hours later. After all the preparations were completed, we stopped to get a quick dinner. "Ma, what time did the phone repairman finish?" Johnny asked.

"He finished about four-thirty. I fed Rusty, let him out, and brought him back inside the house, but guess what happened on my way here?"

I was concerned. "What happened? Did you get a flat tire?"

"No. While I was driving on the Southern State Parkway on my way to Canarsie, about twenty minutes later, I wondered if I put the baby gate up for Rusty leading downstairs. I panicked, knowing the damage he could do. I got off at the next highway exit, turned around and got back on the parkway and headed toward North Massapequa. When I arrived home, I saw that I was mistaken. I did put the baby gate up for Rusty, and he was fine. So I headed back to Canarsie."

"Wow, you did a lot of driving tonight," I said.

"You know, as well as I do that we can't trust Rusty when he's home alone," Ma answered.

Johnny stepped in. "You got that right, Ma. Thanks for going back to check on him. We really didn't need him to destroy the house, not now."

That night when we came home, Rusty sensed something was still wrong. Seeing the sadness on our faces and watching me having my moments of crying, he just stayed on his bed in his new room and left us to grieve.

The following day, the three of us went to Canarsie for Kay's wake, leaving Rusty plenty of food, water, and lights on in the house. Back then, a typical Italian wake usually lasted for three full days, until late at night. Rusty was amazing. He didn't cause any destruction in the house. He didn't even pee or poop in the house even though he was alone for all those hours each day.

When we came home from the funeral, Rusty didn't greet us with the usual playful demeanor that we were accustomed to. Yes, he was happy to see us; his tail wagged, but he was more subdued. Rusty's selfless behavior proved he sensed our loss of his Grandma Kay's passing.

Several days after the funeral, Rusty's character kept improving. Our sympathetic dog was there for us in our time of need. Joe came over to spend the weekend with us and Rusty was excited when he saw him, but he seemed confused. He probably wondered why his Grandma Kay wasn't with his Grandpa Joe; they always came together. Jumping up onto the bay window, he looked toward their car to see where she was and wouldn't stop barking.

Since he looked puzzled, I sat him down and explained to him, "Rusty, Grandma Kay was very sick and she went up to heaven. She can't come over to visit us anymore, so you have to be extra nice to Grandpa Joe."

It seemed that he understood what I said. He looked so sad. Going over to Joe, Rusty put his big red head on his grandpa's lap, offering his wordless comfort as he sensed his loss. Joe kept petting him. "You're such a good boy, Rusty," he said.

Miraculously, Rusty was good medicine for all of us during that difficult time. Displaying his kindness, his compassion, and his sympathy; he demonstrated his huge heart, filled with unconditional love for his entire family.

Chapter 13

Dog Turned Shark

Once we unpacked all the boxes, we started painting the inside of our house atrium white. Actually, I enjoyed painting the walls in the smaller rooms. Johnny's job included painting the ceilings, painting the larger rooms, cutting the edges for me, and touching up all the spots I missed. Johnny knew all too well how clumsy I was and what a sloppy painter he had for a wife. I would get more paint on me than the walls, but between the two us, we had fun and got the job done.

While we painted the three bedrooms, Rusty was content sleeping in his favorite place inside the bay window, staying out of our way. When we were ready to paint the living room-dining room section, we thought it would be better if Rusty wasn't upstairs with us, so I brought him downstairs to stay with his grandma.

A couple of hours later we stopped to take a lunch break. I took the cold cuts out of the refrigerator and the Italian bread out of the pantry. Just to make sure Rusty was still downstairs with his grandma, I called down to her. "Ma, how's Rusty?" I asked.

"He's sleeping."

"Okay, thanks. We're going to take a break and eat lunch."

Johnny was feeling a little uneasy. "Jo, I don't think it's a good idea to leave the paint out. We can't trust him."

"He'll be fine. He's downstairs sleeping."

"I hope you're right."

After we ate lunch, we went into the living room to finish painting, but our mischievous redhead beat us to it. Rusty paw-painted the living room, dining room and everywhere in between. His humongous paw prints were all over the walls, the floors, the furniture, and the TV; you name it, he paw-painted it. *And to think, I was the sloppy painter.* But I must say, the way he arranged his paw prints on the wall looked like a painter's masterpiece, but I didn't think Johnny would agree.

Oblivious to what was going on around him, Rusty was so focused on what he was doing that he didn't even hear Johnny sneak up behind him. "Yo, psychopath! What are you doing?" he shouted at Rusty.

"See, Jo, I told you we couldn't trust him."

I wrong again. Standing in the tray of paint, our redheaded Picasso took his head out of the five-gallon paint bucket with the paint roller still in his mouth. His whole face was covered in paint except his eyeballs; even his long pink tongue was atrium white. If that wasn't bad enough, his long ears were covered, dripping in paint. The expression on his face clearly showed that he knew that he had done wrong. As he ran away from Johnny, he accidently brushed up against the freshly painted walls. The whole right side of his body was covered in paint, and his red hair ended up getting pasted to the walls. "Rusty, stop!" Johnny yelled. "Look what you're doing to our walls, you crazy dog!"

My mom ran upstairs when she heard Rusty getting yelled at.

"I thought he was sleeping," I told her.

"Last time I checked he was. I went into the bathroom for a minute, and when I came out, he was gone. When I didn't see him and it was quiet, I assumed you called him to go back upstairs."

Actually, I couldn't blame her. It wasn't her fault, but I guess I should've listened to my husband.

Instead of going back to painting, it was time to give Rusty a bath, as if we had nothing better to do. As soon as Johnny said it was bath time, Rusty ran straight into the bathroom and jumped right into the bathtub. Rusty enjoyed getting baths. While Johnny was busy bathing Rusty, I was nervous and called the vet. I told him that Rusty had had a paint roller in his mouth that was full of paint, and I asked whether we should be worried. The vet asked me if it was latex paint. I looked on the can, and it was. He wasn't too concerned and told me that latex paint wasn't toxic to dogs. He said Rusty might have an upset stomach for the day, but he would be fine. After the phone call, I went into the bathroom to join Johnny and our crazy redhead.

"Johnny, I called the vet."

"What did he say?"

"He said latex paint is nontoxic to dogs. He'll be fine."

"That's good—one less thing to worry about."

"Yeah, I know."

There was no such thing as a quick bath for Rusty. Because of his large size, the amount of long feathering hair, and his always being full of dirt, or at that time paint, it took Johnny at least thirty minutes to get him clean. Rusty sat patiently while Johnny lathered him up with baby shampoo and conditioner and rinsed him off twice to get all the paint off. Johnny towel-dried him, and then it was my turn to take over. Taking my hair blower, I blew out his beautiful red hair, now free of paint to perfection.

After his bath, we brought him back downstairs by his grandma, and this time he wasn't coming back upstairs until we were ready for him. It took us quite a while to handpick his hair off of the freshly painted walls, clean up the paint that spilled on the floor, and wash his paw prints off of the TV, the furniture, and the floor. Then Johnny had to repaint over Rusty's paw-painting on the walls.

Rusty's relationship with food was chaotically demanding, even though we established a regular meal schedule and many treats for him. Our redhead was no ordinary dog. High maintenance was more his style; that's for sure. Needless to say, the spoiled little brat was persistent and did not like to hear the word "no" when it came to food.

Breakfast on Sunday mornings is one of Johnny's favorite meals, whereas I'm not a breakfast person. However, Rusty was a fan of pancakes. As soon as Johnny took the pancake griddle out of the kitchen cabinet, Rusty knew it was time for breakfast. While Johnny was mixing the pancake batter, Rusty would stand up on his hind legs with his paws resting on the counter, watching his daddy spoon the batter into perfect circles. With his adorable, innocent Irish setter look, he would nudge Johnny. *Daddy, hurry up. I'm hungry and I'm waiting patiently. Can I have my pancakes please?* As usual, Johnny made extra pancakes for Rusty, but our boy would only eat his pancakes with maple syrup. If I didn't pour the syrup on his pancakes, he would sit there, refusing to touch them, and bark. His deep piercing bark penetrated right through our ears until I caved in and gave him the pancake syrup. When our royal redhead's pancakes were acceptable, Rusty wouldn't just eat them, he would inhale them.

When it came to dinner on Sunday's, Rusty loved his pasta and meatballs, but he wouldn't eat it with just plain sauce; he also had to have grated cheese on it. He insisted on Locatelli or Pecorino Romano cheese, and he requested lots of it on top of his pasta, like a typical Italian. One day, I bought a brand of Parmesan cheese in a green container for a considerable amount cheaper than the imported cheese. I figured he wouldn't notice the difference in the flavor; after all, he was a dog. I poured some of the less expensive Parmesan cheese over his pasta and meatballs. After he tasted it, he flipped his bowl over and looked at me with an insulted expression. *Are you kidding me? What is this! You call this grated cheese? I'm not eating this imitation cheese!*

The simple fact was that our redhead was as stubborn as a mule and as demanding as can be. Determined to get what he wanted, he would go over to the refrigerator and try to open the door to get the cheese he craved. With no success, he tried his hardest to communicate with me by barking weird sounds that echoed throughout the house. I threw up my hands. "I give up, you nut! How do you know the difference between the two cheeses?"

Reincarnated? Absolutely! In his prior life, he definitely had to have been a chef or a food critic. What other explanation could there have possibly been for his knowing the difference between the imported cheese and the imitation cheese, as well as pancakes with and without maple syrup? Just to shut him up, I gave him new food and sprinkled the insisted-upon Locatelli cheese on top of his pasta and meatballs. Again, when his highness's pasta was to his liking, he inhaled it.

Aside from making his food-preferences known, Rusty acted as if he had an alarm clock in his stomach. His eating habits had surely changed since he was a sweet little puppy. Promptly at six-thirty every night, Rusty sat in front of his bowl drooling, pushing it with his nose, barking until I got the message that he was hungry. Filling it up with a generous amount of dog food was never enough. Despite eating three cups of dry food mixed with one can of wet dog food, he had a bottomless pit. Our hungry redhead was such a messy eater. He wolfed down his food with gusto. One would think every meal was his last. Time and time again, kibbles went flying out of his bowl and landed all over the kitchen floor. After devouring the food in his bowl, he proceeded to finish the kibbles that he scattered on the floor.

After inhaling his dinner, he would also be the sloppiest drinker on the planet. When he drank water from his bowl just like when he drank from the toilet, he splattered water all over the walls and floor, including the toilet seat, never licking his mouth after he drank. I guess I should've listened to Tommy when he warned us not to let Rusty drink from the toilet; a little too late now.

Rusty sometimes didn't tell the truth and was a good actor. Time and time again while I was getting dinner ready, our hungry redhead would be barking at his bowl. How many nights would Johnny and I repeat the same conversation?

"Jo, didn't you feed Rusty tonight?"

"Of course I did."

"Well, he's acting like he hasn't eaten all day."

"Don't let him fool you. He likes to sit next to his bowl and put on his adorable Irish setter charm. Just look into his eyes and you'll see what I'm talking about."

Johnny would go over to Rusty and sit down next to him. "Rusty, tell me the truth. Did Mommy feed you tonight?"

Rusty would move his face close to Johnny's and looked him straight in the eyes. *No, Daddy. Mommy was busy and forgot to put food in my bowl, and I am hungry. Please feed me.*

"Jo, you are so right. But I guess he's still hungry. I'll give him a few dog biscuits."

"Who has the soft spot for him now?" I said as we both laughed.

His obsession with food was apparent. Rusty was the master of counter surfing. Any food that was on the counter, such as my lasagna, it disappeared in a flash. Although he ate tremendous amounts of food, there wasn't an ounce of fat on his body. He was lean and pure muscle with a fast metabolism that we could only dream of.

In addition to his reputation for overconsumption of food, he was famous for chewing up shoes, socks, slippers, sneakers, and boots. Apparently Rusty had a fixation for items related to feet.

Our dog also had a set of teeth like a shark. You name it; he chewed it. Outside in the yard he was famous for chewing rocks, the patio deck, which was made out of pressure-treated wood, the aluminum patio chairs, the watering hose, and the bottom of the shed, just to name a few items. And let's not forget that he turned Frisbees, tennis balls and footballs into mulch. It was just amazing that he never chipped a tooth.

After we completed the painting in our new home, the walls looked great, but Johnny didn't like the way the parquet floors looked in the hallway and dining room; they appeared to be dull and worn. It was definitely more noticeable with the new paint on the walls, so he decided to re-stain and polish them over the weekend. Rusty stayed downstairs with his grandma while Johnny worked on the floors. When he finished, they looked brand new. He did a great job!

The following weekend, we were going out to dinner with our good friends Sheri and Andy. Whenever we left our house, we had to be on high alert, never knowing what kind of damage to expect from our rascally redhead. When we returned home, without a doubt, Rusty had been at it again. As soon as we walked into the kitchen, Johnny noticed that there were broken pieces of wood on the dining room floor.

"Rusty! Where are you? I'm gonna kill you!"

"Why? What did he do now?" I asked.

"Take a look at the dining room floor, and you'll see what the monster did."

Looking down at the floor, I was in total shock. All I could think of was *Oh no! He's in real trouble.* Our mischievous redhead had done a number on our dining room parquet floor. As unbelievable as it was—who would ever think our dog would take apart a parquet floor—he had done it. He had ripped off a whole section of the wooden planks, starting at the corner of the dining room, and he had chewed six of them. His teeth marks were pretty evident on the wood, and the ends of the planks were ground away.

Johnny was furious. "That's it! I've had it with him. He's outta here!" Grabbing a piece of the parquet flooring, Johnny ran after Rusty, chasing him throughout the house as Rusty ran for cover.

Despite the fact that Johnny worked so hard on the parquet floors, the dining room floor was destroyed. Trying to figure Rusty out, I looked at the floor closely. I noticed that Johnny hadn't put up the new baseboard moldings in the dining room yet. Knowing Rusty, he needed to keep busy, and he saw the small space between the floor and the wall, and that was all he needed to amuse himself. Life with Rusty—there was never a dull moment. *Too bad there was no Internet back then; we may have been able to find a dog psychiatrist. God knows, he needed one.*

That evening, we settled in the living room and got into a heated discussion. "Jo, think about it. There is no way we can keep him. He continues to damage everything inside and outside of the house. This is the second house that he has destroyed. We have to get rid of him. I'm going to ask Gary if he knows someone who will take Rusty off of our hands."

Granted, I knew Rusty messed up, but I didn't want to hear it. "You could forget about talking to Gary about getting rid of Rusty. This is Rusty's home and he isn't going anywhere!"

A few months later, with all the repairs completed, our new house was finally becoming a home. Our next step was finding a formal dining room set. We went furniture shopping and came across a pretty Mediterranean-style wooden set.

That Saturday, Rusty was downstairs with his grandma so that he wouldn't go crazy when he saw the deliverymen in our house. Once the furniture was delivered and set up, the room looked beautiful. When they left, Rusty came upstairs; he walked around the new furniture curiously but didn't give it a second thought. While we were watching TV later that night, Rusty was playing with his toys in the living room and didn't go near the new dining room set.

Upon waking up the following morning, I was excited to unpack my china and stemware and arrange it in my new china closet. While I was unpacking the china, Johnny came in and commented on how nice the furniture looked. Suddenly, he said, "Jo, look at this? I didn't even notice that the pedestal was damaged when they delivered it yesterday."

"That sucks. Maybe we should call the store and tell them about the damage, and they'll bring us a new table."

Johnny crawled underneath the table to look closely at the damage. "Forget about it. The pedestal wasn't damaged when they delivered it; the damage is due to teeth marks! And guess whose teeth marks? Our shark!"

"No way! When did he do this?" I asked.

"When do you think he did it? Probably while we were sleeping," Johnny snapped. *Uh oh, Rusty is in trouble, again.*

We hadn't even owned the dining room furniture for twenty-four hours, and the base of our new dining room table was ruined. Rusty had left his mark—not by peeing this time. Instead, our sneaky redhead had chomped away at the wooden pedestal base that held up the table. There were at least ten large teeth marks straight across, deep into the wood. If that wasn't bad enough, he had also chewed all four corners of the base, until the wood finish was raw, by taking chunks of wood out. Evidently, Rusty had acquired a taste for wood in addition to everything else. Both of us yelled at him, "Bad boy! What did you do?" And the jury reached its verdict: Guilty on all counts!

I had done everything I could possibly do to protect him time and time again, but not that time. For the rest of the day, Rusty was in solitary confinement; we were not letting the fugitive out of his room. Every now and then, Johnny took him out on his leash to go potty, but that was it. Johnny knew Rusty would put on his Irish charm for me and I would give in to our spoiled brat. With him, he would be stern. There would be no running around in the yard, no playtime, and no treats for him that day. The redheaded criminal needed to do some hard time as a convicted felon. We just didn't know what we were going to do with our crazy dog.

Johnny tried as best as he could to match the stain on the wooden pedestal. He sanded it and restained it, but Rusty's teeth marks were still embedded in the table base, and the finish was different from the rest of the dining room table. Even years later, it never looked quite right.

Chapter 14

Absence Makes the Heart Grow Fonder

Ma went to visit my grandparents in Florida in January and February of that year. A few weeks after the dining room table fiasco, we decided we needed a break. We had a three-day weekend for Presidents' Day and thought it would be fun to take a trip to the Pocono Mountains in Northeast Pennsylvania with our friends Anna Marie and Frank. Winter was the perfect time to go the Poconos. There was so much to do, especially skiing.

Our long weekend was going to be our first time leaving Rusty. With his grandma in Florida, we had no one to watch him. The problem was Rusty was going through the terrible twos. That meant endless patience was required, and our relatives saw what a handful he was.

Bridget knew Rusty was a prankster, and sometimes she laughed. Other times she wondered if he would ever grow up. My big sister didn't share my enthusiasm for him. Tommy thought Rusty was the dumbest dog ever and continuously said, "Your dog is from another planet." Truthfully, Tommy disliked Rusty, but Rusty didn't take a liking to Tommy either. Dogs can sense when a person doesn't like them, so they were out as dog sitters.

Andrew tolerated Rusty, but disapproved of the bizarre things he did. He said Rusty reminded him of me when I was young, except for the red hair. He never saw a dog so destructive and thickheaded in all his life. However, Rusty did like his Uncle Andrew. My sister-in-law, Stephanie thought Rusty was beautiful and an airhead, but she enjoyed him. The problem was they had a cat, and, knowing Rusty, he'd probably have scared the cat to death. So they were out.

Next were Cousin John and Delores. Delores was a dog lover, so she was attached to Rusty. Rusty was always excited to see them. Every time they came over, his greeting for Cousin John was almost knocking him over. Our energetic redhead would wrap his paws around him until Cousin John pushed him off. Even though Cousin John would yell at Rusty to get off of him, he would have a big smile on his face, clearly enjoying the greeting he received. My cousin pretended he didn't like Rusty, but we knew better. He loved to provoke Rusty to go crazy, and, of course, Rusty did. Rusty didn't need much to get him going. Our thickheaded Irishman would give it right back to our thickheaded Italian cousin from Sicily. They would've been perfect to dog sit, but they were going up to Saratoga that weekend, so they were out. The only option we had was to board him at the animal clinic where he went routinely for his checkups and shots.

After a three hour drive, we checked in at Pocono Palace, which was a romantic resort with quaint cabins, heart-shaped bathtubs, and breathtaking views of the mountains. The weather was great; it snowed the whole time. For the three days we were there—you name it, we did it. We went skiing, snowmobiling, and ice skating; and we played pool, roasted marshmallows in the fireplace, and enjoyed the huge heart-shaped bathtub. Even though we were having a fantastic time, I couldn't wait to see Rusty. I really missed him. Johnny thought I was crazy. He felt he was finally getting a much-needed and deserved break from our roaring redhead.

Our long weekend flew by. When we arrived at the animal clinic, we were informed by the technician that Rusty had gotten kennel cough while he was there, but that it was under control. I asked him, "What is kennel cough?"

"It is an upper respiratory infection caused by inflammation of the dog's voice box and windpipe. It's a form of bronchitis, and it's highly contagious to other dogs. It will clear up in a couple of weeks. It will not affect his appetite or his behavior, but he will have a persistent dry cough. We are giving you a supply of antibiotics and cough medicine."

Johnny asked him, "How did he get kennel cough?"

For the most part, I could tell that the technician was embarrassed when he told us. "We were unaware that one of the other dogs came down with it," he said.

Upon opening the door, another technician brought Rusty out to us. I was watching him closely as he was hacking away. I felt so bad for him. To make matters even worse, Rusty walked right past me as if I didn't even exist and stood next to Johnny. I went over to him, "Rusty, it's me, Mommy."

All I wanted to do was hug my little boy, but he acted as if I wasn't even there. As Johnny walked him out to the parking lot, Rusty was excited as he jumped onto the backseat in the Celica to go home, but every time I tried to get close to him he turned his head the other way. Rusty wanted no part of me. On the way home, I was racking my brain for an explanation as to why he was acting that way toward me. All of a sudden, Rusty hit my arm with his paw, barked at me, and gave me a look with the evil eye. *Mommy, you abandoned me! You put me in that bad place. What kind of mommy are you? I thought you loved me?*

"Oh my gosh! You're right!" I said.

"Who is right? Honey, what are you talking about?"

"Johnny, I know why Rusty is mad at me. Who was the one who walked him out of the car and brought him into the boarding clinic? Me, not you; you stayed in the car and waited for me."

"Yeah, that makes sense."

"Rusty, I am so sorry. We had no one to watch you, and I thought you would have fun with the other dogs."

The little brat turned his head away from me again, and pouted as Johnny laughed.

At home, I tried to give Rusty treats, and for the first time he refused them from me. At dinnertime, I put the food in his bowl, but he just left it. He didn't eat until his daddy came into the kitchen. He wouldn't even allow me to give him his cough medicine. Johnny had to do it. *Go figure.* I was the one who felt bad dropping him off to board him. I was the one who missed him and couldn't wait to pick him up. Something didn't go Rusty's way, and he decided to forget everything I had done for him. The point being was this: Who was the one who was always covering up for him when he was bad? Me. Who was the one who felt sorry for him because he was always in trouble? Me. Who was the one who always protected him? Me. And, who was the one who loved him unconditionally? Me. What happened to all that loyalty? Gone, down the drain, sell out! Now I was on Rusty's shit list. Was he kidding me?

For two days, Rusty ignored me and Johnny thought it was funny, but I obviously didn't. On the third day, I thought I would play against our temperamental redhead at his own game. I didn't offer him any treats, I didn't even try to pet him. When I left the house, I didn't even say good-bye to him. I could see that Rusty was trying to figure it out as he tilted his head, looking at me puzzled. *You're not going to say good-bye to me and give me a cookie? I thought I was your little boy, Mommy?*

When I came home, I didn't say one word to Rusty. I just started doing my own thing around the house. Not belonging to a gym, I bought myself Jane Fonda's workout videotape, which allowed me to exercise in the comfort of our home. I turned the TV on and put it in the video machine. I started doing the exercises while Rusty was just sitting there looking sad, watching me. *What is mommy doing? Why isn't she playing with me? She always plays with me when she comes home.*

As soon as he saw me lying on my back on the living room floor lifting my five-pound weights, something finally clicked inside Rusty's big red head. He carefully walked over to me and sat on the floor next to me. All of a sudden he showered me with his affection: wagging his tail, smiling, showing his happiness to see me. He started kissing me with slobbery kisses all over my face, not allowing me to exercise. Honestly, I didn't mind. I would rather be playing on the floor with him than exercising anyway. Finally, my little boy wasn't mad at me anymore.

After we rolled around on the floor and had our playtime, I was rewinding the videotape and went to get a glass of water. When I came back into the living room, Rusty was gone. I assumed that since we had our playtime, he went to see his grandma. I thought there was my chance to get some exercising done, so I started the videotape again. *Where are my weights?* I looked all around on the floor, under the couch and behind the recliner. *Could Rusty have taken them? Nah. I don't think he would've wanted to upset his mommy again. Would he?* Noticing that the bathroom door was closed, I turned the doorknob to open the door, but it didn't budge. Standing in front of the door, I heard a weird crunching sound. Pushing with all my strength, I was finally able to open it slightly and peak my head in. Our sneaky redhead was against the door chewing on my weights.

"What are you doing to my weights?" I shouted.

Rusty moved away from the door and I was able to open it. When I saw him, he dropped the weight and kissed me. When I looked at the weights, I saw that his razor sharp teeth had chewed all the plastic coating off the metal weights in just a matter of minutes. I couldn't get pissed off at him because he did drop the weight and apologized to me with a kiss. It could've been worse. Our sensitive redhead could have stayed mad at me and continued to give me the silent treatment.

Once again, he didn't leave me alone for a second; he was glued to my hip and was my shadow. My furry twin followed me everywhere and made up for all the kisses he deprived me of for those two days, and I loved every minute of it. I learned my lesson. We would never board him again. The next time we wanted to go away, we'd plan it when my mom would be home so Rusty could stay downstairs with her.

The one good thing that came out of Rusty's being pissed off at me, was that he became affectionate with Johnny, and Johnny finally warmed up to Rusty. Almost every night, they had wrestling matches on the living room floor, pinning each other down. Rusty always had a big smile on his face with his tail wagging, while Johnny was laughing. Then they started playing a game. Johnny would tease Rusty, and Rusty would answer him back, which sounded like he was cursing Johnny out in doggy talk. Both father and son always wanted to get the last word, but our vocal redhead usually won in the long run.

At other times, Johnny liked to infuriate Rusty when Rusty didn't understand him, but Rusty never gave up. He would bark his head off, determined to compensate for his lack of human language. So there went Johnny, barking right back at him. At first, Rusty looked suspiciously at Johnny. He tilted his head as if he was questioning him with the oddest look on his face. *Daddy, why are you barking at me? You're not a dog.*

It became a ritual between the two of them, cursing each other out and barking at one another. It did get very noisy and comical in the Roseo house.

Chapter 15

Master of Digging

Rototilling was at our service, free of charge, courtesy of our dog. During the summer months, Rusty with a curious nature, got himself into the terrible habit of digging and enjoyed every minute of it. His skills as a rototiller were exceptional. He turned over our soil better than any machine could do. Routinely, he dug holes, ripped up sod, dug up tree roots, uprooted bushes, and scattered debris all over the backyard. He also ate grass, tree branches, and anything else he could possibly find, and then he threw up—not a pretty sight. His humongous paws were going a mile a minute, as if he were digging a tunnel to go back to his roots in Ireland. Our backyard looked more like it had been hit with landmines with all the bulldozing Rusty did. After digging the massive holes in record times, our rototiller would sit in the hole and get as dirty as can be, which meant bath time.

One Monday I was off from work because I had worked on Saturday. While I was cleaning the house, I let Rusty out in the yard to run around. About fifteen minutes later, my neighbor Karen, directly across the street, called me on the phone. "Jo Ann, I'm looking out my window; Rusty is in your front yard trying to crawl under your fence."

"What! That little brat! Thanks, Karen."

Running to the window, I saw that he was already on the other side of the fence. That was the first time he had gotten out of the yard in our new house. Having gotten out before when we lived in Valley Stream, he always came back when I called him, but he was younger and smaller in size then. Racing to the door, I grabbed his leash, flung open the front door, and saw him running in the street. I called for him to come home, but he took one look at me and ran even faster, heading toward Broadway. *The numbskull couldn't run the other way, down toward the dead end on our block? No, instead he had to pick the busy street!* There I went chasing after him. "Rusty, come here! Cookie! cookie!"

Our high-spirited redhead went barreling down Broadway free as a bird. As I was shouting his name, he ran farther and farther away from me without a backward glance. Rusty was on another one of his missions. Therefore, there was no stopping him, as he displayed boundless amounts of energy and athleticism with the speed of a thoroughbred. Finally, I was able to catch up to him about three blocks away from our house. He was rummaging through the garbage in front of a Fairway Food Market, the local grocery store, which enabled me to attach his leash.

Walking Rusty home was far from simple. This time wasn't any different. There was never a time when I could walk him easily, having to constantly pick up the pace to keep up with him. For sure I was his jogging companion, and he kept me fit. As we were approaching the corner of our house, suddenly we came to a dead stop. Across the street in Rusty's view, there happened to be a big black cat. The cat was staring and hissing at Rusty, which caused him to go completely berserk. He erupted into a frenzy of barking to no end and charged toward the cat. Demonstrating his dominance, there was no holding back my crazy redhead. He yanked me in pursuit of the cat in a speed chase. Trying to pull him back was impossible. His strength overpowered me as he dragged me along with him. At first his leash made red indentations on the palms of my hands that really hurt, but as I kept pulling him, I suddenly realized I was holding a leash and collar with no dog. Between his overall strength and my pulling him, one of the spikes on his choker collar came loose, and it opened.

Again, there he went racing down Broadway after the cat as I was frantically running behind him. Suddenly I heard a loud car horn, followed by the screeching sound of car brakes. My heart stopped. The driver swerved and stopped short, trying not to hit Rusty and me. Thank God he didn't. Luckily, the cat got scared too and took off away from Rusty's view. That was a close call. Fortunately, Rusty sat between my legs while I closed the spikes on the collar and put it back on him. I firmly held his leash as we galloped toward home. The realization of me and my little boy coming so close to getting hit by the car had been terrifying to me.

Arriving back home, Rusty tracked in muddy paw prints all over the floors, which was nothing new. "Rusty, come; it is bath time!" As soon as I started running the water in the bathtub, he jumped right in and splashed water all over the place. He drank the water as it was coming out of the faucet, and then he was drinking the dirty, sudsy water. My dog had no class. It took quite a while for me to spread the baby shampoo throughout his long body and lather him up, soaking his paws, rinsing him off, and then applying conditioner.

After his much-needed bath, I started blow-drying him. Enjoying the warmth from the heat of the hair blower, Rusty stood still for me, picking up his paws and his legs so I could get the warm air underneath him until his hair was fully blown and brushed out. Our redhead looked absolutely stunning after each bath. I really got a workout that day! *For digging and running away, he got pampered. For me running after him like a crazy woman and almost getting killed, what did I get? Zero, nothing. A massage would've been nice.*

After his bath, I went outside to check out the hole he dug earlier. *Oh my God!* Looking down, a large portion of the grass was gone, ripped to shreds, replaced with a mountain of dirt all around it. "Rusty, that's it! You are going in the family room in time-out; and don't you dare bark to come upstairs!"

While he was chewing on a bone in the family room, I shoveled the enormous amount of dirt back into the hole. *Like this was what I wanted to do on my day off. It just never ended.* I really didn't want to show Johnny Rusty's latest destruction because I knew the shit would hit the fan, but I had no choice. In any case, I needed his help. I compacted most of the dirt, but Johnny would have to replace the sections of grass that were no longer there. I dreaded hearing those words again—"We have to get rid of him." Of course I would rebut with, "Yeah, right. I don't think so."

I was still pissed off at Rusty, so I didn't take him when I went to pick Johnny up at the train station. When we came home, punishment was over; it was long enough. Johnny and I went downstairs so I could show him the damage that Rusty had done in the yard, and to bring our sly redhead upstairs, but Rusty wasn't in the family room. When we saw no Rusty, we went outside and I called him. "Rusty, where are you?"

As we walked around the yard, we saw that it looked like a war zone. "Holy shit! Look at this yard! I'm gonna kill him!" Johnny shouted.

"I can't believe Rusty dug all these holes," I said.

"Then who else dug these holes? Your precious dog was the only one in the yard. Don't you know him by now? Rusty always has an ulterior motive. He can be calculating and smart when it's beneficial for him."

I guess Johnny was right. It was downright infuriating to me that Rusty dug hole after hole when he was supposed to be in punishment. "Johnny, where is he? Do you think he ran away?"

"No, I bet he was just being spiteful because you punished him. Do you see this yard? It looks like there were a dozen dogs digging it up! Wait till I get him. I've had it with this crazy dog! I'm telling you, we have to get rid of him."

"Not happening." I started walking away to look for Rusty before he could answer me back. Not even a minute passed and he called me. "Jo, come and look at this mess!"

I followed him in the yard and stood startled. "Wow, did Rusty really do all of this damage?"

"Of course he did."

Rusty transformed Ma's beautiful patio area into a lunar landscape. Stones were scattered all over. He even dug up each one of the stepping stones that were her walking path, along with the pretty flowers she planted, and the small bushes that lined her walkway.

"Do you realize how much time, money and effort I spent to make Ma's patio area and walking path as nice as it was? I have had it with this dog! All he does is give me work to do!"

I took out my imaginary violin. *Here we go again.*

After Johnny's reaction to Rusty's latest destruction, I decided not to tell him that he ran away and both of us almost got hit by a car. *It was best to keep that part out, and keep it between me and my redheaded furry twin.*

Searching the backyard, Johnny saw him at the far end of the yard pushing his face in the dirt by the large oak tree. We ran over to see what he was doing and saw that he was covered in ants. Without a doubt, he had hit an ant pile while digging. Rusty kept hitting his nose with his paw, trying to get the ants off; but looking closely, he also had small ants up his nose. "Jo, some of these are carpenter ants." Taking the hose, Johnny was trying to wash the ants off of his face.

"Johnny, how are we going to get the ants out of his nose?"

"A wet rag," he said.

I ran into the house to get the rag. "Got it!" I said. "Now who is going to put their finger up his nose to get the ants out?" I asked.

"Jo, I stuck my finger up his butt how many times? It's your turn now."

"What's fair is fair. Besides, my pinky finger is much smaller than yours. I'll do it."

It was funny, but it wasn't. While Johnny held Rusty, I was pushing my pinky up his nostrils to try to get the small ants out. It was a good thing that Rusty let me do anything to him and that his nostrils were on the wide side. After I took the ants out of his nose, Johnny noticed that an ant head was still attached to the outside of Rusty's nose.

"Jo, I need something small, like a tweezers to get it out. I'll go inside and get one; I'll be right back."

I stayed with Rusty while Johnny went inside. When Johnny came back, I held Rusty down while Johnny took the tweezers and pulled the ant head out. When the ant came off, so did a tiny piece of the skin on Rusty's nose.

"It's my fault, for leaving him downstairs by himself," I said.

"Don't feel bad. That's what he gets for digging up our yard."

"You're right." This time I really couldn't disagree with him.

Going back into the house, all three of us tracked in mud. Rusty ran straight into the bathroom and jumped right into the bathtub. There went Johnny, washing him. The water in the bathtub turned muddy brown and had a bunch of dead ants floating around. *If only Johnny knew this was Rusty's second bath of the day.* After Johnny towel-dried Rusty, he put medicated ointment on his nose.

"Jo, why was he outside? I thought you left him in the family room in time-out?"

"I did. My mother went out this afternoon; I wonder if she let him out when she came home. I'll go ask her."

I went downstairs and knocked on her door. "Ma, did you let Rusty out earlier?"

"Yes, he was barking to go out, so I let him out and he was running around. I figured he would bark to let me know when he wanted to come back inside."

"I guess I didn't tell you. I put him in the family room in time-out because he dug up the yard again."

"Oh no, I didn't know."

"It's okay."

When I went back upstairs, Johnny just finished towel-drying Rusty. "Johnny, I spoke to Ma. She did let Rusty out when she came home. Rusty was barking to go out. She didn't know he was being punished."

"Well, that explains how he got outside."

My poor husband never got a break, but I also had a pretty rough day, too. There was never a dull moment with our rollicking redhead.

Chapter 16

Tools of the Trade

With any projects Johnny was working on around the house, Rusty suddenly became his assistant. Our redhead became intrigued and at Johnny's side. One day Johnny was working on unclogging our bathroom sink. For some reason, my hair constantly wound up in the drain. I always cleaned my hair out of the sink after I blew it dry, but I guess I shed as much as my redhead. *Another trait we had in common.* Johnny's head was under the sink, and Rusty's head was right next to his. "Hey, Jo, look at this. Rusty thinks he's a plumber."

Going behind them, I laughed. It was cute seeing both of their heads inside the vanity doing plumbing work together. Being a good daddy, Johnny explained to Rusty what he was doing, and Rusty listened to every word, fascinated as to what his daddy was telling him. It looked like Rusty and Daddy were finally becoming pals. *It was about time.*

Focusing on unclogging the sink, Johnny didn't notice that Rusty was no longer with him. Reaching for his tool belt, it wasn't there. "Jo, have you seen my tool belt? I thought it was on the floor next to the vanity."

"No, I haven't, but I'll look around." Searching the house, I found his tool belt downstairs in the family room beside our rascally redhead. The screwdrivers were scattered on the floor along with the empty tool belt, and Rusty was busy chomping away on one of the screwdriver handles.

"Drop it!" I yelled. Rusty totally ignored me.

"Come on, Rusty, you'd better give me that screwdriver, or you are going to be in big trouble!"

There went one of Rusty's famous looks with his Irish setter charm. *Mommy, I was just sharpening Daddy's screwdriver for him so it would work better.*

"Yeah, right! You're such a little liar Rusty."

Finally, he slowly opened his mouth and released it, wet and slimy. Picking up the screwdrivers, I put them back in the tool belt. However, I couldn't save the one large screwdriver that Rusty destroyed, making it unusable.

"Rusty, go upstairs and pretend you are sleeping, so Daddy won't know that you chewed the handle on his screwdriver."

Going back upstairs, Rusty raced past me and went straight into his room and went to sleep, or pretended he was sleeping, just as I told him to do. He could be extremely smart if it was beneficial for him. I went outside and threw the chewed up screwdriver across the street so Johnny wouldn't see it; then I went into the bathroom. "Here you go. I found your tool belt."

"Great! Where was it?"

"It was in the kitchen."

"Oh right, I was in there earlier to get a glass of water. Thanks."

"You're welcome."

"Honey, this is odd. The extra long screwdriver is missing. I had the whole Craftsman set. You didn't see it, did you?"

"No, this is all I found." *Here I go again, telling a little white lie to protect my little boy.*

"Oh, I must've dropped it somewhere. I'll look around later."

Whew, Rusty got out of that one, thanks to Mommy, again.

It seemed that Johnny was always fixing Rusty's latest destruction. The more Johnny repaired, the more Rusty destroyed. Surely Rusty kept him busy, and Johnny became handier fixing up all the damages Rusty created. In a way, I guess I should thank Rusty for Johnny's learning experience. I think in Rusty's mind, if he kept Johnny busy fixing everything he had damaged, then Rusty would have more quality time to spend with me.

We all knew that Rusty was obsessed with me and was jealous of my relationship with my husband, and he demanded all my attention. Every time I sat on Johnny's lap or when we kissed, Rusty went wild barking at Johnny. I always felt bad for Rusty, so I would move away from Johnny for just a minute to give my little boy some love and attention. I didn't want him to feel left out.

When Johnny and I would go into our bedroom at night to watch TV or go to sleep, we kept the bedroom door half open since Rusty slept right outside our room. Rusty was practically joined to my hip, so I had to be within his sight at all times. Quite often, we shut the door, not wanting to be disturbed; however, Rusty had a pretty good idea what was going on inside the bedroom. Without a doubt, every single time Johnny opened the door, Rusty gave Johnny a dirty look and grunted and sneered at him. Then Rusty would go between us so Johnny couldn't get close to me. To this day, we still crack up about Rusty's jealous ways.

There was no question that living with Rusty was a lot of fun, challenging, and sometimes a lot of work. No matter how lovable he could be, every now and then we could still expect the unexpected.

My husband was addicted to the TV show *This Old House* which was all about home renovations. During one episode, they were showing the different types of crown moldings. Johnny liked the way they accented the rooms, and he decided to try it in our living room and dining room.

This one Saturday morning, he went to the lumberyard and picked up the crown moldings, and then he was busy cutting away. After lunch he suggested, "Honey, it's a beautiful day. I need a break. Do you want to go for a bike ride?"

"Sure, that's a great idea!"

Johnny went into the shed to get the bicycles and I was going to meet him in the front of the house. "Rusty, Mommy and Daddy are going for a bike ride. We'll see you later." Rusty ran to the back sliding door looking for Johnny. Then he put his head down, turned away and walked upstairs.

While we were bike riding, I mentioned it to Johnny. "Rusty was looking for you when you went to get the bikes; he was really sad when we left the house. Do you know why?"

"Oh, yeah. I forgot to give him cookies. I always give him a handful before I go out. He'll get over it."

When we came home, Rusty wasn't there to greet us. We assumed he was off sulking somewhere. Walking upstairs, Johnny thought he was going to continue working on his project, but out of the blue he began yelling. "Where are you Rusty? You are dead meat! I'm gonna kill you dog!"

"Kill him? Why? What are you talking about?" I asked.

"Look what your dog did!"

When I ran up the stairs and saw what Rusty had done, I was astounded. *Oh no! He's in big trouble again.*

"Well, I guess you should've shut the door, or put your tools away so he couldn't get to them," I said.

If there was a frustrated look, I got it. Evidently, Rusty was pissed off at Johnny because he didn't give him any treats before we left the house. Our mischievous redhead had chewed all of the crown moldings. He destroyed each one of Johnny's tools—his hammer, the electric drill, the circular saw, the miter saw, and, worst of all, his "sacred" Sawzall.

Johnny had such rage in his eyes. As he ran through the house looking for Rusty, the yelling started again. "Where are you, you crazy dog?"

Going ballistic, Johnny ran out of the house. I was curious. *Where is he going?* When he came back inside, he had a baseball bat in his hand. "Where is he?"

"I don't have a clue, and if I did, I would never tell you!" I answered.

At first, I thought Rusty was hiding under Ma's sewing machine, as he normally did when he was in trouble, but her door must've been closed because Johnny found him hiding in the bathroom. "Yo, what did you do to my tools? You psychopath!"

Rusty ran away with full speed and stamina, fully aware he was in big trouble. I ran downstairs to my mom's apartment. "Ma, hurry up. Johnny wants to kill Rusty!"

As a loving mother-in-law, she came upstairs and walked over to him. "Calm down, Johnny. What happened?"

"Ma, I'm done with him! He is the devil with paws. He chewed up all the new crown moldings and all the cords and plugs on my electrical tools. They can't be fixed. Now I need to buy all new ones, and they aren't cheap."

"Oh dear," she said.

As Johnny walked away, my mom pulled me over to the side. "Jo Ann, I've never seen Johnny so angry."

"I know. His patience with Rusty has run out."

Along came Johnny with the baseball bat in his hand. "That's it! He's outta here!"

"No he's not!" I yelled.

"Do you hear me? We are getting rid of him tomorrow!"

I kept my mouth shut because I didn't want to piss him off even more, but I grumbled under my breath. *Over my dead body are you getting rid of him. If you put your stupid tools away in the first place, this never would've happened.*

Johnny went running after Rusty. The energetic game of ring-a-levio was happening inside our house, just like when we played it in the streets of Canarsie. Honestly, Rusty was uncatchable, leaping through the house like a kangaroo. It was amazing how he jumped straight down the flight of stairs, from the top step from our house, down to the landing by Ma's door.

Exceptionally smart, our setter knew I would protect him as he ran behind me for cover. It occurred to me that I needed to get Rusty out of the house and fast, because Johnny was acting so ridiculous.

"Hurry up, Rusty. Come with Mommy."

"Where are you going with that dog?"

"Out!"

Rusty and I raced out of the house through the front door. I slammed the door shut behind me, opened the car door, and Rusty jumped right in. Locking the car door, I sped away, burning rubber to protect my little boy. *What is it with men and their precious tools anyway?*

We rode around for about twenty minutes, and then I stopped at a pay phone and called my mom. "Ma, how's Johnny?"

"Honey, you can bring Rusty home now. Johnny calmed down."

"Are you sure?"

"Yes, he's fine."

When we came back home, the guilt radiated off of Rusty. He knew he had done wrong, big time. Johnny didn't have to say one word to him. Rusty lowered his head, and, looking toward the floor with his tail between his legs, he walked straight into his room and stayed there the rest of the night.

As usual, Johnny got over it quickly. The following day he went to the store to replace his power tools and crown moldings. When he came home, he was so excited about showing me his new tools. My husband looked just like a little kid at Christmas. *Go figure.* Our credit card balance did increase substantially that day, but who cared. Rusty was still a part of our family, and that's all that mattered.

Throughout all Rusty's craziness, I found it rather amazing that Johnny always threatened to kill Rusty or get rid of him after every single episode of his destructive or bizarre behavior. But the truth is, Johnny was all talk. Although he did curse Rusty out and put him in time-out over and over again, he never once laid a hand or baseball bat on my furry twin, not that I would let him anyway. Apparently, there had to have been a bond deep down in Johnny's heart for our mischievous redhead.

Chapter 17

On the Lookout

Everyone needs a place to hang out, including dogs. In our North Massapequa home, Rusty's safe haven was inside the bay window in our living room. He enjoyed taking the sun as it shined on him through the southern exposure, but, most importantly, he was on the lookout. His alert nature proved he was an excellent watchdog. As our burglar alarm, he would have a warning button that went off inside his head. At any given moment, our boisterous redhead would get into a barking frenzy to let us know when someone was passing our house or if something looked out of the ordinary. Even though he saw the mail carrier and UPS trucks on most days, he went nuts until they drove away, clear of his view.

During the winter months, we received the oil deliveries to heat our home, and that was the worst. As soon as Rusty heard the fuel truck arrive, he ran to every window and door, barking his head off to get outside, actually scaring the deliverymen. They had access into our yard to pump the fuel into our tank and pumped it in record time and then they hurried out of our yard. I often wondered if we got shortchanged on the oil since they were in and out so fast.

Rusty tolerated the sanitation workers as long as they were across the street from our house, but as soon as they touched our garbage pails, our territory, he flipped out with powerful, excessive barking. There was also a landscaping nursery across the street from us on Broadway that he could view from "his" bay window. Each time the nursery received a delivery, Rusty let loose an explosion of noise, barking for one straight hour after the truck drivers drove away. No matter how many times we yelled at him to shut up, it was useless.

In any case, Rusty's instinct was to protect his family; one couldn't blame him for that. He had a special need to feel superior, so he displayed his aggressive bark, wanting to scare people he felt threatened us. On the one hand, I always felt safe with him around, and on the other hand his barking drove me crazy.

One Saturday morning, it was extremely cold; the temperature was only in the teens. Rusty was lazily stretched out on the cushion inside the bay window when he saw a man approaching our front door. Being on the lookout, Rusty went into defensive mode. The man at the door happened to be my brother, but Rusty didn't recognize him because he had a beard. At the time, Andrew worked outside in New York City. He was stationed on the electrical poles in front of the Twin Towers doing his job as an electrician. Trying to stay warm that winter, he grew a beard to protect his face from the bitter cold and gusty winds.

Jumping out of the bay window, Rusty ran straight to the front door, barking like a maniac, believing there was a stranger at the door. If Rusty didn't recognize you, there was no getting past him. Apparently he didn't recognize Andrew, with his beard and the black ski hat he was wearing. He went into such a protective state that he tuned out my brother's voice. Andrew kept yelling through the door as he took his ski hat off. "Rusty, it's me. Look, it's Uncle Andrew. Let me in!"

I ran to the door, grabbed Rusty's collar, and held him down. "It's okay, Rusty. It's Uncle Andrew. You like Uncle Andrew. Let him in."

Finally Rusty saw that I didn't feel threatened and calmed down. It took our roaring redhead a few minutes to stop barking so I could open the door to let my brother inside the house. While Andrew walked up the stairs, he just shook his head. "Jo, your dog is nuts; he needs help."

Laughing, I told him, "Yeah, I know. But you gotta love him."

He looked at me as if I were crazy. "Maybe you do Lucy, but I don't."

I started to giggle. "Hey, brother, remember all the crazy things I did? You wanted to kill me how many times, but you still love me, don't you?"

Andrew put his arm around me. "I have no choice. You're my sister, and I'm stuck with you, but your dog is another story."

"Wait and see. You will love Rusty one day." Andrew just laughed and walked away.

Rusty's bay window

Rusty was my canine bodyguard. It was beneficial for me to have such a large dog with a deep bark, especially with Johnny working long, hard hours and commuting to and from New York City. Like clockwork, Rusty knew the exact time we had to leave to pick Daddy up, and he would be all revved up and ready to go. By the time I put the key in the ignition and put my seatbelt on, Rusty had already jumped from the backseat to the front seat and obediently had taken his seat riding shotgun next to me.

Rusty and I arrived at the train station a little past eight o'clock every night. While we were waiting for Johnny, Rusty was the perfect protector sitting next to me. Anytime someone would pass our car as they were walking toward their car in the parking lot, Rusty jumped up against the window and started growling and barking at them. Especially in our compact Celica, I'm sure his appearance looked even larger, causing them to move away from our car rather quickly. He could've woken up the dead with his deep, aggressive, penetrating bark. But as soon as the train slowly rolled into the station, excitement kicked in for Rusty as his eyes focused on the platform searching for his daddy.

Once Rusty saw Johnny walking across the upper level of the platform, he jumped from one seat to the other with his big feathery tail slapping me in the face. Each time Johnny entered the car, Rusty, the copilot, landed on his lap as if Rusty was going to drive us home. Johnny always laughed and pushed him into the back so he could take control of the car.

Anyone who is a dog owner knows that there is nothing better than the way your dog greets you with utmost excitement and unconditional love and affection for you. No matter how many times Rusty got yelled at or was put in time-out, which was quite often, he was always happy to be reunited with us. Honestly, it didn't get any better than that.

Chapter 18

Thunder Roars

In dog world, Rusty ruled. We were all-too familiar that he had his own agenda, didn't listen to us, and did whatever pleased him. With Rusty, he was all about having fun, even though it could be dangerous for him. Anytime the sky opened up—it could be snow, light rain, hail and especially a thunderstorm—he went into a frenzy of excitement with a bout of boisterous barking.

At times when it hailed, large pellets of ice looking like golf balls fell out of the sky, and our curious setter just had to have them. It was funny watching Rusty experience the joys of frozen precipitation as he was jumping up in midair to catch the hailstones. Certainly, he was amusing himself to see how many pieces of ice he could actually catch, and then he went crunching away.

Before Rusty even heard the pitter-patter of the raindrops on the roof, he would get a glimmer of mischief in his eyes, as if he knew that the rain was on its way. And then the barking would begin. As reckless as he was, upon the first clap of thunder and the crackling surge of energy, our rascally redhead raced to each window, smashing his big red head on the door to go out. *Who does that?—Only our kooky redhead.*

For some crazy reason, during a thunderstorm, Rusty would never turn his back on Mother Nature. He would go into his out-of-control, destructive mode—from ripping the curtains off the windows, to knocking things over, and scratching the glass on the sliding doors to get out as he continued barking. It was as if the lighting and thunder were calling him. Some little voice inside his big red head seemed to whisper to him. *Come out and catch us if you can.* I would presume it was Mother Nature's way of communicating with Rusty, or maybe it was Rusty's way of communicating with Mother Nature. Who knows what went on inside his crazy head?

Any time it rained heavily, we tried our best to put up with his excessive barking and reckless behavior to keep him in the house, as good dog parents would do, but after a while we just couldn't deal with it. Rusty was so stubborn that we ended up giving in to him so we could have some peace and quiet in the house. If you think about it, it was as if a switch went off in his brain and was turned on. As long as the lighting and thunder were still going strong, there was no possible way to turn it off. If only he had had a reset button in his big red head, that would've been great!

At night, forget about it. That was the worst. Fearless Rusty would wake us up in the middle of the night every single time the thunder roared to let him outside in the backyard. If we didn't let him out, his barking became endless. His loud barking was the last thing we wanted to hear while we were trying to sleep, so we would let him have his way and let him out in the yard. Johnny and I would stand on the patio deck watching our nutty redhead running fast as lighting while we were in our pajamas half asleep.

"Johnny, look at him. I thought dogs were afraid of thunder. I never heard of a dog who liked thunder," I said with wonder.

"Ya think? Oh, by the way, I spoke to Gary at work about it the other day. I told him how crazy Rusty gets when there is a thunderstorm. He said dogs hearing are much more sensitive than humans. It is about twenty times greater than ours, meaning they could hear the thunder far in the distance much sooner then we can. Barking is his way of expressing his desires and emotions. Dogs also sense the changes in the weather. They could smell approaching storms before we can since their noses are much keener than ours."

"That makes sense."

"Anyway, Gary also said that Rusty's wild behavior and physical energy in reaction to thunder could be an escape for his anxiety. Some dogs are afraid, and they hide; but other dogs, like Rusty who are strong-willed, have to escape."

Yawning, with my eyes half-closed, I said, "As long as the lightning is far away, he should be fine. We just have to watch him and make sure it's not too close, or we'll have to drag him inside the house, which isn't going to be easy."

"Honey, don't worry; I'll get him inside the house."

As bolts of lightning flashed in the distance, Rusty went running back and forth chasing the gusty winds and bark at the thunder. The bright flashes of lightning turned our backyard into daylight, displaying his glowing red coat. He looked like he was part of a team of wild mustangs, and boy, did he look gorgeous. Our next-door neighbor would yell from his bedroom window, "Yo, will you shut that stupid dog up already?" I was always too tired to even respond.

Eventually, when all was quiet after the rumbling stopped and the rain subsided, Rusty came back into the house soaking wet. He shook off and splattered water all over me, the kitchen walls and floors. I even had to squeeze the excess water out from his long ears. Forget about blow-drying him; that was the last thing I wanted to do in the middle of the night. So instead Rusty got towel-dried.

Finally, Rusty succeeded in having fun and wearing himself out. Our crazy redhead fell asleep, meaning we could get some sleep. There was never a dull moment in the Roseo house, but Rusty did keep us entertained.

Chapter 19

Let There Be Light

Fridays were my late nights to work at the bank; typically I came home after seven o'clock. It was too early to wait for Johnny at the train station, so I would go home, let Rusty out, feed him, and then we would head out.

During the winter months as the days grew short, darkness set in early. Pulling into the driveway one Friday night, I noticed that the light in the entrance foyer was on. It was peculiar because I knew I wouldn't leave it on during the day, especially since it had eight candelabra light bulbs in it.

On our way home from the train station, I asked Johnny, "Did you put a timer on the foyer light?"

"No, why?"

"Well, the light was on when I came home from work tonight."

He looked a little confused, "No, I only leave a small night-light on in the kitchen and living room for Rusty."

"Hmm, that's odd. Maybe my pocketbook accidently hit the light switch on my way out the door this morning."

Not thinking anything of it until the next Friday night; I came home from work at the same time, and the light in the foyer was on again. *Okay, now this is getting a little weird.* After getting a blissful greeting from my little boy, we rolled around on the living room carpet, and I got plenty of wet kisses from him. Then we went downstairs, and I let him out. As he ran around the yard exploring, I went back upstairs and snooped around the house to see if Johnny was playing a trick on me. It was strange because I didn't see any timers. I knew my mom wasn't putting the light on because she was in Florida visiting my grandparents.

The following Friday night when I came home from work, the foyer light was on again. It was puzzling to me that it was on for three consecutive Friday nights. *Could it be that there's a ghost in the house?*

The last Friday of the month, it was my turn to leave work early. As it was getting close to dusk, I wanted to see for myself what was going on. That time, I didn't pull into the driveway as I normally did. Instead, I parked my car in the street out of Rusty's view. I took notice that he wasn't lying in the bay window, which meant he was up to something. I crept up to the house, waiting to see if the light would go on. As I tiptoed up the concrete steps, I hid on the right side of the front door. On the left side of the door, there was a side panel of glass that I covered with a sheer curtain, but looking in closely, someone could see in the entranceway. After a few minutes, I peaked in and saw with my own eyes as Rusty jumped up against the wall. With his right paw he hit the light switch up in the "on" position, wagged his tail and proceeded back up the stairs.

See, I knew I wasn't going crazy. Someone was putting the light on, and that someone was Rusty. My dog cared so much about me that he was doing this so I wouldn't have to walk into the house in complete darkness. Or maybe he was afraid of the dark like me; my furry twin took after me in mostly everything else. The mystery was solved. I was so excited that I couldn't wait to tell Johnny how smart Rusty really was.

When I picked Johnny up at the train station, he was talking about the busy day he had had, so I waited to get home to tell him the good news.

"Guess what? I know how the light in the foyer goes on every Friday night."

"Oh really? Is there a bogeyman who puts the light on?"

"No, it's Rusty."

"Rusty? Are you kidding me?"

"Listen, I saw him do it with my own eyes tonight."

Johnny took my hand and brought me down to the foyer. "Let's be realistic. Look, his claw marks are on the wall. He must've jumped up on the wall because he saw an ant or a spider."

"Come on, Johnny, four weeks in a row? I don't think so. Granted, his claw marks are on the wall, but I don't see any spiders or ants now, do you? Maybe the first time he saw something, he hit the light switch accidently; but once he figured out how to turn the light on, he continued to do it when it started to get dark."

Johnny laughed. "There is no way he would remember to put the light on week after week."

"Whatever. You just don't want to admit that Rusty is intelligent."

"Intelligent? Are you kidding me? He just has big paws and he could jump really high."

"That's not nice. My little boy is extremely smart."

"You must be dreaming."

"No, I'm not. Rusty is an Irish setter, and they are really smart dogs."

"I know that Irish setters are smart dogs, but not this one."

"Yes, he is!"

"I swear, the way you stick up for him, he could be your son."

"That's right. He really cares about his mommy. You just don't get it."

To me, it was pure genius on Rusty's part even though Johnny didn't agree with me. The way dogs learn is through repetition. See, Rusty did have some brains, retaining something he learned all by himself. The bump on his head continued to prove that it was the knot of knowledge, as I had said all along. Only Rusty and I know the truth about the light in the foyer and who was right. Since Rusty couldn't speak for himself, I think Mother knows best.

The following Friday I came home from work at seven o'clock, and guess what? The light was on in the foyer. Feeling safe, I knew our brilliant redhead put it on for me. Case closed.

On one of my early Fridays, I decided to cook a romantic candlelight dinner for us. I made baked muscles, jumbo shrimps stuffed with crabmeat, and pasta with pesto sauce. I kept the food in the oven to stay warm while Rusty and I went to pick Johnny up.

Rusty and Johnny were starting to bond more at times. Actually, Johnny knew he had no choice but to put up with Rusty, because he knew he was stuck with him. Each night when we walked into the house from the train station, Rusty was right there beside his daddy. Johnny always ruffled Rusty's ears and the top of his head since Rusty looked forward to it. Our redhead loved all the attention he could get. Then playtime began. They would go on the living room floor and have a wrestling match. After playtime, Johnny would go into the bathroom to wash up while Rusty followed him.

Putting the final touches on our meal, I lit the candles for our romantic dinner. I turned my back, and all of a sudden our inquisitive dog was standing on the kitchen chair with his head and paws on the table. "Rusty, what are you doing? Get off the table!"

Ignoring me, he took his paws and pushed one of the onyx candlesticks toward him. Our rascally redhead started eating the flames on the candles. "Rusty, stop that!" I yelled.

Calling Johnny, I said, "Hurry up. Come into the kitchen. You gotta see this!"

Unbelievable as it was, we stood there and watched our kooky redhead catching the flames from each candlestick. Taking a bite of the flame from the first candlestick, he moved on to the next candlestick and took a bite out of that flame.

Johnny grabbed Rusty. "What is wrong with you dog? Are you that crazy?"

"Who eats fire? I told you, Jo, he's a psychopath." As usual, I laughed. Rusty could be very comical.

Johnny pushed Rusty off of the chair and away from the table, but not before he grabbed one of the candlesticks and took off. He held it as if it were a gigantic rawhide bone as he ran out of the kitchen. Johnny went chasing after him through the house. "Let go of that candlestick. Drop it!" Johnny shouted.

Watching our nutty dog running around the house with a ten-inch candlestick in his mouth was hilarious; it was his, and he was not giving it up. All of a sudden, we heard a door slam shut. Either there was an intruder in the house, or it was our sly redhead. We opened the door and found Rusty stretch out on the floor in the bathroom chewing away. Johnny pulled the candlestick out of his mouth. The candle was gone, chewed up and swallowed. The onyx candlestick now had teeth marks embedded in it. *Well, so much for bringing back a beautiful, handmade, souvenir from our honeymoon.*

Being a possessive little boy, evidently Rusty was pissed off at Johnny and barked for one straight hour. There went our quiet, romantic dinner. Surprisingly, Rusty didn't get burned, or if he did, he didn't show any signs of pain. Our rascally dog was strong as a bull and immune to pain. Stubborn as he was, only Rusty could do something as bizarre as that. We never knew what to expect next from him. If he were a female, we would've named him Lucy, after my namesake.

Given the fact that our romantic dinner was ruined, the following day Johnny and I were in the mood for calzones for lunch. Buying fresh pizza dough from the bakery on Broadway, Johnny rolled it out, and then we placed the Italian cold cuts and cheeses on top of the dough. Putting the gas flame on high, I heated the oil to make sure it was nice and hot before placing the calzones into the frying pan.

"Jo, come downstairs. I want to show you a project that I started."

"Do we have time? Aren't the calzones going to burn?"

"We'll only be a few minutes. They need time to cook anyway."

"Sure, I'd love to see it."

Going downstairs in the family room, he showed me the wooden bar he was building. The color of the wood looked good with our furniture.

"What do you think? Do you like it?" he asked.

"It's looks great! The bar really isn't taking too much space away from the family room. Nice job."

All of a sudden, we heard Rusty barking from upstairs. Then it sounded like a stampede of horses coming down the stairs. Racing toward us, he was still barking and tilting his head to follow him upstairs.

I shouted, "Oh no! The calzones!"

Running upstairs, we saw that the oil was bubbling over the frying pan onto the burner, and the flames were shooting out from the gas burner. The calzones were totally burnt. Apparently, I put too much oil in the frying pan and we left the calzones in longer than we should have.

"Honey, I got pre-occupied showing you my project that I totally forgot about the calzones. I guess you were right. I should've waited to show you the bar until after lunch."

Yes! Finally it wasn't me or Rusty this time.

Opening the sliding window next to the stove, Johnny took the frying pan with the calzones in it and threw it out the window, hitting a pile of dirt.

"Well, there goes our calzones," I said. "I'll go down the block and pick up a pizza?"

"Sounds good to me; I'll clean this up while you go to the pizza place," Johnny said.

Fortunately, Fire Marshal Rusty was well aware that this fire was potentially dangerous and alerted us. I'm pretty sure that he knew the fire from the stove was different from the flames he ate off of the candlesticks. Rusty saved our kitchen from going up in flames. Even though Rusty could drive us crazy at times, his instinct about any kind of danger was always impressive.

Chapter 20

Grooming Our Redhead

At two years old, Rusty was fully grown, weighed eighty-five pounds, and was absolutely stunning—an oversized dog who walked with his elegant head held high, displaying his elongated neck, gorgeous feathered coat, and long ears. His gleaming red coat and imposing structure were a sight for sore eyes, displaying the external beauty that his breed was known for. Every time I took Rusty for a walk, or, as he preferred, a run, through the neighborhood, passersby stopped and commented that he was such an exquisite-looking dog. Feeling like the proud mother, I would boast. *That's my boy!*

Anyone who looked at an Irish setter could see that the color of its coat is one of the most distinguishing features besides the long ears. Because the Irish setter's coat is so unique, so are the requirements of grooming one. Maintaining Rusty's beautiful coat required some work, but I enjoyed it. I kept an assortment of brushes, a regular comb, a metal flea comb, scissors, nail clippers, toothbrush, and toothpaste. I brushed his long, red coat every other day, including his feathered tail, long ears, chest, and legs to keep his glamorous appearance. In addition, I also added a tablespoon of olive oil to his food daily to keep his coat silky and shiny.

Sitting still for me to groom him was never a problem. From the time he was a puppy, he sat straight up for me with his head raised so I could brush and comb his hair. He was one dog who absolutely loved to be pampered. His favorite part of the home grooming process was when I held his long ears in the palm of my hands and caressed each one as I was brushing it. Taking my time, I looked for fleas and any dry flakes. Actually, we were lucky; he hardly ever had any fleas. Then I took the fine metal comb and removed any dry flakes to stimulate the natural oils in his coat. We still needed to have him professionally groomed every eight weeks, or his long hair would mat, especially around his ears.

The grooming salon was located on Broadway, two blocks north from our house. Rusty had a set appointment on Saturday mornings at eleven o'clock. Initially, Rusty didn't want me to leave him, putting on a sad face and barking. It's ironic because he could act like such a baby yet display this big and tough appearance.

Maria and Marge were the groomers, which was good because Rusty preferred women over men anyway. Maybe he felt powerless with men, and with these two women he could put on his Irish charm and get the attention he needed—or demanded. When I picked Rusty up, Marge told me that he was difficult; he was stubborn and extremely strong. They hoped once Rusty got used to them, it would be easier to groom him. I thanked them for putting up with him and for doing a beautiful job.

When I told Rusty we were going to the groomers for his second visit, he became excited, sitting at attention and waiting patiently for me to attach his leash to his collar. Then we headed down Broadway, and he knew exactly where the grooming salon was. He ran right inside as soon as I opened the door. I could see that he felt more comfortable, as he realized I was coming back to pick him up. As time progressed, Maria told me that Rusty listened to them, and he became very lovable toward them, but he did need to have his selection of treats. With each bath, they trimmed, shaped, and feathered his gorgeous red coat, only shaving a small area of his neck and under his ears.

After a few grooming sessions, Maria asked me, "Could you bring Rusty in at eight o'clock in the morning for now on, before the other dogs come in?"

Uh oh, what did he do now? "Of course I can. Is there a problem?"

"Rusty is fine when he's alone with us, but when the other dogs start coming in, he becomes too much to handle. He constantly barks and scares the other dogs; they are afraid to come inside. Plus, we feel we can take our time and do a better job if he's the only dog in the salon."

"I am so sorry. Of course I can bring him in earlier." *Rats! Now I can't even sleep in on my day off.*

I was fully aware of Rusty's sporadic behavior, and I understood completely. Surely another groomer would've turned him away after seeing how difficult he could be. Luckily, they had patience with him and allowed him back in the grooming salon. Maria and Marge said they got their workout from him, but they enjoyed grooming him because they took pride in the way he looked. They made him look magnificent. Both women said Rusty was the most beautiful dog they had ever groomed; they even displayed an eight-by-ten photo of him in the salon.

Every time I brought Rusty to the salon for the next three years, they did a superb job, feathering him to perfection. After they groomed him, they sprayed him with cologne and sent him home with a new bandana, which Rusty refused for me to take off. Walking him home after each grooming session, he pranced down Broadway just knowing he looked stunning. Rusty was such a ham, literally posing, displaying his beauty and his healthy self-esteem. While the neighborhood people were going in and out of the local stores on Broadway, they stopped to admire him. Maybe our dog didn't have much in brains, as some family members said, but his startling beauty was undeniable. And that's a fact!

In between his professional groomings, cutting his nails was a piece of cake. "Rusty, give Mommy your paws." He gave each one to me without any hesitation. I held it as Johnny clipped his nails. Then onto his feet, "Rusty, now pick up your foot." He picked up each foot, and Johnny clipped those nails, too. Of course, we had to have a handful of treats on hand.

Brushing his teeth was a little extra work. No one wants a dog with bad breath or ugly brown tartar on its teeth. Johnny held Rusty down and held his mouth open while I took the toothbrush and brushed his teeth. The only problem was that Rusty liked the taste of the toothpaste, making it difficult to brush his teeth while he kept eating it. But as a team, we were able to brush them successfully each month, showing off his big pearly whites, and it showed in his appearance.

Chapter 21

The Dog Show

It was time for Rusty's annual checkup and vaccinations, which I dreaded. Anytime I took him to the vet, he behaved so inappropriately; I couldn't wait to get him out of there. When he saw a cat, the saliva started foaming from his mouth as he barked ferociously at it, throwing himself into a deep frenzy. Rusty only related to the large dogs, similar to his size. We could never stay in one area in the waiting room. Every time we sat down, we had to keep moving seats, playing musical chairs, to get to an empty area because Rusty was always starting trouble with the other dogs. All of the dogs sat next to their owners, but not mine. Our redhead was exceptionally strong and uncontrollable, constantly pulling me to make his rounds to the other dogs. He was such an embarrassment, having no manners at all.

While we were sitting in the waiting room at the animal clinic, a woman with a beautiful Gordon setter walked in. The only empty seat was next to us. *Just great! Now Rusty will start trouble with her dog.* The woman introduced herself to me as Mary, and her dog was Oscar. I introduced myself and Rusty to her. It was hard to believe, but Rusty and Oscar formed a connection. With both dogs being males and large dogs, I was concerned Rusty would misbehave, but they actually played well together. With Rusty staying busy playing, I had the opportunity to have a conversation with someone at the animal clinic. Normally, I had to apologize to everyone for my dog's behavior issues.

Mary surely had a knack when it came to dogs, and I could see that she liked Rusty. I took notice of the way she was observing him and interacting with him. In chatting with her, I learned that she was a hard-core dog lover. I was amazed when she said, "I show Oscar in the local setter shows. Based on what I see of Rusty's beauty, his rich red color coat, and his overall appearance, he may qualify for showing."

"Sounds great, Mary, but my dog is temperamental, thickheaded, and crazy as can be. He doesn't listen to anyone, and he has a mind of his own. I don't think he's suitable for showing."

"I used to feel the same way about Oscar, but many of the male setters are known to be energetic and thickheaded. It's a trait, but once they are in the ring, they become totally different dogs."

I wondered. *Could this be true? My Rusty a show dog? Nah.*

"Jo Ann, you should come to one of the local setter shows in the area. There is one next Sunday in Huntington. You can watch them perform and see what showing is all about."

It surely seemed interesting to me. "It sounds like fun, Mary, but let me check with my husband to make sure he didn't make plans for next weekend."

"Great! If you can make it, bring Rusty, too. He'll enjoy it."

"I don't think so. Rusty could get pretty crazy."

"Take it from me. He'll be fine once he sees the other dogs."

"Are you sure, Mary?"

"I've never been wrong about a setter."

Mary and I exchanged phone numbers. She said she would call me during the week to see if we could make it, and, if so, we'll make arrangements to meet.

That night, I couldn't wait to tell Johnny about the conversation Mary and I had had.

"Guess what?" I said.

"What did Rusty do now?"

"Nothing. Actually today was a good day for him. I met this really nice woman at the vet today. She owns a Gordon setter. Rusty and her dog were playing while we were talking."

"Rusty was good at the vet?"

"Yep. He played nice with her dog."

"That's a first."

"Anyway, Mary shows her dog in the local setter dog shows. In fact, she invited us to a show in Huntington next Sunday to see her dog and other Gordon setters and Irish setters perform. Do you want to go?"

"Sure, it sounds like fun."

"She also said to bring Rusty."

"No way. We can't bring that nutcase."

"She liked Rusty. She thought he was beautiful, and she said he'd be fine. In fact, she encouraged us to bring him."

"I don't know, Jo. You know how crazy he gets. He'll destroy something and embarrass us."

"I know. That's what I told her, but she thought it would be good for him to be with other setters."

"Okay, I hope she's right. If he starts any trouble, we are outta there."

"Fine. I'll ask my mother if she wants to come with us."

A week later as we were pulling into the parking lot of the dog show, Rusty was quite taken back. I could see the excitement on his face when he saw the setters walking into the building. Dog scent was everywhere. Moving around in an excited fashion, he was well-mannered. Who knows? Maybe he felt he was in his own element, seeing so many setters like himself. Rusty was always fascinated by the way he looked. He was very vain, and he would stop to admire himself in our full-length mirror in our bedroom, especially after he was groomed. It was perfect timing that the dog show was that Sunday, because we just had Rusty groomed the day before and he looked absolutely beautiful.

Walking into the exhibition area we saw the groomers busy scissoring the pronounced areas of the dogs, brushing and blowing their feathering coats. Each dog we saw was a sight for sore eyes. There had to be at least two dozen Irish setters and Gordon setters. The Gordon setters were beautiful dogs, but I was partial to the Irish setters since I was a parent to one. Each Irish setter was exquisite, portraying something unique. The females had smaller frames, similar to Rusty's biological mother.

While we were observing the dogs, Mary walked over to us with a bright smile and petted Rusty. I introduced her to Johnny and my mom. "I'm so happy to meet you. I apologize for not greeting you as soon as you came in, but on the day of the show, a handler's job is never done. I'll be happy to show you around in a little bit."

I was excited to be there and pleased that she went out of her way to greet us and wanted to show us around. She waved and called out to a man nearby. "Chris, come here." He walked over to us. "Chris, I'd like you to meet John and Jo Ann, and Paula, Jo Ann's mom. This is Rusty, their Irish setter. This is the first show they're attending."

He extended his hand courteously to Johnny and petted Rusty. *What a friendly gesture.* "Hi, guys. Nice to meet you," he said.

Ma, Johnny and I replied, "Nice to meet you too, Chris."

Chris was the owner of Charlie, one of the most beautiful Irish setters I had ever seen. Mary told us that Charlie had won numerous ribbons in the local competitions and had champion bloodlines. Chris and Johnny chatted for a while, and then Chris said he'd catch up with us after the performance. He needed to get Charlie ready for the show.

Meanwhile, since we were only spectators, we wanted to keep Rusty at a low profile, knowing how rambunctious and embarrassing he could be. I dreaded getting kicked out of the dog show and, worst of all, hearing Johnny say, "I told you so." Fortunately, Johnny was able to get Rusty to sit still while we took our seats to watch the dogs perform. Attending the dog show as a novice was enjoyable, especially watching all the different categories of showing. Mary was right; Rusty was acting on his best behavior surrounded by the other setters. He really impressed us.

While Charlie competed, he stood as still as a statue when the judge examined him. Mary, sitting next to us, explained that some of the things the judge was inspecting were his overall appearance, structure, height, weight, ear shape, bite and dentition, alertness, temperament, and, of course, his coat. I was fascinated listening to her. She also explained that the setters in the ring must be outgoing and personable. Shy or hostile setters are at fault, and points are deducted. The judge asked Chris to gait Charlie. Mary said that the setter's gait (the quality of walking) should be big and effortless, and, of course, Charlie's was. After the judge completed his inspection of each dog, he instructed all the handlers to gait their dogs around the ring so he could make his final selection. I was in awe, watching these gorgeous redheads walking with their heads held high and their red coats flowing.

Charlie was exceptional and won Best in Show, adding another ribbon to his collection and earning more points to go on to bigger and better competitions. When the ribbon was placed around Charlie's neck, he preened with pride. Watching him pose for the pictures, he was a total professional and an exquisite dog.

As soon as Chris led his redhead out of the center of the ring, Charlie became just as crazy as our redhead, jumping on his master and taking off and running around the ring as if he were chasing a squirrel. We couldn't believe it; there was another Rusty. It looked like Rusty had a twin brother.

"Johnny, is that the same dog? How could Charlie be so perfect in the ring and act so crazy out of the ring?" I asked.

Chris overheard me talking to Johnny. "Take it from me guys, that's an Irish setter for you," Chris said with a laugh.

Mary came over to congratulate Chris with Oscar at her side. Oscar looked amazing and came in second place in the Gordon setter category.

After the show, Chris came over to us and started petting Rusty. "I find Rusty's appearance rather striking. His flowing red coat is shiny and feels like silk. His feathering looks good, and his body is in proportion, displaying his long-limbed elegance. For the larger-size setter that he is, his weight is ideal for his size. His teeth are impeccably white, and his gums look healthy. Your dog is the ideal picture of one masculine canine. It looks like Rusty may have the qualities and potential of competing in dog shows."

"Really?" I exclaimed.

"Absolutely. Rusty is a beautiful Irish setter."

Feeling overjoyed, I said, "Wow, he sounds too good to be true."

"Do you know if Rusty has champion in his bloodlines?"

Johnny answered, "I don't think so. We bought him from a backyard breeder."

"Let's see what Rusty can do," Chris said.

Johnny and I were skeptical as we looked at each other. It was highly unlikely that Rusty would behave for Chris, but Chris wanted to give it a try, so why not. Chris walked Charlie over to sit with us, and then he took Rusty's leash and walked toward the center of the ring. Charlie went right over to my mom, nudged his head on her lap, and stayed with her while we watched Chris giving commands to Rusty. I whispered in my mom's ear, "Is he kidding me? This is going to be so embarrassing. I hope Rusty doesn't poop inside the ring." My mom was laughing as she was petting Charlie.

Chris decided to gait Rusty around the ring. Rusty was totally focused on Chris and followed his lead. Their eye contact was incredible. Acting confident and observant, Rusty tilted his raised head showing his accentuated neck as if he were the king who ruled the ring as we watched in wide-eyed amazement. Excitedly, I said, "Who is that dog? Is he really our Rusty?"

"Can't be," Johnny said.

While Rusty was under Chris's control, we were fascinated as he walked around the ring with him. Rusty stopped when told to stop, he sat when told to sit, and the biggest shocker was that he stayed when told to stay. While Chris walked around Rusty observing him, Rusty didn't move. I would like to believe when Rusty saw the other dogs standing still, he thought, *I can do that.* As Chris held a treat out for him, Rusty didn't try to snatch it until Chris said it was okay. Watching our handsome, masculine redhead gaiting around the ring with Chris was surreal. To me, Rusty did look like a show dog. *Go figure.* "Way to go Rusty!" I said with pleasure.

I couldn't have been more proud as a dog parent. Our amazing Rusty never ceased to amaze me. James, the obedience school trainer, would never have believed this in a million years. I was so upset that I didn't bring my camera with me. It seemed that both Rusty and Charlie were under some kind of hypnosis with Chris—not to mention Rusty's enthusiasm for his new experience in the ring. His behavior in this ring was quite different than his behavior in the ring in obedience school.

Chris returned with Rusty. I hugged my little boy, "Rusty, Mommy is so proud of you. You did great in the ring. You were such a good boy."

Chris smiled. "Rusty did exceptionally well for his first time. His posture and his stride were really good. I can't emphasize enough that your dog may be a good candidate for showing, with the proper training."

I was beaming. What impressed me was that Chris thought so highly of Rusty. Johnny wasn't as sure. "Chris, this is a fluke," he said. "Rusty is totally nuts and thick-as-a-brick."

"I know how you feel. You saw a few minutes ago my redhead's rambunctious behavior when he got out of the ring. But when he's performing, he knows what is expected of him. It took a lot of time and effort, and now he is one of the top Irish setters in the state. I can fill you in all about showing if you're interested."

The thought of showing Rusty was really enticing to me. At that moment, I fantasized gaiting my handsome redhead around the ring, winning ribbons, and watching the audience give him a standing ovation.

"Johnny, what do you think? Wouldn't it be cool if Rusty could be a show dog?" Johnny rolled his eyes and looked at me like I was crazy.

Mary stepped into the conversation, "Dog showing is great! It's a lot of fun and an absorbing hobby. It has so many rewards for dogs and their owners that last a lifetime."

I was certainly intrigued and eager to try it. Chris saw how excited I was. "Guys, showing is great, but I have to be honest with you. It's also a big commitment. What you have to consider is the extensive groomings, trainings, hiring a professional handler, traveling, photo shoots and other hidden costs that are invested in showing. But let me tell you, it's definitely worth it."

I knew at that point, that my dream of Rusty being a show dog was over. While Rusty and Charlie were playing, Chris and Mary were talking to each other about the show. Johnny took me to the side. "Jo, think about it. We both work full-time, and we want to have a baby soon.

When will we have the time? Plus, it will cost us a fortune, and I still have my doubts about him."

"I know. You're right, but it was fun to imagine."

We walked over to Chris and Mary. "Chris, I know my wife would love to show Rusty, but we discussed it, and it just isn't feasible for us right now; maybe down the road."

"I totally understand. Here's my phone number. Call me if you change your mind. I'll be glad to help. It's been really nice meeting you. I hope to you see you guys at the next show."

"Definitely," Johnny and I replied.

We thanked Mary for inviting us and told both of them that we had a great time. All in all, it was a delightful afternoon and very enjoyable for us, Rusty included. It was truly special to see Rusty interact with Chris, Charlie, and the other setters in a civilized way. I always knew there was hope for him.

Chapter 22

The Christmas Trees

Peace on earth—yeah, right—not at the Roseo house. During the holiday season, we enjoyed decorating our house for Christmas. Johnny hung the white lights on the tree, and I hung all the Christmas ornaments and Christmas balls. He also attached strands of multicolored lights all around our front window in the living room, making it look very Christmassy.

Initially, Rusty was afraid of the Christmas tree. I could only assume that the large tree inside our house felt overpowering to him. The only time Rusty went into the living room was when Johnny and I were with him. Otherwise, we would see him curiously looking in the living room at the tree, but he wouldn't enter the room.

Again, he proved us wrong. One night, Rusty's interest got the better of him. While Johnny and I were putting groceries away, all of a sudden we heard his bark coming from the living room.

"What now?" Johnny asked.

"I have no idea."

We ran into the living room, and there was our rascally redhead, causing trouble, again. One of the strands of Christmas lights from the tree was hanging from Rusty's mouth as he was chewing on the little white bulbs.

"Rusty, stop that! Bad boy!" Johnny yelled.

Thankfully, he didn't get electrocuted. This meant it was time to "Rusty-proof" the Christmas tree. After we scolded him, Johnny nailed the baby gate to the entranceway to the living room to keep Rusty out. I assumed that, during the day, Rusty would find another window to look out since he was blocked off from the living room, but that didn't happen.

Coming home from work a few days later, I took Rusty for a long walk. When we came home, it started getting dark. I went into the living room to turn the Christmas lights on and was startled. "Seriously, Rusty?" The baby gate was down, and the strands of multicolored lights from the window were on the couch, hanging down to the floor. Our beautiful nativity set was destroyed. Mother Mary's head was completely gone, probably chewed up. The lower half of Saint Joseph's body was missing, and the top of the stable turned to mulch. Fortunately, baby Jesus was still intact on the opposite side of the living room. I was upset, but what was I supposed to do? He had done the damage earlier.

A year went by—nothing new. The following Christmas I thought Rusty wouldn't bother with the Christmas tree since he was a year older. Wrong. We bought an eight-foot blue spruce tree and put it in front of the bay window in our living room. Taking us a couple of hours to decorate the tree, we attached beautiful glass multicolored balls, ornaments, and hundreds of clear lights. It looked very magical, especially from outside through our bay window.

That night Johnny and I were in the kitchen finishing dinner. I glanced out of the corner of my eye and saw Rusty standing in front of the Christmas tree picking his leg up. *Oh no. He isn't going to do what*

I think he's going to do. Noticing the expression on my face, Johnny quickly turned his head and looked toward the living room as Rusty started peeing all over the Christmas tree. Johnny jumped up and yelled, "Holy shit! Is he for real?"

Johnny ran after Rusty as his pee was squirting out of him. It seemed as if he hadn't peed all day, it just wouldn't stop. Besides peeing on the Christmas tree, he also peed on the carpet and parquet floors as he ran away from Johnny. I was laughing so hard I almost peed in my pants. My husband's disbelief was obvious, but I found it rather amusing.

"Now what am I supposed to do with a Christmas tree full of dog pee? I am so done with this dog! I'm going to drop him off at the animal shelter tomorrow."

I tried to talk without laughing. "Chill out and stop being ridiculous."

"Ridiculous? Are you nuts? Did you see the amount of pee that came out of him? He was peeing like a racehorse!"

I was trying to get a grasp of the situation. "Let's give Rusty the benefit of the doubt. I'm not a dog psychiatrist, but let's face it; our Christmas tree is a real tree. How is he supposed to know the difference between trees in the yard versus a tree in the house? He probably thought if he could pee on the trees outside, why not pee on this one? In fact, did you forget? We do have a blue spruce tree in front of our house, and Rusty and I pass it every day when I walk him."

There was only so much I could do to protect my little boy. Johnny just shook his head. "You are always making excuses for him."

"No, I'm not always making excuses for him. Give him a break."

"Are you kidding me? He is always giving me work to do."

There was not getting through to him. "Whatever."

In my opinion, it wasn't Rusty's fault. He's a dog; no one can really blame him for that. His defense did make sense to me, but not to

Johnny. Another comical moment in the life of the Roseo's—thanks to our redheaded comedian.

We began taking all of the Christmas balls, ornaments and lights off of the tree. Then Johnny took the tree out of the stand and dragged it across the living room, down the steps, through the family room, and out into the yard, leaving a trail of pine needles behind. On that extremely cold night, Johnny started hosing the tree down with water and Pine-Sol to get the scent of pee out, and he was really pissed. For me, I was upstairs staying warm in the kitchen, washing each Christmas ball and ornament with soap and hot water. Once he brought the freshly cleaned Christmas tree back into the house, we let it dry over night. The next day we redecorated the tree. We hoped it would stay up without anymore traces of Rusty marking his territory. Little did we know that Rusty's pee wasn't the only problem we would experience with the Christmas tree.

The following weekend Johnny and I were in the living room watching a movie on TV and Rusty started barking like a lunatic. Looking out from the side of the bay window, I saw that the neighborhood kids were playing in the street in front of our house. I'm pretty sure as soon as Rusty heard them, he wanted to go outside and play with them. Since Rusty's view from the bay window was obstructed by the Christmas tree, he couldn't see the kids. He ran to all the other windows to search for them. Front to back, side to side, each window was full of dog slobber. He ended up back at the bay window trying to look out from the side, and suddenly the Christmas tree came crashing down. Rusty stood on top of the tree looking out the window as if he were Rin Tin Tin.

"Rusty! What is wrong with you! Get off of that tree!" Johnny yelled.

The amount of broken glass all over the floor was endless. Again, I had to hear my frustrated husband. "Does he ever stop? Another mess I have to clean up. Just look at all these broken Christmas balls!"

I took out my imaginary violin. *Here we go again.*

In the meantime, I wanted to take the blame for buying them. "Johnny, I don't think it was a wise decision buying glass Christmas balls and ornaments."

"Honey, what are you talking about? You spent an awfully long time picking them out."

"I know, but think about it. When we have a baby, the baby may grab them. God forbid they break in his or her hands. I think we should buy the unbreakable ones."

Nodding to me, he said, "Okay, whatever you want."

I was so happy he had finally calmed down and that I had persuaded him that Rusty wasn't totally at fault for breaking them. So we went back to Pergament Home Center to purchase more lights, unbreakable Christmas balls, and more ornaments. We redecorated the tree and hoped that it would stay up until Christmas.

While Christmas shopping, I wanted to find the perfect presents for our family and, of course, Rusty. One night Johnny was working and I decided to wrap some of the presents. All of a sudden, Rusty grabbed the bag of bows. "Rusty, give me those bows!" He refused to give them up until I did an even exchange with him. "Okay, Rusty, I'll give you a bone if you give me the bows." *You have a deal, Mommy.* Releasing the bows, he grabbed the bone and went on his merry way. Again, I had to give in to the spoiled brat. Finally, after wrapping all the presents and putting the bows on each one, I placed them under the tree and arranged them perfectly around our "new" nativity set, wondering how long they would look that way.

Over the course of the next few days, it was incredible that the Christmas tree was still standing and the presents were untouched when I came home from work each day. I guess I spoke too soon.

A little over a week later, our crazy redhead was at it again. On my way home from work, I stopped at the mall to do some more Christmas shopping and I came home later than usual. As soon as I walked into the house, I saw that the tree was down on the floor. "Rusty, come on now. How did you knock the Christmas tree down?"

Rusty gave me one of his sweet, innocent Irish setter looks and kissed me. I could just read his mind. *Mommy, I'm so happy you're home; the Christmas tree fainted.*

"The Christmas tree fainted? Yeah, right. You're such a little liar Rusty."

He didn't fool me for a minute. Apparently, the Christmas tree was still in the way of his territory. I'm sure he didn't mean to knock the tree down, but the bay window was his favorite place in the whole house to be on the lookout. I had a feeling that my husband would tell me that he was really going to be ready to get rid of Rusty this time, but I was prepared to put the guilt trip on him. *You can't get rid of him during the holiday season. Who does that?*

I knew I'd better hurry and clean the mess up before I had to leave to pick Johnny up at the train station. Presents were spread all over the place. Boxes were torn open and ripped apart, and the clothing was tossed aside. The wrapping paper, ribbons, and bows were shredded into pieces, scattered all over the living room. Of course, Rusty found two of his presents under the tree and tore them apart. That time he chewed the material off of the new satin Christmas balls. I could only assume that after Rusty accidently knocked the Christmas tree down, he was bored since I came home later than usual. He was a full-grown dog, with puppy-like enthusiasm, only wanting to play and have fun.

Single-handedly, I moved the tree and put it back in place in front of the window. It was a pretty difficult task, given that the tree was big and heavy. Then I put the ornaments back on the tree. At least Rusty didn't touch the strands of Christmas lights. I never would've been able to put them back in place. I sucked at putting the lights on the tree, whereas Johnny always did a great job. *What am I going to do with all these damaged Christmas balls, broken boxes, and ripped wrapping paper? If I put it all in the garbage pail, Johnny would see it, and Rusty would be in trouble again.* Picking everything up, I put it all in a trash bag. I walked across the street and put the trash bag in my neighbor's garbage pail. As usual, I had to protect my little boy.

After I picked Johnny up at the train station, Rusty was a little standoffish when we came home. Maybe he was feeling guilty for what he had done earlier, and he knew he would be in trouble. As we were eating dinner, we heard Rusty crying from the living room. That was a first. Rusty never cried except when he was a baby, and then again during the Shamu episode. *What did our mysterious dog do now?* We ran over to him, bent down next to him, and saw blood on his tongue. I shouted, "Where is the blood coming from?"

Forcing his mouth open, Johnny looked inside his mouth. "Jo, the metal hanger from the top of the Christmas ball is stuck in the side of his cheek. I'll have to pull it out."

"Oh no! I wonder how that happened." *I really knew, but of course, I played dumb.*

Johnny stuck his hand in Rusty's mouth while Rusty sat still for him, knowing that his daddy would help him. Thankfully, Johnny was able to pull it out. After he dabbed peroxide on Rusty's cheek, he walked over to the tree, inspecting it as if he were looking for gold, sensing Rusty had been up to no good. Rusty was so smart, knowing I would protect him as he hid behind me.

"Honey, it looks like some of the Christmas balls are missing."

"No, they are all there. What must've happened was when the branches opened on the tree, it created more space, so it looks like there are less Christmas balls."

"I guess you're right. Next time I go to the store, I'll pick up another package of Christmas balls so the tree won't look so empty."

"Good idea." *Yes! Rusty got away with it.* I couldn't help smirking. Johnny glanced at me, kind of doubtful and with a sly smile indicating that he knew somehow that I mysteriously held Rusty's secret. Of course I did, but I would never own up to it.

Sounding truly concerned, Johnny asked me, "How did the top of the Christmas ball wind up in his mouth? He could've been seriously hurt if he had swallowed it. This is no joke."

Wow, that was a first! Johnny was really concerned about Rusty's health and well-being. *Did I see an attachment forming between Daddy and Rusty?* That being said, Rusty never went near the Christmas tree again. It was a tough lesson, but maybe it was a good lesson to learn. However, he claimed another window—the dining room window—to look out of during the holiday season. Of course, the window was filled with slobber, but it turned out to be a very nice, enjoyable Christmas for all of us. Rusty was happy with all of the Christmas presents he received from Santa and Mrs. Claus.

One of Rusty's Christmas Presents

Chapter 23

Hormones Run Wild

Johnny and I wanted to take a nice vacation before we started our family. Ma was going to watch Rusty, which was a big help since we could never board him at the vet again. I learned my lesson when we went to the Pocono Mountains. Looking through brochures for destinations, we decided on Hawaii, and a few of the Hawaiian Islands.

Hawaii was amazing. Starting off in Oahu, we visited Pearl Harbor, which was very moving and informative. Then we flew in a small plane that was really scary to the Islands of Maui and Kauai. Renting a jeep, we had a fantastic time exploring the islands. In Maui, we went to Haleakala National Park which covers the summit area of the larger of the two volcanic mountains. Standing above the clouds and looking down at the Haleakala Crater, the view was absolutely breathtaking. We went to a luau, met some of the natives and really enjoyed ourselves. We were having an awesome time on our vacation until the last two days. When I woke up the morning after the luau, I was so nauseous. I thought I may have gotten sick from the food that I had eaten the night before, or maybe, I came down with a stomach bug.

At the airport on our way home, the airline upgraded us to first-class since they had extra seats available, at no extra charge. I thought it was going to be so cool. We would sit in the larger seats and relax for the long flight home, and eat good food, but that didn't happen for me. Instead, I was in the tiny lavatory hanging over the toilet bowl on the verge of throwing up for most of the flight, whereas Johnny enjoyed first-class. He ate filet mignon, shrimp cocktail, lobster tails, crabmeat salad, and he drank some red wine. At least he enjoyed first class.

When we returned home, I was still feeling sick. Two days later, I went to the doctor,—Surprise! Surprise! I was already eight-weeks pregnant with our first baby. We were ecstatic, but I had to stop working earlier than we anticipated due to the awful morning sickness I experienced. Honestly, why do they call it "morning sickness" when it lasts twenty-four hours a day? I wasn't able to eat or drink anything except for saltine crackers, ginger ale, and sometimes grilled cheese sandwiches for the first five months of my pregnancy. Any food smell, including Sunday sauce, was nauseating to me.

Being overjoyed about our baby and wanting to know everything about being pregnant, I bought a pre-motherhood book that explained the growth and development of the fetus growing inside of me, along with illustrated pictures from the date of conception all the way up to the fortieth week. I would look in the mirror and compare my belly with the pictures in the book while Rusty also took notice of my growing belly. Then Rusty and I would have our talks, and I would tell him about the baby's development. After all, he was going to be the big brother. I read poetry books and sang nursery rhymes to the baby, hoping he or she would hear me. The funny thing was Rusty thought I was reading and singing to him. He sat next to me and listened, just like when I would sit him down and explained things to him, or when I told him stories of the crazy things I did as a kid. It seemed as if he understood everything; he was incredibly intelligent—when he wanted to be.

At the end of my fifth month I was able to eat again, but I was craving chocolate chip cookies. For some reason the cookies had to be Entenmann's; other cookie brands didn't cut it. I don't know if it was the pregnancy or what, but I became the cookie monster.

One autumn day, Rusty and I were outside in the yard playing Frisbee. He looked so pretty running through the beautiful colored leaves on the ground, blending with the coloring of his flowing coat. Diving into the leaves, he attacked them with enthusiasm. Picking the leaves up, I sprinkled them all over him as he caught the leaves and went crunching away.

After our playtime, we went into the house. A little while later, I was in the mood for chocolate chip cookies. I went into the kitchen and looked on the counter, and I didn't see any cookies. I looked in the pantry, and I didn't see any cookies. *They have to be here. Johnny just bought them, and I didn't even open the box yet.*

The house was quiet, and my darling redhead was nowhere in sight; usually he was glued to my hip. I didn't want to believe it, but I had a good idea who took my cookies. I tiptoed around the house and found him hiding in the bathroom just as I expected. I grabbed my stubborn redhead and got into a tug-of-war with him. Even though he tightened his jaw, I finally forced it open. I stuck my face right in his face, and he had cookie breath! Inside his mouth there were tiny pieces from the cardboard box spelling out E-N-T-E. I screamed at him, "You little rat! You stole my cookies!"

My hormones were running wild, I was pregnant, and I was craving my Entenmann's chocolate chip cookies. Only my dog would eat the whole box of cookies, crumbs, and wrappings. As I was screaming at him, he was looking at me as if I were crazy. I probably was at that moment. Once this expectant mama calmed down, I sat Rusty down for one of our talks.

"Rusty, I'm going to tell you a story about when I took chocolate chip cookies when I was a little girl. It was summer vacation, and my best friend, Sara, and her family went to Montauk Point for a few days. Sara's mom, Rosa, made the best chocolate chip cookies. While they were away, I was playing hopscotch with my friend, Terri, who lived next door to Sara. A little while later we were hungry, so we went in Sara's front yard and started picking figs. Then we got thirsty and started drinking water from the hose which was above their kitchen window. We looked through the window and saw the chocolate chip cookies in a plastic container on the counter and we just had to have them. There was a small window on the side of Sara's house leading to the basement bathroom. Having no fear, just like you, I opened the window and we jumped down. We walked into the kitchen and took lots of cookies. On the way back to the bathroom window, we started eating the cookies. When Sara came home, she called me to go over and play. Right away, Sara's mom came toward me. She was talking to me in Italian and broken English, asking me if I knew what happened to the chocolate chip cookies. I didn't say a word. She grabbed me by my ponytail and showed me the trail of cookie crumbs on the floor, and my long dark hair that was stuck on the bathroom window. Then Rosa pointed her finger at me and told me to never do that again, just like I told you to never take my cookies again. What you did was wrong, and what I did was wrong, but since I took the chocolate chip cookies without their permission, I understand, and I will let you slide this time. But remember, taking things that don't belong to you is bad. We do not do that."

It seemed that my little boy understood, and I got one big kiss full of cookie breath.

After I told Rusty my story, he was busy playing with his rubber hotdog. I went into the nursery to admire the new carpeting we just had installed the day before. A few minutes later, along came my little boy. As soon as he entered the nursery, he started heaving. The sight and sound of a dog or human heaving makes me gag, pregnant or not pregnant, but being pregnant made it even worse. Then my dog erupted like a volcano, puking his guts up. Everything from the kitchen garbage pail and the bathroom wastepaper basket, including the chocolate chip cookies, exploded out of him, right on top of the brand new carpeting. I ran into the kitchen to get Pine-Sol and paper towels and went back into the nursery. When I walked past Rusty's puke zone and bent down to clean the carpeting, the smell was so deadly that it caused me to puke right on top of his. It was like a chain reaction. He threw up; I threw up. He threw up again, and I threw up again. The new carpeting had piles and piles of puke on it. I called down to my mom. "Ma, come upstairs. I'm sick."

In a panic, she ran into the nursery. She thought something was wrong with me or the baby. She took one look at the carpeting, and said, "Did you throw all this up?"

"No, Rusty threw up first, and when I tried to clean it, I threw up on top of his throw up, and then he threw up again, and I threw up again."

Ma laughed. "It sounds like the two of you in a throwing-up contest. He must've eaten something outside that made him sick. Do you want me to clean this up?"

"Please, I can't do it, or I'll throw up again."

Luckily she was patient with me and cleaned it up. It is just amazing what mothers do for their children.

Later that night, when Johnny came home from work, I had to tell him about this last incident. "You are never going to believe what happened today."

"What did Rusty do now?"

"I was craving my chocolate chip cookies, and our hungry redhead stole the box and devoured them."

"You mean the cookies you sent me out to Dairy Barn at eleven o'clock last night for?"

"Yep, those are the ones. Anyway, we were in the nursery, and he threw up twice. I tried to clean it, and I threw up twice on top of his throw up, and my mom had to clean it all up."

"Throw up on the brand new carpeting—nice going. You two couldn't pick another place to throw up?"

"I didn't plan it. He must've eaten something outside that made him sick."

"How are you feeling now?"

"Much better."

"I'm glad you're feeling better, but after dinner, I'll go to the store and rent a carpet cleaner. I need to get all the germs out of the carpeting from you and your redheaded furry twin."

"That's a good idea. Thanks."

"Did you take Rusty to the vet today?"

"No. He just threw up twice, and then he was fine all day. Believe me, if he was sick, you know I would've taken him to the vet in a heartbeat."

"Did you know that chocolate is poisonous to dogs?"

My heart stopped. "No, I had no idea."

"Honey, just to make sure he's okay, I'll call vet before I go to the store."

While Johnny dialed the number, I was so nervous.

"Jo, the vet wants to know if Rusty had diarrhea today."

"No, he pooped once, and it was normal."

I watched as Johnny was writing something down. After he got off the phone, he said, "Jo, do you want to know what the vet told me?"

"Of course I want to know."

"He said that chocolate contains theobromine, a stimulant found in the cocoa bean that is toxic, depending on the size of the dog and the amount of chocolate it ate. Usually after the dog eats the chocolate, it immediately has diarrhea, which could last all day. Based on Rusty's large size, that he only vomited twice, and that he had no signs of diarrhea, it meant he was pretty lucky."

I started to cry. "Oh my goodness, I could've killed my Rusty!"

"Honey, he's fine. You know he has a cast-iron stomach. Just keep him away from chocolate."

"I promise; from now on, I will hide anything with chocolate away from him. You're such a good daddy for calling the vet to make sure he was okay. See, you really do like Rusty."

"Don't push it."

"You can't fool me. I know you pretty well."

Johnny just smiled and walked away knowing I was right.

Chapter 24

The Rollicking Runaway

All it took for our rascally redhead to calm down was for me to stay at home with him and give him all my attention, or so I thought.

As my pregnancy progressed, I was always tired. While Johnny was at work, every afternoon Rusty and I watched the (ABC) soap operas on our "new" queen-size bed. Both of us couldn't watch TV without our snacks, so I was munching on my chocolate chip cookies, and my furry twin was enjoying his variety of dog biscuits. After the soaps, we napped together. As the weather was getting cold, I pulled the covers over me as my little boy snuggled next to me, sharing my pillow. Rusty developed a fondness for our bed, and he was one happy dog; but when Johnny came home from work he carried on. "That mutt was in our bed again! Do you see all that red hair in our bed? He does not belong in our bed!"

I took out my imaginary violin. *Here we go again.*

"What's the big deal? He keeps me company."

"Can't you and your furry twin watch TV in the living room, like normal people?"

"No, Rusty gets distracted when he hears noises outside. In our room he's calm. And, I am pregnant and our bed is comfortable."

My husband knew he couldn't argue with a pregnant woman, so he walked away. Okay, granted, Rusty did shed, but lots of dogs shed, and he was being a good boy. So what's a little hair? Plus, he was my constant companion throughout my pregnancy. I told Johnny I'd keep him out of our bed, but, of course, I didn't.

One Sunday morning while Johnny was asleep, I was in the mood for hot bagels, so I decided to go out to the bagel store. I didn't take Rusty with me because I knew it would be crowded and he would bark like a lunatic.

About twenty minutes later, I returned from the bagel store. When I walked into the house, Rusty wasn't there to greet me; instead, I heard yelling. *Uh oh, he's in trouble again. What did he do now?* Walking toward the commotion, I asked, "What's going on?"

"I'll tell you what's going on. Your dog was in our bed again. And to top it off, he was under the covers with his head on your pillow and his body was stretched out. He was pretending to be you. I rolled over to cuddle, and guess who looked straight into my eyes?"

I burst out laughing. "Are you serious?"

"Do I look serious?" He continued to rant. "I thought I was going to kiss you good morning, and instead I felt a cold black nose on my lips!"

"Chill out. Maybe he wanted to stay warm under the covers."

"I don't want to hear it. Our bed is covered in dog hair. I don't ever want him to come in this bed again."

Yeah, yeah, yeah. I did feel for Johnny, but I also knew that Rusty would still come in our bed when he wasn't home, and that was that.

"I'm here now. You can kiss me."

"Forget about it. I'll pass."

"Fine."

Honestly, I think Johnny was more embarrassed for not realizing sooner that he had wrapped his arms around Rusty and tried to make out with him instead of me. Of course, I was to blame because I let Rusty in our bed every day and spoiled him. Oh well. I thought it was pretty funny, but then again, I thought a lot of stuff my little boy did was funny.

See, it really wasn't Rusty's fault. He liked to hug and he liked to be hugged. Rusty was used to wrapping his arms around anyone he greeted, so I assumed it felt comforting to him when his daddy wrapped his arms around him in bed earlier.

Without question, I was the one who Rusty hugged the most. When my little boy stood on his hind legs and wrapped his paws around my neck, he was almost the same height as me, which enabled him to become my dancing partner. Anytime I put the stereo on, as soon as Rusty heard the music, he wanted to dance, and we did the Rusty Rumba. When my husband and I would dance, he would say that I stepped on his feet. Disco dancing, I was pretty good at, but when it came time to the other stuff, Johnny was right, I had two left feet. But Rusty never complained; he enjoyed our dancing time together, and so did I.

As the winter grew colder and my pregnant belly grew bigger, we began to shop for furniture for the baby's nursery. We decided on a very pretty, light wooden canopy crib. It came with a matching dresser which could be used as a changing table, and a four-drawer chest. The problem was we could only put down a deposit to hold the furniture. My mom, being an old-fashioned Italian, insisted that I didn't have a baby shower or set up the nursery until the baby was born. Superstition I guess, but I was disappointed that I didn't have a baby shower.

For one of my Christmas presents, Johnny bought me a beautiful wooden rocking chair that matched perfectly with the nursery furniture we selected. But thanks to Italian superstition, again, the rocking chair wasn't allowed upstairs, so it stayed downstairs in my mom's bedroom.

One day, Ma and I went to Brooklyn to visit with Bridget. When we returned home, I pulled into the driveway and didn't see Rusty lying in the bay window. That meant trouble. As soon as I opened the front door, Rusty was coming up the stairs. I asked him, "What were you doing downstairs in Grandma's apartment?"

Looking at me, my mom said, "I think he was up to no good."

We went downstairs and looked around to see if Rusty did any damage while he ran to his room. Everything looked good until we walked into her bedroom. Then I screamed, "Oh no! My rocking chair!" I sat on the floor next to my rocking chair and cried. Apparently, he feasted on my brand new rocking chair, chewing two of the bottom legs down to the raw wood. Either he still loved the taste of wood, or he was pissed off at me for being out for most of the day. Usually I was flattered by Rusty's persistent demands for my undivided attention, but maybe Johnny was right—Rusty was becoming too demanding of me. Or maybe I was getting too tired of his escapades at the end of my pregnancy. I was furious and I ran upstairs, dragged him downstairs, and put him in the yard in time-out.

While Rusty was outside, I got into the "nesting" phase of my pregnancy. I suddenly got the urge to clean everything in sight.

While I was cleaning, Ma called up to me. "Jo Ann, I am going out to meet my friend Vicky."

"Okay, I'll see you later."

As I was cleaning the dining room window, all of a sudden I saw Rusty running full speed in the yard. Unexpectedly, he leaped over our five-foot fence into our neighbors' yard and out to the street. Panic exploded throughout my body when I saw him running down the busy street. I was terrified that he would run away just like Duchess and never come home.

I looked for my car keys but I couldn't find them. Frantically, I ran out the front door, grabbing his leash that was hanging on the railing. I was in such a hurry that I forgot to put my winter coat on, and headed in a desperate search for my nutty redhead.

Running as fast as I possibly could in the bitter cold, I was holding my belly since I was visibly nine-months pregnant. *Dr. Plotkin, my ob-gyn, suggested mild exercise, but I'm sure running down Broadway wasn't what he meant.* It was early January, and all I was wearing was a pair of maternity jeans, a gray and red maternity sweatshirt that said "Baby," and a furry pair of blue slippers. Strong winds started blowing, and I began to shiver.

After a frantic chase, I saw Rusty in the distance down Broadway. I yelled, "Rusty! Cookie, cookie! Please come to Mommy. I am not mad at you." If anyone heard me, the person must've thought I was nuts. Rusty took one look at me and went running full throttle down Broadway, looking like the smaller version of the greatest horse of all time, Secretariat. *Where did my hyperactive dog get all his energy from?* It was as if running around in the yard a hundred times a day wasn't enough for the beast. Each time I got close to Rusty, he ran farther away, leaving me in tears. It was useless; he was out and enjoying his freedom. No longer did I have the energy to go after him. Plus, I was starting to get a sharp pain on my right side, which was concerning me.

It was pretty evident that I wasn't going to catch him. The only conclusion I could think of was to walk back home, look for my car keys, get my coat, and drive around until I found him. Just as I was turning the opposite way to walk home, I saw a glimpse of our rascally redhead about a half a mile away. *Thank you, God. Now, please let him stay put.*

I didn't call his name because I didn't want him to take off again. I ran on the opposite side of the street so he wouldn't see me. There he was, stopped on another one of his missions, pulling a massive tree root with all his power, showing every muscle in his body. I dashed across the street, snuck up behind him, and grabbed him. Fortunately, his collar was still on, and I attached his leash to it. Hugging my furry twin, I looked him straight in the eyes. "Rusty, don't you ever run away from Mommy again!"

If it wasn't for the tree root giving me the opportunity to catch up to him, I may have lost my little boy forever. I was so happy I finally found him, but I also wanted to kill him. To make matters worse, he couldn't walk home normally; he pulled me along in every direction but straight ahead. *Why couldn't I have a nice leisurely walk with my dog like most people?* Dragging our eighty-five-pound, thick-as-a-brick, energetic redhead back home, I was out of breath, and my heart was beating so fast. First, I was freezing, and then I started sweating, trying to keep up the pace with him. Truthfully, I didn't know if I was going to make the half-mile walk back home. I was totally exhausted. Plus, being pregnant and carrying an extra twenty-five pounds didn't help. I hoped I wouldn't get pneumonia because of my crazy dog. I didn't have that nice red coat to keep me warm that he had. All I wanted was to get my crazy little boy home and get to the warmth of our house.

Suddenly, I stopped. My stomach started cramping. *Oh no! I hope these aren't contractions.* I sat on the curb for a few minutes and waited for the cramps to subside. Surprisingly, Rusty sat still, watching the cars going by. A few times, the pain was so severe that I actually felt as if the baby was coming. I could just hear it on the local news: *Woman gives birth on the sidewalk in North Massapequa while Irish setter watches.*

I was trying to figure him out. What was he thinking running away, especially from me? He always treated me as though I was the love of his life. He had a great home, all the food he wanted, including homemade Italian specialty dishes, and plenty of toys. Besides, he had a big yard to run around in, and he was spoiled rotten. God only knows what made him tick and what went on in his mind.

Arriving back home, we walked up the steps, and I brought my flaming redhead back into the house. I detached his leash and filled up his water bowl, from which he drank to the last drop. Then I collapsed on the recliner, trying to catch my breath. Now what was wrong with this picture? What was I thinking? I should've taken care of myself first. But no, to me my redheaded furry twin always came first. For sure I was at his beck and call, and he was always one step ahead of me.

At that point, I decided I needed a break from him. I brought him downstairs in the family room so he could look out the glass sliding door and not bother me. "Rusty, you were a bad boy today. Mommy is going to take a nap. You are staying down here in time-out. Be good; I'll come and get you later."

As I was going upstairs, Rusty was busy chewing on a toy and I went to take my much-needed nap, without him. The best part was I was done going out for the day. With the baby arriving any time now, Johnny purchased a Jeep Cherokee for himself. He knew it would be too much for me going back and forth to the train station with the baby. He also traded in the Celica for a Chevrolet Monte Carlo. We felt we needed a larger car with the baby.

A couple hours later, Johnny surprised me and came home from work early. He kissed me hello and knew from the expression on my face that Rusty had done something again.

"Where's Rusty?"

"He's in the family room in time-out."

"What did he do now?"

"You don't want to know."

"Just spit it out."

"Okay. First, he chewed up the legs on my rocking chair."

"He what!"

"I put him outside in the yard in time-out. Then he got out of the yard and ran away."

"Are you shitting me? I hope you let him go."

"No, I would never let him go! I ran my ass off going down Broadway in the freezing cold to catch him."

"Have you lost your mind? Why didn't you drive to look for him instead of running after him?"

"Because I couldn't find my stupid car keys, that's why!"

"You know you shouldn't do anything to jeopardize our baby."

"I know. I really thought he was only a couple of blocks away when I went after him. Sometimes he sits outside the grooming salon when I walk him waiting to see the other dogs. By the way, Dr. Plotkin said I should get exercise."

"Yeah, by taking leisurely walks. Not running down Broadway after a thoroughbred in twenty degree weather."

"Listen, I had no choice. I wasn't going to let him run away."

"When will you ever stop protecting that dog already?"

"Never."

"I just don't get it. Why do you let him control you? You are the parent here, not him. Remember, you are nine months pregnant. You need your rest."

"Rusty doesn't control me. We have a lot of fun and I do take naps."

"You call running down Broadway after him fun and resting?"

"Well, it doesn't happen that often," I said.

"Anyway, when we came home, I was exhausted and I needed a nap, so I put him downstairs in the family room in time-out for the second time."

"So, where is he now?"

"He's still downstairs; I just woke up before you came home."

"Okay, let me get out of my work clothes, and then I'll look at the rocking chair, and then we'll bring the nutcase upstairs."

"Fine."

Even though I knew Johnny had a valid point, but the fact was, Rusty was still my little boy, and if he had run away and didn't come home, I would've been devastated. In spite of Rusty driving me crazy at times, I still adored my redheaded furry twin and loved him with all my heart.

Chapter 25

And Baby Makes Four

During the weeks leading up to my due date, I was so uncomfortable and felt like a beached whale. Heartburn had set in, and my hands and ankles were swollen. Most of the time, Johnny even had to help me get off the recliner or the couch each day.

We were so excited about our baby arriving soon, but my family was concerned about what Rusty's reaction would be toward the baby. I had to hear the sarcasm and ridicule from my brother-in-law, Tommy as he kept telling us to get rid of Rusty. "After all, the baby is going to be my godchild, and as godfather I need to protect the baby. Get rid of that dog already."

"No way, Tommy; we are not getting rid of Rusty. I'm sure he'll be fine once the baby arrives."

My brother-in-law could be just as thickheaded as Rusty. "Jo, you're not taking me seriously. I'm warning you. If I don't like the way that dog looks at the baby, I will take him out and get rid of him myself."

"Tommy, Rusty isn't going anywhere. This is his house, and that's that!"

"I'll talk to Johnny. He'll listen to me."

There was no reasoning with him; he was taking his pre-godfather duties a bit too seriously. However, it did show me that he would really be a good godfather, caring so much about our baby's well-being, but I would never tell him that.

"Fine, go talk to Johnny," I said.

Silently, he shook his head and walked away.

After Tommy left, Johnny sat me down. "Jo Ann, we need to talk."

When Johnny calls me Jo Ann that means he's serious. "I guess Tommy spoke to you."

"Honey, Tommy is right. When he's right, he's right. Listen, Rusty is a really big dog. He's extremely strong and energetic. And, he is used to getting all of your attention. It is possible that he may be jealous of the baby."

"Jealous of the baby? Are you kidding me? No way. He will love the baby, you'll see."

"Remember, obedience school? You couldn't control him no matter how and you tried. How are you going to handle him and take care of a baby?"

I listened to what Johnny was saying, but the point was, Rusty wasn't going anywhere. No doubt Rusty was accustomed to receiving all my affection. My feelings were that when the baby arrived, I would lavish Rusty with even more of my love and keep spoiling him, and he would be fine.

The following day, when Johnny came home from work, he seemed troubled. "Is something wrong? Did something happen at work today?" I asked.

"Work was fine. Here's the deal, Jo. I talked to Jimmy at work today. His parents live in upstate New York, and their house is on five acres. Jimmy spoke to them, and they said they would be willing to take Rusty."

Just hearing what Johnny was saying was ripping my heart out as I started crying. "No way! You are not getting rid of my little boy!"

"Look at it this way. Worst-case scenario—only if Rusty starts acting crazy. It is possible that he will start destroying the baby's things. The two of you are inseparable, and once the baby comes, he will have to share you. I'm telling you, he is not going to be happy. At least Jimmy's parents are also Italian. That means Rusty would still have his Sunday pasta with meatballs. It wouldn't be too much of a shock for him."

I was fuming, practically spitting out venom. "Over my dead body! No one is going to take Rusty away from me and his home!" I stormed out of the room before Johnny could even respond to me.

Wondering how to acclimate Rusty to the baby, I had to come up with a plan, and fast. *This is going to be tough.* After all, Rusty had been the baby of our family for two and a half years, and my little boy was spoiled rotten, thanks to me.

The following day, I drove to Toys "R" Us and started browsing through the variety of diapers and baby toys. While I was in the store, something clicked. *Let me buy a doll that looks like a baby.* I found the perfect doll. It was a girl, and she resembled a newborn. The package on the box said that the doll cried and even came with a bottle that had make-believe milk moving around in it. *This may work.* I was curious to see what Rusty would do when he saw me take care of the infant doll. I hoped that he liked the doll and my plan would be successful.

Coming home, I was delighted from the greeting I received from my furry twin. He was so happy to see me, as if he hadn't seen me in a month. It didn't get any better than that. I took the infant doll out of the package and brought it into the nursery while Rusty followed me. A month earlier, Bridget had given me a few of my nephew's receiving blankets, which I hid from my mom. Spreading one blanket on the floor, I put the doll on it, pretending the doll was a real baby. I undressed the doll, rubbed baby lotion on her, dressed her, and wrapped her in the receiving blanket, all while Rusty stood there watching me.

I then sat him down for one of our talks. "Rusty, this is a make-believe baby. Mommy is going to have a real baby. Watch how Mommy takes care of the baby."

I was showing Rusty step-by-step everything I was doing with the infant doll. Rusty looked curiously at me and the doll, back and forth. It was great that I had his undivided attention and that he was interested to see what I was doing with the doll. Next, I carried the doll in my arms and sat on the recliner in the living room as Rusty followed me. I showed him the baby doll up close. I wanted him to get used to the scent of the doll with the baby lotion. He sniffed it gently. When I shook the doll, she cried. "Rusty, look, the baby is hungry. The way you eat food from your bowl, the baby has to eat from her bottle. See how nice she drinks her bottle."

At times Rusty reminded me of a child; he was so inquisitive. Much to my surprise, he kissed the doll on her foot. "You need to be a good boy when our baby comes home, just like you're being a good boy right now," I said. "Mommy is really proud of you. You're a big boy now."

I practiced the baby exercise with him several times a day for about two weeks, and it seemed that Rusty was enjoying the special time with me and the baby doll. I was optimistic that he wouldn't forget when I went into the hospital because his life with me in our home depended on it.

I was waiting anxiously to go into labor; it was a week past my due date. Johnny and I started going for bumpy car rides, and of course we took

Rusty with us. We also did a lot of walking in the cold trying to bring on the labor, again taking Rusty with us. Finally, at eleven-thirty on a cold Thursday morning in late January, I went into labor. Our big day had finally arrived. I called Johnny at work. "This is it! Today is the day!"

Johnny sounded so nervous. "How are you feeling? Are you in any pain?"

"No, I'm fine. I don't have any pain and no contractions yet. I'll call Dr. Plotkin, and Ma will drive me to the hospital."

"Okay, I'll catch the first train and meet you at the hospital. Jo, I love you."

"I love you, too. We are going to be parents. Wow!"

I ran downstairs to tell my mom. "Ma, guess what? I'm in labor."

"Finally. How are you feeling?"

"I feel good."

"Do we need to go the hospital now?"

"No, I'll call Dr. Plotkin first. I'll let you know when we have to leave."

I went back upstairs, and at noon I called Dr. Plotkin's office. His nurse gave him the phone. "Jo Ann, are you having any contractions?"

"No, not yet."

"Okay, then meet me at the hospital in one-hour. Who will be driving you?"

"My mom."

"Good. I'll see you at one o'clock."

"One o'clock it is. Thank you, Dr. Plotkin."

Instead of relaxing and taking it easy, I was doing my normal routine around the house. At one o'clock, instead of going to the hospital I made my lunch and started watching *All My Children* with Rusty. I wasn't having any contractions yet, so, to me, what was the rush? This was my first baby, and I had heard that it could take several hours before anything happened. Besides, I really wanted Johnny to be there from the beginning. At one-forty-five, Dr. Plotkin called me on the phone. "Why aren't you are the hospital young lady?"

"I'm not having any contractions, and I wanted to eat my lunch first."

"Finish your lunch, and then go straight to the hospital."

Oops. "Okay, we'll leave soon." *I couldn't tell Dr. Poltkin that I was watching one of my favorite soap operas.*

When *All My Children* was over, I called down to my mom. "Ma, Dr. Plotkin said we have to leave now."

"Okay, I'll be right up. She came upstairs and took my bag to drive me to the hospital, which was close by.

I was so happy about having our first baby, but I was also worried about the pain I was going to experience giving birth. Although we had attended all of the Lamaze classes and knew the routine, a few friends of mine had told me that they were in labor for over twenty-four hours, and that scared me.

Now was the dreaded time to say good-bye to my little boy. Mommy, Daddy, Rusty, and now baby would make four. "Rusty, Daddy will bring you a toy if you are a good boy while I'm in the hospital and another toy when Mommy and Daddy bring the baby home. Now, don't forget what I taught you with the baby doll."

I gave him a nice long hug and kiss, fighting back tears. In return, I got a bunch of wet kisses and a wagging tail, and my heart melted. I really hated leaving him. Too bad he couldn't come with us and stay in the waiting room. I just had to stay positive and keep hoping Rusty would like the baby. Then I took one last look at him and walked out of the front door with my mom.

Perfect timing! Johnny made it to the hospital in record time. He arrived at the hospital at exactly the same time as we did. When he got out of his car, he saw us walking into the hospital and he ran after us. "Jo, wait up!"

After he kissed me hello, he asked, "Honey, I don't get it. I ran my ass off trying to catch the local train, and I just missed it. I ended up getting a cab to take me to Penn Station. Why are you and your mom just getting here now? I thought Dr. Plotkin wanted you here by one o'clock?"

"He did. But I really wanted you to be here with me. And *All My Children* had a really good episode today, and I didn't want to miss it."

"You mean you really wanted to watch the soap opera."

"We're here now, so what's the big deal?"

"What would've happened if you had the baby at home?"

"Oh, stop. I'm feeling fine and the hospital is only ten minutes from our house."

At that point, the nurse came with a wheelchair and wheeled me to a private labor room.

"Hey, Johnny, there's a TV in my room. This is so cool. Could you put *One Life to Live* on?"

"Jo, are you kidding me?"

"Ma, what are we going to do with her?" My mom just laughed.

"Are you here to have a baby, or watch soap operas?" My husband asked.

"Chill out. I'm here to have a baby, but if the soaps are on, that's good for me. Maybe watching TV will take my mind off of the labor pains I'm going to have."

"I don't know who is more nuts, you, or your dog."

"Whatever."

All of a sudden, Bridget walked into the labor room. "Hey, what's going on here? I thought you would've been hooked up to the monitor and having contractions by now?"

Before I could even answer, Johnny stepped in. "Ask your kooky sister."

"Jo?"

"Everything is fine," I said.

"Okay. You look great, so that means everything is good with the baby. Is this another one of your goofy episodes? Let's hear it."

"No, it's not another one of my goofy episodes. I was just late coming to the hospital because I wanted to finish watching *All My Children*."

"You were watching *All My Children?* I can't believe it. I missed watching my favorite soap opera to drive here to be with you, and you got to watch it."

"Well, one of us had to watch it," I said with a giggle.

Bridget shook her head and laughed. "So how was it today?"

"It was really good; I have so much to tell you."

Johnny started cracking up. "That's my wife."

During labor, I was thirsty and wanted a snack; but the nurses said I wasn't allowed to. All they gave me were ice chips to suck on. The four of us were waiting anxiously in the labor room, but nothing was happening. I had a few contractions here and there for the first five hours, sometimes strong, but no big deal. Then all of a sudden, I shouted, "Holy shit on a stick!"

"Honey what's wrong; are you okay?" Johnny asked.

"No, I'm not okay. These contractions are really hurting."

Johnny was amazing. He started massaging my shoulders and rubbing my back to keep me calm. We started doing the breathing each time I had a contraction. Honestly, the breathing technique we learned in Lamaze class did help, and my husband was a great coach.

For the next two hours, the contractions were coming fast and nonstop. Suddenly, I wasn't interested in snacks any longer, but something else sparked my eye. "Johnny, look! *Knots Landing* is on."

"Cool. I like that show."

"By the way, it is a night-time soap opera, just so you know," I said as Bridget and I were laughing.

At the final stage of my labor, the contractions were really painful, but I was a trooper and toughed it out. Then Dr. Plotkin examined me and said, "Your baby is ready to be born."

We only got halfway through *Knots Landing* and it was time to take me to delivery. Johnny hurried and put on his surgical gown, surgical cap, and shoe coverings since he was going to be in the delivery room with me. As they were wheeling me on the gurney, I wore my pink booties, hoping for a baby girl and yelled out to Johnny, "Don't forget the camera."

"I got it," he answered.

After ten minutes of my pushing, Dr. Plotkin announced, "It's a girl!"

I looked at Johnny and shouted, "Yes! A baby girl!"

Having become first-time parents, Johnny and I were beaming with joy. Kristine Marie weighed seven-pounds, five-ounces, and thank God, she received a clean bill of health. So alert, she looked directly at us with her big brown eyes and a full head of black hair. While I held our baby in my arms, I was enchanted by the fact that Johnny and I had created this miracle; it felt surreal. Johnny whispered to me that he had hoped for a baby girl, too.

Kristine was absolutely beautiful; no words could describe the pure excitement I felt holding her for the first time and hearing her first cry. Johnny stepped out of the delivery room to tell my mom and Bridget. My mom was very happy and had had a feeling I was having a girl by the way I carried. After having had four boys, Bridget was jumping up and down screaming in pure excitement, "It's a girl, it's a girl, it's a girl!" At that moment, I could actually feel my mother-in-law, Kay, looking down smiling at the baby. It was ironic that she knew we would have a baby girl, and she had wanted a granddaughter more than anything. It really saddened me that she wouldn't be with us to see her granddaughter grow up.

The following morning, Johnny came to visit me. "How's Rusty?" I asked.

"Jo, he's so sad. All he is doing is moping around the house looking for you. I even took him out in the yard to play, but he wanted to go back inside and look out the window."

"Tell him I'll be home tomorrow with the baby."

"I will. Later, when I pick up the baby's furniture, I'll let him stay in the nursery with me while I get the room situated."

"Great idea. I'm sure he'll like that."

On that Saturday morning, Kristine and I were released from the hospital. Something very important was going to happen shortly. Rusty was going to meet his baby sister for the first time. On the car ride home from the hospital, all I thought about was my Rusty. *Please behave; please be a good boy; please adjust to the baby.* I kept hearing Johnny reiterating his warning. *If Rusty shows any kind of jealousy toward the baby, or acts crazy, he will go to another home.* I couldn't be happier about our baby girl, but it physically made me sick to imagine that Johnny would give Rusty to Jimmy's parents if he didn't take kindly to the baby.

When we came into the house, Rusty was downstairs with his grandma. Johnny and I went into the living room with the baby. I took off the white sweater, bonnet, and booties that Ma had crocheted for her. It was time to introduce Rusty to his baby sister.

I sat down on the recliner and Ma brought Rusty upstairs, holding him by his leash. Taking the leash from her, Johnny brought Rusty over to me and the baby. Johnny explained to him, "Rusty, this is Kristine, your little baby sister. You need to be very gentle with her and be a good boy. Your job is to be her big brother, to love her, and to protect her."

At first Rusty looked at her inquisitively up and down, and then he looked at me and Johnny for approval. Approaching the baby hesitantly, he slowly started wagging his tail. All of a sudden, he gently kissed her right across her tiny hand. We were happily surprised. To our amazement, he was subdued with the baby, gentle as a lamb. Unbelievably impressed with Rusty, it seemed my training him with the infant doll had really paid off. Then he started kissing me and wagging his tail while I hugged my little boy. "Rusty, you're such a good boy. Mommy is so proud of you."

The joys of parenthood suited us beyond our wildest dreams. We had our beautiful, healthy, precious baby girl, and our spoiled, but lovable redheaded dog. Immediately, Rusty started fulfilling his role as the baby's protector. Everywhere we went with the baby in the house, Rusty tagged along during all hours of the day and night.

Johnny was an incredible husband and new dad, wanting to spend as much time with the baby as he could, letting me get much-needed sleep. Sharing the middle-of-the-night-feedings, I slept softly as Johnny and Rusty paced the floors with the baby. I heard him explaining every detail about the pictures and paintings on the walls to her. Johnny would sit on the recliner and sing to her while Rusty was right at their side. As Johnny told me, it was his bonding time with his baby girl and his dog. Honestly, I don't know how he worked all day and stayed up much of the night with the baby, but he did and never complained. I believe he looked forward to it.

Once Kristine came into our family, Rusty's life changed radically for the better. Kristine was a good, happy baby, only crying when she was hungry or had a dirty diaper. Rusty set up camp right next to her. If she made any little whimper, Rusty barked to alert us. His bed didn't exist anymore. Whether she was sleeping in her bassinet in our bedroom or in her crib in the nursery, our protective redhead was always right there watching her.

It still amazed me how fast our spoiled dog grew up and took the role as her big brother. I guess Rusty knew he no longer was the baby of the family; he was a big boy now. Not much earlier, there had been talk about sending Rusty to a new home. See, everyone was mistaken. He didn't need to live with Jimmy's parents. I was right all along. I could see that Tommy was impressed with Rusty's good behavior too, but he would never have admitted it.

Remember the parquet floor, the dining room table, and our bull-dozed kitchen? Those crazy, bizarre episodes were only a little over a year prior to Kristine's birth. Now Rusty had no desire to cause any destruction. There was no more going into the wastepaper basket looking for sanitary napkins or dirty tissues, or even in the garbage pail in the kitchen looking for food. Soiled, smelly diapers didn't even faze our redhead. Rusty's high-spirited puppy days were over. It was on to bigger and better things.

The only time Rusty slept was when Kristine slept, but he always slept with one eye open protecting his baby sister. Although he still had plenty of spirit, his temperament definitely softened after she was born. Johnny was very happy with this new behavior from our dog and finally liked him. Rusty must've sensed Johnny's feelings and continued to warm up to him. *Life was good!*

Chapter 26

Let the Winter Fun Begin

Out of the four seasons, winter was definitely Rusty's favorite. The freshly fallen snow looked breathtaking. It was very pristine and shimmery-looking, like sparkles as a reflection from the sun. Opening our front and back doors, it surely looked like a winter wonderland. A fresh blanket of snow covered our entire property. Snow was everywhere, including all the rooftops. That winter, it was really cold and wet, with snowfall after snowfall, and then two blizzards hit to top it off. In some areas, the snow was much higher due to the snowdrifts; they were at least six feet high.

At the first sight of the newly fallen snow, Rusty had a sudden burst of excitement. Racing to the sliding glass door, I couldn't open it fast enough for him to frolic in the snow. With each new snowfall, his adrenaline kicked in as he raced around the yard. Lucky for me, my mom stayed inside with the baby so I could play with my little boy in the snow. I made perfectly round snowballs, threw them at him, and he snagged them in midair and devoured each one, chewing them until they disintegrated in his mouth. In every part of the yard, Rusty found something to do—from catching the snowflakes that fell from the sky to eating the frozen icicles that hung from the patio table. His mouth was constantly moving. Seeing the snowdrifts, Rusty ran and crashed into the highest one and came out wearing a white coat. Watching him having fun, I joined him freefalling in the same mountain of snow. My redheaded furry twin and I were always acting silly, rocking and rolling around in the snow like two little kids. Once our high-spirited dog got ahold of the snow, there was no stopping him. Rusty dug all the holes he wanted to without getting dirty or getting into trouble.

As our professional snowblower, Rusty threw the snow everywhere. With his paws going full speed, he plowed paths in the yard leading to nowhere. Tiring himself out, he would jump on the patio table, spread out on the blanket of snow, take a break, and take off again, dashing through the snow. After a while, when I thought he had had enough of playing in the snow, I would bring him into the house. Since he was fully covered in snow, I took my hair blower and thawed him out, melting the snow off of him, while Johnny was busy shoveling the snow.

When Johnny was finished, he came inside, relaxed for a while and then it was playtime for him and our rollicking redhead. Taking Rusty outside again, Johnny too chased him around in the snow and threw snowballs at Rusty. The best part for Rusty was the sleigh riding. As soon as Johnny took the wooden sled out of the shed, Rusty jumped right on it. Sitting straight up, smiling and showing his big pearly whites, he was pulled by Johnny all around the yard where there weren't any snowdrifts. Once he brought Rusty back inside, I had to blow-dry him, again.

When Johnny bought his Jeep Cherokee, it also came with a snowplow that enabled him to clear our driveway. Always being helpful, Johnny even snowplowed a few of our neighbors' driveways as Rusty proudly sat shotgun. Our neighbors offered to pay Johnny, but he wouldn't accept money from them. He just wanted to be neighborly. So instead, our neighbors gave Rusty a bunch of dog biscuits, and he was one happy copilot.

When the sanitation snowplows arrived in the middle of the day to clear the snow off of the streets, they literally pushed the snow against our driveway, as well as our neighbors' driveways. Our cars ended up being blocked in by at least three to four feet of snow. Most of the time, they came around when Johnny was at work, so he couldn't shovel the snow to another area. If I needed to go to the grocery store, I couldn't get my car out of the driveway, so I would take Rusty with me and we would walk down Broadway while Ma watched the baby.

Once the sidewalks were shoveled and it stopped snowing, the dusting of snow turned to ice. My redheaded furry twin and I would begin our slipping and sliding routine. I did the slipping, and my little boy did the sliding. Rusty had a fascination with ice. When there was ice on the ground, he ran so he could slide, most of the time crashing into the fence. My fun-loving redhead just had to see every single ice patch, pulling me along as we went sliding. Time and time again, I slipped and landed on my ass. I don't know how he did it, but this dog never went down. A courteous and respectful dog, Rusty always waited for me to grab on to him and pull myself up.

At times, when he saw our house, he took off, leaving me holding on to him for dear life. The way he ran, it was as if he were a sled dog and I was his passenger, but without the sled. Before we crash-landed into the snowdrift the first time, I closed my eyes, not knowing what to expect. When I opened my eyes, Rusty looked at me, smiling, wagging his tail. I could always read his mind. *Mommy, please, can we do it again? This is so much fun.*

Of course, I would give in. "Okay, Rusty, one more time, and that's it."

And off we went. Actually, it was fun. He took off running and sliding, as I wrapped my arms around him until he crashed right into the mountain of snow again head-on. It was pretty scary at times, but we made it home safely every time.

Rusty the Snow Dog

At the end of March, after a long, snowy winter, Johnny and I brought Kristine and Rusty downstairs by their grandma. We wanted to walk around the backyard to check on things and spruce it up before Kristine's christening. The outside area by the sliding door looked good; there was just some frozen snow on top of the grass and dirt. But walking a little farther into the backyard, there was an awful smell? I thought there was a dead animal in the yard. Thankfully, we didn't see one, but instead we saw massive amounts of Rusty's dumps, or, more politely, poops. No, forget about it. Poops are small, dumps are big, and Rusty's dumps were humongous.

"Jo, look at this! Our whole yard is covered in dog shit!"

"Well, what do you expect? With all the food Rusty eats, it has to come out somewhere."

Johnny was annoyed and rolled his eyes. Pile after pile of poop was everywhere. We didn't even have an area to walk in without stepping in dog poop. Our backyard was the Shrine of Poop.

Johnny looked at me, and I looked at him. "Johnny, I thought you were cleaning it up?"

"Honey, I thought you were cleaning it up," he answered.

"Oh well. I guess neither one of us were cleaning it up," I said with a laugh.

During that extremely cold winter and being busy with the baby, we didn't take Rusty for walks, so the yard became Rusty's bathroom. All we had to do was open the sliding door in the family room, and Rusty went outside to do his business in his designated area. Little did we know his designated area became our whole backyard. We held our breath to stop ourselves from choking, being overcome by—the only way I can describe it—toxic fumes.

"Johnny, what are we going to do?"

"Don't think I'm putting all his shit in trash bags. The sanitation workers may think there's a dead body in them and they will call the police on us. Let me think about this for a minute."

I was wondering what kind of idea he was going to come up with. Then he suggested, "We can put it all in the wheelbarrow."

"Wheelbarrow, and do what with it?"

"You'll see. I have a plan, but I need your help."

Getting his wheelbarrow out of the shed, I held it while Johnny scooped up and tossed two months supply of Rusty's dumps into the wheelbarrow, filling it to capacity. The smell was deadly as we were gagging the whole time. All of a sudden I lost my grip, and the wheelbarrow tipped over. Dog poop was all over the ground, and we just burst out laughing.

"Well, at least it's all in one area. We don't have to walk all around the yard to pick it up again." I just had to say.

"What happened to my relaxing weekends? Aren't we supposed to spend quality family time together, instead of doing this?"

"I would think so, but shit happens."

"Honey, you got that right."

"Seriously, Johnny, what are we going to do with a wheelbarrow full of Rusty's dumps?"

"We'll put it down the sewer across the street."

"Aren't people going to see us?" I asked curiously.

"No, we'll wait until it starts getting dark."

"If you think it will work, it is fine with me."

Cold and exhausted, we went back into the house, washed our hands, and checked on the baby. Kristine was happy looking up at her mobile in the portable crib in Ma's apartment, and Rusty was looking out her patio door. We hung out downstairs for a little while, and I told my mom, "We have to go back outside for a few minutes; we'll be right back."

"Where are you going?" she asked.

"We have to finish what we started earlier. We won't be long."

It started to get dark. I opened the stockade gate while Johnny pushed the wheelbarrow through the opening. I grabbed the other handle, and off we went.

As we were passing the front of the house, Ma came out on the steps and was going to ask us what was in the wheelbarrow, but she didn't need to. The smell was overwhelming. Standing on the front steps, she started laughing. "I was watching the two of you from the window wondering what in the world you were doing with the wheelbarrow. It looked like Johnny was gagging as he was holding his flannel shirt over his face, and it looked like you were gagging too, covering your face with your ski hat. Now I know why both of you were gagging. If I didn't see this with my own eyes, I would have never believed it. This definitely belongs on an episode of *I Love Lucy*."

I was hysterical laughing. "Ma, this crazy idea wasn't mine. This time it was Johnny's. But I guess you can add this episode to the list of the crazy things I've done."

Holding the wooden handles of the wheelbarrow, I held it tight as we were walking down Broadway, hoping not to tip it over again. I was on the lookout while Johnny shoveled all of Rusty's dumps into the sewer. It took him quite awhile until the wheelbarrow was completely empty. Then we went back to the yard for round two and back to the sewer.

Mission accomplished! It was to our advantage that no one saw us. It would've been pretty embarrassing. Two wheelbarrows full of Rusty's poop were floating in the sewer system on Broadway. Hopefully, it didn't get clogged that day. We vowed to never let that happen again, no matter how bad the weather was. Every Saturday for now on, both of us as a team would be on poop patrol.

Rusty always kept busy in the winter, snow or no snow. Each month Johnny ordered a cord of firewood to use in our fireplace and had it delivered to our house. The delivery workers did a great job of stacking it up in the corner of our backyard, close to the family room for easy access. The pile of firewood was approximately four feet high by eight feet wide by four feet deep. The wooden logs were neatly piled high until our curious redhead got hold of them.

One day, I was in the family room cleaning when I noticed from the window that Rusty was climbing on the fresh load of firewood. I stood there shaking my head. *What a piece of work he is.* Yelling out the window, I said, "Rusty, get off of there!"

He jumped right off the pile of firewood, but not before he pulled one log off, causing all the logs to tumble down. Taking the log with him, he went to the other side of the yard and started ripping it apart, chewing it piece by piece, scattering it all over. Watching him in action, I had to laugh; but I knew Johnny was going to flip out when he saw the logs all over the ground.

Again, my redheaded furry twin took after me. In mishaps similar to what Rusty had done with the wood, I also had the habit of being clumsy when things were piled high. Just a few days before, I had gone food shopping. When I reached for a bottle of Coca-Cola that was on the pyramid display—with my luck—just by removing one bottle, just as Rusty had removed one log, I caused them to start tumbling down. Watching about fifty bottles of soda rolling all over the floor in the store, I couldn't pick them all up, so I just walked away. *Good thing no one was around at that moment to see the destruction I had made.* Therefore, I couldn't fault Rusty for taking the log out of the pile of firewood, because I basically had done the same thing.

Chapter 27

Two Peas in a Pod

Being busy with the baby all day was rewarding, but it also was a full-time job, especially since Kristine didn't sleep as much as infants usually do. She was very alert, inquisitive and was always looking around instead of sleeping. It seemed like she didn't want to miss anything, just like our dog.

One night when Johnny came home from work, he told me that he had to be at work for an early meeting the next day. I told him I would get up during the night to give Kristine her bottle. *It was the least I could do, since he helped me so much with the middle-of-the-night feedings.*

Through my sleep, I heard Kristine crying at two o'clock in the morning. With my eyes half opened, I went into the kitchen to warm up her bottle. Suddenly she stopped crying and fell asleep. I sat down on the rocking chair in the nursery, which was right across from our bedroom, knowing she would wake up at any moment and I'd get her bottle and have it ready for her.

Like a roar of thunder, Rusty started barking vigorously. Hearing the sound of his loud footsteps, I opened my eyes and saw him charging into our bedroom. Rusty was standing next to our bed hitting Johnny with his paw. Startled, Johnny jumped out of bed, and then I jumped out of the rocking chair. We followed Rusty and ran into the kitchen, smelling something coming from the gas stove.

"Oh no! Kristine's bottle!" I shouted in a panic.

All of the water evaporated and melted the plastic bottle. The smell of the burnt plastic was nasty. Johnny turned off the gas burner, threw the pot into the sink and opened the kitchen window to air the room out.

"Johnny, is Kristine going to be okay? Should I call her pediatrician?"

"No, she's fine. The smoke is contained in the kitchen. There is no smell anywhere else in the house, but I'll open the dining room and living room windows, just to play it safe."

"Thank God the nursery is at the other end of the house," I said.

"Honey, what happened?"

"I don't know. Kristine woke up really early this morning, and she was fussy all day. I must've been in a dead sleep when she cried for her bottle. After I started warming up her bottle, she stopped crying. I went in the nursery and sat down on the rocking chair waiting for her bottle to be ready, but I must've fallen asleep."

"Well, thank God, Rusty alerted us. I'll put the burnt pot outside. Since Kristine is still sleeping, go back to bed. I'll make her another bottle when I come back inside."

"Johnny, are you sure? I thought you have to wake up really early tomorrow?"

"It's fine. I'm up now anyway. You need sleep more than I do."

"You are so sweet. No wonder why I fell in love with you. Thanks."

I went over to Rusty and hugged him. "Rusty, thanks for calling Daddy. You are such a smart boy. You are the best dog ever!"

While we were asleep, our noses hadn't detected the scent of the burning plastic on the gas stove in the kitchen, but Rusty had smelled disaster in the making if he hadn't woken us up. Our smart setter saved our lives with his keen sense of smell and quick response to danger.

For Kristine's baptism, Bridget, as godmother, bought her a beautiful white satin christening gown with eyelet flowers and a matching bonnet and booties. It was a lovely ceremony, and Kristine only cried when the priest poured the holy water on her forehead.

With thirty people in the house for the christening party, our redhead was on his best behavior, but anytime our friends and family wanted to see the baby, they needed Rusty's approval. While Kristine was in her crib catnapping, Rusty lay in the doorway blocking the entrance so no one could enter and disturb her. As always, Rusty was faithfully at Kristine's side and there was no getting past him. His priorities clearly had changed. Being her protector, he didn't leave her alone for a minute; we were impressed and so proud of him.

After Kristine woke up, my sister was giving her her bottle while Johnny and I were mingling with our guests. Suddenly, Johnny noticed that Rusty was sitting by himself in the corner of the dining room, which was odd.

"Hey, Jo, look at Rusty. He's making weird faces. He must've swiped someone's drink and gotten drunk."

We went over to Rusty as he was making clattering noises. He was sticking his tongue out, moving it side to side and up and down. Johnny bent down and opened his mouth, "Oh no! Rusty has a beer bottle cap with the ridges stuck in the roof of his mouth!"

For a moment, everyone in the room froze and looked at Rusty. With his fingers, Johnny pulled and pulled, but the bottle cap wouldn't budge. "The bottle cap is embedded too deep. I'll have to use my pocketknife to get it out," Johnny said.

Reaching into his pocket to get his pocketknife, he turned to Cousin John. "Could you hold Rusty down while I try to get the bottle cap out?"

"Of course I can." Cousin John kneeled down next to Rusty and held him while Johnny took the point of his pocketknife and pushed it under the bottle cap. The bottle cap came out and some blood dribbled out, but at least it was out. Rusty was pain-free and happy. Thankfully we didn't have to take him to the emergency animal hospital during the christening party. Daddy had saved the day.

After a long, cold, snowy winter, spring finally arrived and the weather was getting warm. I was so excited to take Kristine for a walk in her new carriage. At first, I thought about taking Rusty with us, but I didn't think I could handle him and push the baby carriage at the same time. Right after we left the house, I heard Rusty barking at us from the bay window. I looked up, and he looked so sad.

The following day, I decided to take him and see how it went. "Rusty, do you want to come for a walk with me and the baby?"

With a huge smile on his face, tail wagging, he was all ready to go. I grabbed his leash and fastened it to his collar as he sat patiently. "Now, Rusty, you need to walk nice and slow with us, or I'll have to bring you back home."

Surprisingly, Rusty walked obediently beside me. His eyes were intently focused on being the leader, the protector of his baby sister. *Who is this dog?* It felt refreshing to finally take a stroll in the neighborhood with my Irish setter, and it became a daily habit. Neighbors came over to see the baby while Rusty sat straight up at attention next to the carriage. No jumping, no barking—just observing every movement they made. Our dog became a pleasure. Anywhere Kristine was, our beautiful redhead was—right next to her. His heart was full of so much love, not just for me as it always had been, but for his baby sister, too.

On those beautiful spring days, I also took Kristine in the yard. Seeing how content she was in her carriage with Rusty right beside her always brought a smile to my face. The fresh air outside helped her fall asleep. Once Kristine was napping, Rusty, the sun-worshiper, jumped on the patio table to take some sun, which was another one of his favorite things to do. No more digging, no more uprooting bushes—those days were over. Of course, he did mosey around in the yard, but our backyard never looked so good. His destruction had finally ended.

Rusty sunbathing

Rusty was obsessed with his baby sister. When Kristine started sitting up, I put her in her windup swing while Rusty lay underneath her. Once Kristine was ready for her walker, she scooted all around the house as Rusty followed her, never leaving her out of his sight. When she began eating solid food, I would put a handful of cheerios on the tray of her walker. As soon as Rusty saw Kristine turn away, his tongue went right across the little tray, and he scooped all the Cheerios, gone in one shot! The Cheerios became entertainment for them. Each time I put more Cheerios on the tray, Kristine tossed them with her tiny fingers to the ground so Rusty could eat them. She clapped her hands and giggled as he ate them all up.

With summer arriving, Johnny decided that the Jeep Cherokee had done its job over the winter snowplowing, but it was getting old, so he traded it in for a Ford Bronco. It was a newer SUV, and the back area was more spacious for Rusty. Almost every weekend, Johnny was outside in the driveway washing our cars. My little boy, my baby girl, and I would go outside to join him. Kristine was either in her stroller, or in her walker watching her daddy while Rusty sat right next to her, with no leash. He wasn't taking one step away from his baby sister. Just a few months earlier, Rusty without a leash was unheard of, but now he acted as her parent. It was incredible how attached our baby and our dog were, and how special was the bond that they shared.

Kristine and Rusty

A month before Kristine's first birthday, she developed a terrible cough. I took her to her pediatrician, Dr. Aiello, who was only ten minutes away. He prescribed infant cough medicine and suggested I put a humidifier in her room. The following night, I didn't like the sound of her cough; it sounded different. As soon as Johnny walked in the door after work, I said, "I'm so glad you're home. Kristine's cough has gotten worse. I just took her temperature and it's 103 degrees. I'm going to call Dr. Aiello."

Johnny took Kristine from me as she held her arms out to him. "You're right. She's burning up."

It was after-hours when I called, so the answering service picked up. The woman who answered the phone told me she'd give Dr. Aiello the message. Within minutes, he called me back. "Mrs. Roseo, Dr. Aiello here. What's going on with Kristine?"

"Doctor, we are really concerned. She has a temperature of 103 degrees, and her cough sounds worse."

"Okay, meet me at the hospital. Don't go to emergency; go straight up to pediatrics. I'll see you there."

I called down to my mom. "I just spoke to Dr. Aiello. He said we have to take Kristine to the hospital."

"I'll be right up. I'm coming, too."

Johnny went outside to warm up the car. When he came back inside, I was bundling Kristine up in her snowsuit since it was really cold outside. Concern was written on Rusty's face as he saw us hurriedly leaving the house.

When we arrived at the hospital, Dr. Aiello examined Kristine. He told us they needed to take some tests. I was a nervous wreck holding Kristine in my arms. While we were waiting for the small gurney, the receptionist came into the room. "Mrs. Roseo, I need you to complete this paperwork while they bring your daughter for testing."

"I'll fill out the paperwork later. I am going with them."

"No, you cannot go with them. You need to come inside the office and complete the paperwork."

"I am not leaving my baby. I'll do it later."

She was adamant. "We cannot run any tests until you complete the paperwork."

"Well, you could forget about it. I am not going anywhere but with my baby."

Dr. Aiello saw how distraught I was and told the receptionist, "Mr. Roseo will fill out the paperwork. Mrs. Roseo will be coming with us while we run the tests on their daughter."

After Johnny completed the paperwork, they waited anxiously for us to return. About twenty minutes later, we came back, and Dr. Aiello told us the results. "Your daughter has a very bad case of bronchitis and a touch of pneumonia."

"How did she get bronchitis and pneumonia?" I asked. "She is in the house most of the time."

"It's not unusual for babies to come down with this infection during their first two years, especially during the cold winter months."

"Doctor, how will you treat her?" Johnny asked with concern.

"I need to keep her in the hospital for forty-eight hours."

"Two days?" I asked.

"Yes, we need to treat her by placing an oxygen tent that fits over the crib to help her breathe, along with medication."

"Dr. Aiello, I can't leave. Please, I need to stay with my baby."

"That's fine Mrs. Roseo. There is a recliner in her room that you can sleep on."

"Great! Thank you."

When the nurse carried Kristine into the oxygen tent, she looked scared. She started crying and held out her arms to me, "Mama." I slipped my finger through a small opening in the tent and held her tiny hand. She tried to come out, but then the nurse gave her cough medicine, and she fell asleep within minutes. My mom and Johnny left the hospital at eleven o'clock that night, and I just sat up in the chair watching her for the rest of the night.

The following morning Johnny came back to the hospital. He brought me my toothbrush and a change of clothes. Kristine was happy to see Johnny, and thankfully her cough was quieting down, but she still needed to stay in the oxygen tent for another day.

After she fell asleep, I asked, "How's Rusty?"

"Not good. I think he's going through a state of depression. He didn't sleep at all last night. All he did was look around for you, and then he lay down in front of Kristine's crib and didn't move. He didn't eat a thing this morning; all he is doing is moping around. I took him in the yard and threw the football to him, but he didn't even want to play. When I go home later, I'll take Rusty for a ride in the Bronco; he likes looking around at everything that's going on in the neighborhood."

"Aww, my poor little boy. Could you also make him pancakes, or give him a two-by-four, or something to chew on?"

"Sure, I feel bad for him too."

Later that day, Ma came by the hospital. "Kristine is looking so much better. When can she come home?"

"Dr. Aiello said tomorrow."

"That's good news because I don't think Rusty could take another day without the two of you. He is very sad. He doesn't want to come downstairs by me, so I stay upstairs with him so he won't be alone."

"I know. I really feel bad for him."

When Johnny came back later that night I asked him, "How's Rusty?"

"He still hasn't eaten, not even one dog biscuit. I took him in the yard to play, but he wanted to go inside the house. He didn't even want to go in the Bronco. You and Kristine better come home tomorrow because this dog will die of a broken heart."

"Could you ask the nurse if you could bring him in the hospital to visit us? You can say he's a therapy dog."

"Honey, he's not a golden retriever. He's our big, kooky Irish setter."

"Well, it was worth a shot."

The following day, Dr. Aiello came into Kristine's hospital room. "Mrs. Roseo, I am very pleased with Kristine's progress. I am discharging your daughter. Keep her at home for a few days, and she'll be fine."

"That's great! Thank you, Dr. Aiello."

Excited to go home, I couldn't wait to see my little boy. As soon as we walked through the front door, Rusty exploded with joy at the sight of Kristine and me. He ran right over to us. I gave him a big hug, and he started crying. Then he had the biggest smile on his face. His tail was wagging a million times a minute, and there he went, kissing Kristine and then me. His family was back together.

Chapter 28

The Perfect Gentlemen

One particular great quality Rusty had about him was his love for children. Rusty was drawn to kids with the hope that each one would be his playmate. He may have instinctively known it was his job to protect them. At first, when we walked Rusty down the block, the little kids were afraid to touch him. His size must've been intimidating to them, but once they saw that he was a gentle red furry giant, they didn't stop petting him, and Rusty loved it.

Bridget and Tommy would come over and visit often. Their four boys, Little Tommy, Danny, David and Andrew were Rusty's pals. Always delighted to see the little cousins, Rusty's body would wiggle in delight. Everywhere Kristine and the boys would go, whether in the house or outside in the yard, Rusty was right there with them running around and playing.

During the summer, the little ones would go in Kristine's plastic kiddy pool and started splashing water at each other. Rusty saw them having fun and he'd jump right in the pool to join them. Once Rusty plopped in the pool, there wasn't much room for the kids to move around. Getting back at Rusty for hogging up the pool, they filled up their plastic beach pails and poured the pool water on top of Rusty. The funny thing was, Rusty sat there and enjoyed it while he was also drinking the pool water. When there was hardly any water left in the pool, I put the sprinkler on in the yard for the kids to run through. Of course, Rusty was the first one to run through it, as the kids followed him. Rusty was too funny; he acted like he was just another one of the kids, running back and forth through the sprinkler.

One of Rusty's favorite games he played with Kristine and her cousins was hide-and-seek. The kids would hide, and Rusty would try to find them. He'd run into every room, looking behind the furniture, underneath the beds and behind all the doors. When they played outside, he squeezed through the bushes, looked under the outdoor furniture, and under the patio deck stairs. This dog was on a mission, and with his extraordinary sense of smell, he always found each one of them. The kids would be "out," and Rusty would win the game of hide-and-seek. No matter how hard the kids tried, they just couldn't outsmart our setter.

I spent many afternoons strolling along outside with Kristine and Rusty. Suddenly, I was concerned. This time it wasn't about Rusty, it was Broadway. Broadway seemed so much busier with traffic than when we bought our house a few years earlier. I mentioned it to Johnny, and he was already on the same page.

A few days later, we put our high-ranch house up for sale. With that sale, Rusty was allowed to stay in the house when the Realtors showed it; he had calmed down significantly, and finally became a docile dog, like Duchess.

Our house went into contract within weeks. Fortunately, we found a really nice four-bedroom, split-level house close by in Massapequa Park, another pretty suburban town on the South Shore of Long Island. The new house was on a quiet block, not on a main street. It was the third house in from the corner, and the Bethpage State Parkway was down the block. All the bedrooms were upstairs and the kitchen and dining room was huge. Downstairs in the family room, there was a beautiful stonewall fireplace; and there was also a cute apartment for my mother. Her apartment had another private side entrance, but we also had access behind our family room. This house also had an in-ground swimming pool, but Rusty still had plenty of room in the backyard to run around in.

Getting accustomed to his new environment and surroundings, Rusty went exploring, inspecting each room and every nook and cranny. He was eager to rock and roll. Our foyer was spacious for our active redhead to run back and forth, from the front entrance to the back sliding doors, and up and down the two split levels of stairs.

Claiming his territory in the backyard, Rusty ran around and peed on every tree and bush and even Kristine's swing set. The only thing he didn't care for in the new house was the in-ground pool. Walking to the edge of the pool, he sniffed it once, and that was it. He ran as far away from the pool as he possibly could.

Later on, Johnny tried to walk Rusty down the steps leading into the pool, but Rusty pulled back with a strong force. Even though Rusty loved his bath time and getting squirted with the hose and running in the rain and hail, he wasn't comfortable near the pool. Seeing his reaction, we didn't force him to go in. I'm pretty sure as soon as he sniffed the chlorine, he remembered how horrified he was when he saw our pool in Valley Stream tumbling down. It's funny how dogs don't forget.

Each holiday, I worked very hard to make each one special when our relatives came over. I always put out a good spread of food. Our favorite celebration was Christmas Eve, which in Italian tradition is the Feast of the Seven Fishes. There was no meat on the table that day, just amazing seafood and, of course, pasta. My mom was also busy making the best seafood salad and homemade pizza. She always gave Rusty some of her pizza, even with her secret Sicilian ingredient in the pizza sauce. Midnight was when the meat came out—the sausage and peppers, steak and chicken. Rusty was always on his best behavior while our family sat at our dining room table eating up a storm, the Italian way.

That Christmas, my brother, Andrew, my sister-in-law, Stephanie, and my niece, Melissa, had brought their dog, Chuckles, a French poodle over to spend Christmas with us. Over the years, Rusty had gotten along well with Duke, but he had never been with Chuckles before. I was a little leery since Chuckles was so small and Rusty was so big and strong, but Rusty shocked us all. They played well together, and he wasn't rough with Chuckles at all. It was just amazing to watch how good Rusty was with the little dog.

Rusty knew he would receive many presents from Santa and Mrs. Claus. I gave him one of his presents, and he was excited, but he didn't open it. Instead, he sat waiting patiently on the living room floor right next to Kristine, watching her open all of her gifts. Once he saw her playing with her new toys, he realized she had finished opening her presents, and it was time for him to open his.

Rusty's Christmas destruction was finally behind us. He was such a good boy, the perfect gentleman. Luckily, I still have those precious memories on video.

Watching my little boy and my little girl growing up together was priceless. One of Kristine's Christmas presents was a Cabbage Patch plastic tea set. It had a tea pot, four little cups, four saucers, a plate, and four tiny spoons. She placed her tea set on her little round wooden kiddy table that came with two little chairs.

"Rusty, come here and play tea party with me," she said sweetly to him.

Walking over to her, Rusty wagged his tail in excitement. In all actuality, he couldn't sit on the little wooden chair, but Kristine was such a bright little girl that she moved his chair away from the table so he could sit directly in front of his place setting.

I watched in amazement as he sat straight up and they played tea party together. She poured the tea for herself and for Rusty; it consisted of apple juice and water. She also put a few animal crackers and dog biscuits on the plate in the center of the table. Rusty understood every word Kristine said to him and willingly followed her instructions. *How is it that he listened to a two year old, but he never followed my commands in obedience school?* Sitting in an upright position, with his right paw on the little table, Rusty acted just as a person would, but he had a red fur coat on.

In her squeaky little voice, she asked him, "Would you like some tea, Rusty?"

Rusty moved his paw toward her.

"You're welcome. The tea tastes good, right?"

Rusty barked a "yes."

"Do you want a dog biscuit or animal cracker?"

Rusty barked two "yeses."

"Good boy. Have an animal cracker, I like them, too."

So much for the dog biscuits. However, Rusty did finish them after he ate the animal crackers.

When it came to Easter Sunday, my sister and I alternated the holiday. Of course, we had Easter egg hunts with the little ones. Rusty was right there alongside the kids searching for the Easter eggs.

Our caring redhead noticed that Kristine was having a difficult time finding the colored eggs. The boys were a little older than her, and they were always one step ahead of her; so Rusty stepped up to the plate for his little sister. With his impeccable scent, he would find an Easter egg, pick it up with his mouth, never breaking it, run over to Kristine, and drop it into her Easter basket. Then off he went, squeezing under the furniture to find more eggs to bring her.

Little Tommy always found the golden egg, but Kristine usually won the Easter egg hunt with the most Easter eggs in her basket, with Rusty's help. *I guess that's what you get when two play for the price of one.*

While Kristine was getting into everything as a toddler, Rusty was always right behind her. Luckily, her terrible twos weren't as bad as Rusty's terrible twos. What she did like to do, was take each toy out of her toy chest and throw it to Rusty so he could catch it. Then she moved on to Rusty's toy basket, and threw each one of his toys to him. Every day there were piles and piles of toys on the floor; whether it was her toys, or his toys, our floor was always full of toys.

Rusty loved pleasing his little sister. Our toddler and our dog were inseparable. He let her pull on his ears, pull his tail, and basically he let her do anything she wanted to do to him. She would even climb up on him, and try to ride him as a pony. There was never any complaint about Rusty when it came to his relationship with Kristine. He was just amazing with her.

Every afternoon at three o'clock, *Sesame Street* came on TV, and at four o'clock, it was *Mister Rogers Neighborhood*. Sitting on the couch, Kristine would be focused on *Sesame Street* and enjoyed learning new things. But during *Mister Rogers Neighborhood,* she would get off the couch, go on the floor and used Rusty as a pillow. She watched the show for a few minutes, then her eyes would get heavy and she would fall asleep. It must have been the song—*Won't You Be My Neighbor?*—which started, "It's a beautiful day in the neighborhood." To me, the song sounded like a lullaby.

Meanwhile, Rusty was such a good sport that he stayed in that position and didn't move until *Mr. Rogers Neighborhood* was over and she woke up.

Kristine was overjoyed every time they played together. I will never forget her words: "Mommy, I love Rusty. He is my best friend in the whole wide world."

Best friends Rusty and Kristine

Chapter 29

Rough Days Ahead

April showers were all gone. By early May our rose bushes were in full bloom. One spring afternoon, I called Rusty to come outside with Kristine and me. His response was strange; he didn't come to me. I went looking for him and found him in the family room sleeping. "Wake up, Rusty. Come on, let's go outside and play with Kristine."

Opening his eyes for a second, he looked at me and went back to sleep. Rusty's behavior was highly unusual. Normally he jumped at the chance to go outside with us.

Later, when I was preparing dinner, Rusty got up and walked around the house, but something wasn't right. I looked in his water bowl, and he had hardly touched it all day; usually he drank a few bowls throughout the day. At the time, I assumed he probably had a stomach bug from eating something in the yard that made him sick.

For the next two days, his strong appetite diminished. Rusty wasn't acting at all like himself. Even Kristine tried playing with him, but all he wanted to do was sleep. This was so not like him. Something had to be wrong. It really was concerning to me to see our energetic dog acting so peculiar.

The following day, I took Rusty to a local vet. We had used this animal clinic before for his shots and when he had an ear infection. When the vet examined him, he told me that Rusty was dehydrated and that he had a urinary tract infection. He gave me antibiotics and said to give him plenty of water. After ten days on the antibiotics, Rusty wasn't getting better. In fact, he started losing weight and began coughing. On that Friday night during dinner, Johnny asked me, "When do you take Rusty back to the vet?"

"On Monday," I answered.

"Can you call the vet tomorrow morning and see if they're open on Saturday? I want to take him back tomorrow; Rusty has been sick for over a week now. Something is not right with him."

When I called the vet the following morning, the receptionist gave us an appointment at eleven o'clock that day. Arriving at the animal clinic, they tested Rusty for heartworms and it came out negative. Then the vet asked me, "Mrs. Roseo, does your backyard have grass?"

"Of course our backyard has grass. Rusty is in the yard all the time."

"It looks like your dog may have allergies to certain grasses."

"So what can we do to make him better?"

"You can buy Benadryl over the counter. Give him two caplets three times a day for his allergies. You can also buy Robitussin cough medicine for his cough. Keep him inside for a few days. He'll be fine."

When Johnny and I left the animal clinic, Rusty was still hacking away. "Jo, do you trust this vet?"

"I don't know. Should we try the Benadryl and the cough medicine and see if it works?"

"Jo, I think this vet is a quack. How could a dog that's been playing in the grass his whole life suddenly develop an allergy to grass? We need to find another vet."

"I think you're right."

A few minutes after we arrived home, Rusty collapsed and fell down on the floor. His whole body started shaking. I started screaming, "Johnny! What is happening to Rusty?"

In a panic, Johnny said, "It looks like he's having a seizure!"

As fast as the seizure started was how quickly it subsided. Rusty stood up and seemed disoriented. Then he sat down. I sat on the floor with him and petted him on his favorite spot between his eyes. For the longest time, he looked at me with his big empathetic eyes, as if asking me to help him. My poor little boy looked so frightened.

"What is wrong with him, Johnny?"

"Honey, I have no idea, but we need to get him to another vet, like now."

I tried calling our friends who had dogs to get the phone number of their vet, but they weren't home. I started looking through the *Yellow Pages* when the doorbell rang. Cousin John and Delores had stopped by to visit while they were in the neighborhood shopping. Rusty didn't even get up to bark at the sound of the doorbell or jump on Cousin John, his normal greeting. Johnny escorted Delores into the kitchen while I stood in the foyer with Cousin John. "Hey, what's up with Rusty? No crazy greeting for me? I'm insulted."

"We think he had a seizure a few minutes ago," I said.

Cousin John looked shocked. "What do you mean he had a seizure?"

"He hasn't been himself for almost two weeks now. We took him to the vet twice already. As soon as we came home from the vet today, he collapsed and his whole body was shaking."

"What did the vet say?"

"The first visit, he said that Rusty was dehydrated and had a urinary tract infection. The second visit, today, he said that Rusty has allergies to grass."

"That's absurd! What about the seizure he just had?"

"I didn't call him yet. Actually, we need to find another vet. We don't think this doctor is too swift."

Cousin John said, "Listen to me. I know this dog pretty well—since he was a puppy. He's always been a pain-in-the-ass, but there is definitely something more seriously wrong with him than the vet is telling you."

Dolores overheard us. "I know of two excellent veterinarians with impeccable reputations," she said. "They also deal with unusual cases. Their names are Dr. Alan Baum and Dr. Gary Baum. They are brothers, and they are located at Crawford Animal Hospital on Merrick Road in Lynbrook." She went into her pocketbook. "Here, Jo Ann, I just happen to have their card."

I gladly accepted the card from her. "Thank you so much, Dolores."

When I called to make the appointment, the receptionist asked me, "Are you an existing patient or a new patient?"

"New patient," I answered.

"I'm sorry, but Saturdays are our busiest days; we are totally booked. I'll look to see what available appointments we have for next week."

"Please, we need to see the doctor right away. Our dog has been to a vet twice already and he has gotten worse. In fact, he just had a seizure fifteen minutes ago."

"I will speak to the doctor. Please hold."

She came back on the phone. "Dr. Baum said you can bring your dog right in."

"Thank you. We will be there within a half an hour."

Rusty was weak, and Johnny needed help from Cousin John to get him into the Bronco. After Johnny and I left with Rusty, Cousin John and Delores stayed at the house to visit with Ma and Kristine. I sat in the back of the Bronco with my little boy while he lay across the whole back seat with his head resting on my lap. Usually Rusty jumped from window to window barking at strangers; now it was complete silence.

The moment we arrived at Crawford Animal Hospital there were at least a dozen dogs in the waiting room. However, as Johnny carried our eighty-five-pound redhead in his arms, the receptionist must've noticed how sick Rusty really was, and even though the waiting room was packed, she was kind enough to bring us right in. "Just wait in this examining room; Dr. Alan Baum will be right with you."

At first glance, Dr. Alan Baum was young, kind, and compassionate. I explained to him the symptoms Rusty was having, plus the seizure he had had earlier. I told him what the prior veterinarian diagnosed him with, and gave him the list of medications that he prescribed for him.

"Folks, you are telling me that your dog was being treated for a urinary tract infection, allergies, and a cough?"

"Yes," I replied

From the negative expression on his face, Johnny and I could tell it was the wrong diagnosis.

During the examination, Rusty went into another seizure. That time, his eyes started to roll back. Foam came out of his mouth, and a few drops of blood started coming out of his nose. Dr. Baum called out the door, "Gary, room one stat!"

Dr. Gary Baum rushed into the examining room. He was also young and looked concerned. Dr. Alan Baum filled in Dr. Gary Baum about Rusty, and then they both examined him. After they completed their examination, they spoke to each other quietly in the corner of the room. I could see the grimness on their faces. As soon as Dr. Alan started to speak, I detected something in his voice that wasn't good. "Gary and

I came to the same conclusion. Rusty is showing signs of neurological dysfunction."

"Neurological dysfunction. You mean brain damage?" I asked.

Dr. Alan replied, "Yes, I'm sorry. Your dog is very sick. We need to run blood work on him, but we won't be able to get the results for three days. With this being a Saturday, the blood tubes won't get sent out until Monday and we need the results right away. Your dog may not make it three days."

Tears filled my eyes, and I started crying. This news was too agonizing to hear. My eyes were pleading to Johnny to help Rusty as he stood there in shock himself. I looked back and forth at both doctors in blind confusion. I burst out, "I'm not hearing this; this can't be happening. What happened to him?"

While we were standing in the examining room, I had my arms wrapped around my little boy while Dr. Alan made a phone call. Listening to him, he explained to the vet on the other end of the phone about his findings, and how urgent it was that Rusty be seen. After he hung up the phone, he said to us, "I just spoke to a friend of mine at the Animal Medical Center in New York City. You need to take Rusty there immediately. They are going to run the tests on your dog. I told him we need the results right away. They are expecting you."

Johnny questioned him. "What kind of tests are they going to do? And what type of animal hospital is it?"

"It is a specialty teaching animal hospital; they are open seven days a week and they handle all kinds of emergencies. The facility has the necessary laboratories and equipment to get immediate results from the blood tests we ordered. We also requested X-rays, which Rusty will be sedated for."

Trying to comprehend what he was telling us, I asked, "X-rays?"

"Yes. They will look for any inflammation of his brain, spinal cord, and lungs. They will also run a specific blood test called a PCR, which is a fairly new test, in combination with a test for antibodies. Typically this is the most accurate way to make a complete diagnosis."

I was so desperate to save my little boy that I took off my marquise diamond engagement ring as I cried to both Dr. Alan and Dr. Gary. "I don't care how much money it costs. Here, take my engagement ring; it is probably worth about five thousand dollars. Please do everything you can do to save my Rusty; I'm begging you."

Dr. Gary put his arm around me with comfort and said, "There's no need for that, keep your ring. We'll try everything we could possibly do to save him, but I have to tell you there are no guarantees."

Dr. Alan gave Johnny the address and the veterinarian's name to see once we arrived there. "You may be there for quite a few hours since they will have to sedate your dog to run the proper tests. They will call us with the results upon completion of the tests."

"Dr. Alan, if Rusty has to be hospitalized will he stay there, or do we bring him back here?" Johnny asked.

"It's their call. They will let you know when Rusty is awake. If they want you to bring him back here, we'll get instructions and treat him," Dr. Alan responded.

Suddenly I panicked and looked at Dr. Alan. "What happens if you are closed when we get back?"

"No need to worry. Gary or I will be here for Rusty, as long as it takes."

Before we left Crawford Animal Hospital, Dr. Alan gave Rusty a mild sedative to relax him for the car ride. A technician carried Rusty out to the Bronco, placing him on the back seat. I sat next to him, put his head on my lap, and cradled my furry twin. Silently and in shock, we drove straight to New York City while Rusty slept.

With all the traffic on a Saturday, it seemed like an eternity by the time we arrived there. Hurrying inside, Johnny carried Rusty in his arms. I told the receptionist that Dr. Baum sent us there. The staff was extremely nice and caring. Rather quickly, two technicians came out and took Rusty into the examining room as we followed. The veterinarian came in and introduced himself. He also introduced two students who were doing their residency. He gave Rusty a quick examination. "Dr. Baum informed me of their findings. We will run the proper tests that he ordered. You will be here for a couple of hours. Meanwhile, you can have a seat in the waiting room."

"Thank you," Johnny replied.

At that point, the technicians put my little boy on a gurney, and wheeled him away as the doctor went with them. Sitting in the waiting room, I stared blankly at the floor in disbelief of what was happening. Minutes ticked by, turning into hours as we waited. For the life of me, I couldn't think coherently as we sat in silence. I prayed to St. Francis, the patron saint for animals, to make our Rusty well again.

Eventually, one of the technicians came out and brought us into a private office. The veterinarian came in. "The tests are completed. I spoke to Dr. Baum. We all feel it's in the best interest for Rusty to bring him back to Crawford Animal Hospital for treatment."

"Doctor, what are the results? What is wrong with him?" Johnny asked.

"Mr. Roseo, one specific blood test we ran will take at least another hour to get the results. You can head back to Lynbrook. Meanwhile, I'll go over all the tests results with Dr. Baum. He'll have them for you when you arrive there."

Johnny shook his hand. "We can't thank you enough. We really appreciate you seeing Rusty and running all the tests."

"You're welcome. I'm glad I could help."

A few minutes later, one of the technicians brought Rusty to us. He was still groggy from the anesthesia. He carried Rusty out to the Bronco and placed him on the backseat. Looking at Johnny, I said, "I don't think it's good news. He probably didn't want to tell us."

"Honey, maybe it really does take time for all the results to come back, and he doesn't want to jump the gun. We will find out when we get back to Crawford Animal Hospital."

"Okay, you're probably right."

I sat in the back holding my little boy, just watching him sleeping.

We arrived at Crawford Animal Hospital at seven o'clock; there was no staff or any other pets in the waiting room. Technically they were closed, but Dr. Alan was at the front door waiting for us. Dr. Alan held the door open for us while Johnny carried Rusty inside and put him on the examining table. Dr. Gary was already in the examining room.

Dr. Alan spoke. "We went over the results from the tests that we ordered. It appears that Rusty tested positive for Ehrlichia."

"What is Ehrlichia?" Johnny asked.

"Ehrlichia is a type of rickettsial disease. It is a tick-borne infection. It is spread by the brown dog tick. When a dog is bitten by this tick, it passes the organism into its bloodstream."

"Brown dog tick?" Johnny replied. "I don't understand. He always wore his flea and tick collar. I change it monthly."

"Apparently, it didn't work. This type of organism inhabits the body's white cells and destroys the cells lining the vascular system, causing hemorrhage and swelling of the central nervous system," he explained.

"Can you help Rusty?" I asked.

Dr. Alan responded sadly, "I'll be honest with you. We don't know. This type of bacteria can be fatal. The delay in the diagnosis and the initiation of the incorrect antibiotics contributed to the development of his neurological problems. It was determined that he also has fluid in his lungs, which was detected in the X-ray. Usually proper treatment needs to be started within five days after being infected with the brown dog tick. The chances of surviving are pretty good, but at the chronic stage of this disease, it can cause multiple organ failures and impending death."

I wanted to express my understanding as to what he was saying, but I couldn't get the words out. Holding hands, Johnny and I stood there horrified, and then Johnny asked him, "Do you know how long he's had this disease, and is it in the chronic stage?"

Dr. Gary responded, "There are two scenarios of this disease. Either the disease could've been dormant for a few months, and he didn't have any symptoms, and suddenly they appeared, or it is an acute form of the disease."

Suddenly, my knees went weak and panic tightened in my throat. I grabbed Johnny's hand, squeezed it as tight as I could, and whispered to him, "What about Kristine?"

"I was just going to ask the same question." Johnny turned to both doctors. "Is this disease contagious to humans? We are really concerned for our daughter. She is two and a half, and she is always lying on top of Rusty, and he is always kissing her."

As we waited for an answer, I felt a wave of nausea pass over me as I started sweating. Thankfully, Dr. Alan put us at ease. "No, dogs do not transmit the bacteria to humans. Let me assure you, the only way a human can get this disease is if that person was bitten by the same infected brown dog tick, which is extremely rare. You have nothing to worry about. Your daughter is fine, but for your own peace of mind, you can have her pediatrician run blood work on her. But I know it will be negative."

My mind was spinning in circles. I felt all kinds of emotions all at once—relieved that Kristine wouldn't get the disease, but devastated about Rusty's diagnosis. I just burst out crying. Johnny held me as I tried to stop my tears of happiness and grief, but it was impossible. I was a pure basket case. Johnny and I knew that both doctors were very knowledgeable, but we were going to have Dr. Aiello run the blood test on Kristine right away, just to make sure.

"Mr. Roseo, in answer to your question, I am very sorry, but yes, Rusty's disease is already at the chronic stage. The damage is extremely severe, and his chances of surviving are slim," Dr. Alan said with sadness.

Clamping my hand over my mouth, the reality hit me that my furry twin wasn't invincible, and he could actually die. Hearing this horrific news was devastating. I started screaming, "Johnny, please, they can't let my little boy die. Help him!"

Dr. Alan and Dr. Gary looked at us with sorrowful faces. Then Dr. Alan said, "Based on all the facts, you will need to make a decision. Treatment could be costly, and there are no guarantees that he will make it; but mainly, we don't want the animal to suffer. We can discuss euthanasia, or we can hospitalize him and try our best. Think about it; we'll be back in a few minutes."

I was numb as I was thinking. *Our Rusty is so young. He doesn't even have one gray hair. It simply isn't possible that our indestructible redhead, who ruled the world, could die. This is just a bad dream. This can't be happening.*

"Johnny, are they giving us the option of ending Rusty's life?"

"Honey, I hate to say this, but yes they are."

My husband's face was pale as he took me in his arms. He knew this news was killing me, and he couldn't do anything about it. Needless to say, this wasn't the answer we had hoped for.

When they returned, Dr. Alan asked us, "Have you guys made a decision?"

Me, I was unable to respond. I couldn't swallow the lump that was in my throat. Truthfully, it felt like my heart was being ripped out of me. Even though Rusty's prognosis wasn't good, I wouldn't give up on him. A tiny part of me still held out hope.

Johnny just looked at me. I didn't need to say one word—the devastation and agony were written all over my face. Johnny questioned them, "You said his chances are slim; but if there is even the slightest chance that he can recover, please try whatever you can to save him. I promise you, I will not let him suffer."

Dr. Alan gently touched Johnny's hand. "Mr. Roseo, are you sure? It's a long shot."

"Yes, we're sure."

Processing what both Dr. Baum's told us, Johnny and I were fully aware that it was going to be an emotional journey for us, but we were willing to take it. As long as the odds were slim and not none, there was still a chance of Rusty surviving; it was definitely a road worth taking.

Johnny glanced over at me and then at Dr. Gary. "Doctor, out of curiosity, do you know how Rusty came in contact with this disease?"

I was extremely angry and yelled out to them. "I'll tell you how this happened! That incompetent vet we took him to in the neighborhood. This is his fault for diagnosing Rusty with a urinary tract infection and then an allergy instead of running the correct tests. The medical board should take his license away!"

Dr. Gary nodded and said, "The only thing I can say is that the brown dog tick comes from a wooded area. We don't know how long he's had this disease. Like I said, he could've had it for a few months and it was dormant, or he could've contracted it suddenly."

As they were going over their paperwork, Johnny looked troubled. "Jo, let's think back. A wooded area? Our house is down the block from the Bethpage State Parkway. There are woods that run all along the parkway. Did he ever go there?"

"Yes, he did, about a month ago. I walked Kristine over to my friend Gina's house so she could play with her son Michael. Their

JO ANN ROSEO

house is right across the street from the Bethpage State Parkway. When I was leaving Gina's house, I saw Rusty coming toward the end of the block. Evidently, he got out of our yard and went looking for Kristine. When he saw me, he must've known he would be in trouble, so he ran to the wooded area. I was so afraid he would run onto the parkway and get hit by a car, so I ran like crazy to catch him, but I couldn't. By chance, Gina's husband pulled into their driveway; he saw Rusty and was able to catch him. Then I brought him home."

"Right, I remember you telling me. And that weekend we took a ride upstate to Ellenville to my parents' summer house. The property is surrounded by several hundred acres of state land. While we were sitting on the front porch, we let Rusty run on the front of the property since that area was fenced in."

"Johnny, what about the New York State Thruway?"

"Oh yeah. Going upstate, Rusty slept in the back of the Bronco, but going back home he was awake when I stopped to pay the toll. He went berserk, barking at the attendant to the point of almost breaking through the side window to get out. He was mesmerized by the toll booth attendant behind us, barking for one straight hour. Then we stopped at a rest area. I thought if I took him for a walk he would calm down; but he didn't. Back in the Bronco he faced the rear view window and barked for the whole ride home."

Thinking back of how crazy Rusty was that day, we both had to laugh. "He sure did give us all a headache," I said.

"You got that right," Johnny answered.

Based on where he had been, we realized he could've gotten the tick bite in any of these wooded areas.

Dr. Alan said, "First we are going to stabilize him. We'll start an intravenous drip to rehydrate him, along with the correct antibiotics and steroids to try to kill this disease."

"Do you think he has a chance to survive?" I asked him.

"If all goes well and he responds to the treatments, only time will tell. We need to keep him here for at least ten to fourteen days. We are also going to administer a blood transfusion. It is possible that he may be bleeding internally. Again, we can't make any promises; it still may result in a fatal outcome. We will do everything we possibly can, but if he does not respond to the treatment, we will have to discuss the alternative."

"Dr. Alan, as I said before, I give you my word; I will not let him suffer," Johnny said.

Just thinking about what Rusty was going through was breaking my heart. I was his mommy, and I was supposed to help him, but there was nothing else we could do. I knew Rusty was in good hands with Dr. Alan and Dr. Gary. We could only hope and pray that the treatments would start working soon.

Later, when we came home without Rusty, Ma knew from the expressions on our faces that the news wasn't good. Kristine was in the family room watching the TV show *Fraggle Rock*. As soon as she heard the door open, she ran out of the family room into the hallway. "Mommy, Daddy, where's Rusty?"

"Rusty has a boo-boo; he is in the doggie hospital. The doctors are trying to make him better," I said.

"When is he coming home?"

My eyes started to tear as I turned away. Johnny continued answering her questions, seeing how upset I was. "Honey, the doctors want Rusty to stay in the hospital for a few days, but they said we can visit him."

"Can we go visit Rusty now?"

"No, Rusty is sleeping. We will visit him in a few days."

"Good, I can't wait to see him. I am going to bring Rusty a toy."

"Rusty will like that very much when he's feeling better," he said.

My heart was aching listening to her concern for her precious dog. Knowing how much Kristine loved Rusty, if he didn't survive this illness, how were we going to tell her that he wasn't coming home? I had to stay positive; I couldn't think that way. I refused to allow myself to think like that. My little boy was going to make it! My mom hugged me, as she was feeling just as distraught. "What can I do to help?" she whispered to me.

"Say a prayer that Rusty gets better. I'd like to go upstairs and lie down for a little while. Johnny has to go to Dairy Barn for milk. Could you watch Kristine?"

"Of course I can. Go upstairs and rest."

I really needed to be alone with my own thoughts. Since it was a warm spring evening, I opened our bedroom window. I wanted some fresh air to clear my mind. Then I went to lie down on our bed. I just couldn't accept the fact that my little boy could die. I just let it out and couldn't stop sobbing. It was even difficult for me to catch my breath.

After Johnny came home from the store, Ma came upstairs. "Close the window, Jo Ann."

"Why do I have to close the window?"

My mom looked at me lovingly. "You are crying so loud, I heard you from downstairs. The neighbors could probably hear you."

We sat on the bed and spoke for a while about Rusty's disease and what the doctors were going to do to treat him. She seemed to calm me down a little.

Later that night when I got into bed, I was unable to sleep. I just lay there staring mindlessly at the TV for the longest time as I was trying to block out this horrific news. I was struggling with a way to come to terms with how serious Rusty's illness really was. The love that Rusty and I had for each other was eternal. It was just tearing me apart. As I was finally drifting off to sleep, a part of me was at the animal hospital with my redheaded furry twin.

The following morning, I told Johnny that I was going to church to pray for Rusty. After sitting through the mass, I lit a candle and begged God to make my little boy well again.

When I came back from church, Johnny and I went to visit Rusty. He was awake but wasn't able to stand up. He was just lying there help-lessly. Dr. Alan suggested that we not bring our daughter to see him until he was stabilized. Even though Rusty seemed relaxed with the medication, he was looking at me with his sad eyes. I could hear his thoughts in my mind. *Where am I? Who are these people? Where are Kristine and Grandma? Why am I so sick?*

I was furious with myself. I felt that I was a terrible dog mom and inadequate pet owner. Owning up to the fact that Rusty's delayed treat-ment was because of me, and feeling guilty as sin, I cried to Johnny, "Why did I take him back to that stupid vet twice and not go to some-one else for a second option earlier? What is wrong with me?"

"Honey, stop beating yourself up; this isn't your fault. You have been the best mom to Rusty from day one. He's lucky to have you as his mother. All you have done his whole life was protect him, spoil him, and love him."

Johnny was being sweet, but I couldn't accept what he was saying. Instead I wanted to kick myself as to why I took him to that incom-petent vet in the first place. Rusty wouldn't be suffering like this if he had been diagnosed and treated with the correct antibiotics sooner. If only we had gone to Dr. Alan and Dr. Gary from the beginning, Rusty wouldn't be so sick.

At home, I knew I had no choice but to act as if everything was okay. I had to try to go on with everyday life for Kristine, which I knew wasn't going to be easy. All I was doing was thinking about my beautiful redhead and trying to block out the worst-case scenario. Every few hours, I called the animal hospital for updates on Rusty's condition. It felt strange in the house without him. I had never realized how much noise he made barking to go out and trotting up and down the stairs. Since Rusty was so big and clumsy, he constantly knocked things over, making a racket throughout the house. The most upsetting was that Kristine called Rusty's name a hundred times a day, and I wasn't hearing that now.

Chapter 30

On the Road to Recovery

Two days later, Dr. Alan called. "Rusty is stabilized. His vitals are improving. He ate a little food last night and again this morning. Miraculously, he stood up today. He also drank a good amount of water. This is a very good sign. Everyone can come and visit him."

I can't tell you how happy we were. From that moment, Ma, Kristine, and I visited Rusty every morning and afternoon. Johnny visited him straight from work every night. On the weekend, we hung out at Crawford Animal Hospital for most of the day. When Rusty was awake, we visited with him and he enjoyed seeing us. When we saw he was getting tired, we would leave and go grab a bite to eat. After we came back, we sat in the waiting room until he was awake and ready to see us.

The following week, Dr. Alan said I could bring him food—not dog food, but bland people food. On his advice, I cooked broiled chicken breasts with peas and carrots for the next few days. When the technicians brought Rusty out to the reception area to me, he walked slowly, as if he were heavily medicated. After sniffing the chicken, he normally would have inhaled it, but at that time he had a very little appetite, so I hand-fed him one piece at a time. Dr. Alan advised me to take Rusty for short walks in the back of the parking lot, but after five minutes, he turned around and walked toward the animal hospital. I was so worried, and I felt so bad for him, but I had to stay positive.

By mid-May, Rusty was looking so much better, but he had lost more weight. When we visited him, he was excited to see us, and we were thrilled. Next door to the animal hospital there was an auto collision shop. During our daily walks, the radio played on the loud speaker for the mechanics, but anyone outside could also hear it. Everyone knows how the radio stations are—they overplay the new hit songs. The hit song at that time in May of 1985 was "Everybody Wants to Rule the World." This song I didn't mind hearing over and over again. It was a great song. Listening to some of the words, it sounded as if the song was meant for our Rusty.

Several days later, during one of our walks, I was singing along with the song to Rusty and he was wagging his tail. I guess he liked the song, too. When we brought him back inside the animal hospital, Dr. Alan said, "Good news, guys. Gary and I are very pleased with Rusty's progress. His seizures are under control, and his vital signs are good. We've done everything we could do here. He is ready to go home."

Our prayers were answered. Kristine started jumping up and down. "Yaaay, Rusty is coming home!"

We were all ecstatic. The smile on my face was from ear to ear as I thanked Dr. Alan and gave him a hug. Then I ran inside to the other room, thanked Dr. Gary, and gave him a hug. After I came back from thanking Dr. Gary, I saw the concern on Dr. Alan's face. "Mrs. Roseo, may I speak with you and your husband privately for a minute?"

Suddenly I got nervous. While my mom and Kristine stepped outside, Dr. Alan said, "Rusty has improved significantly, but remember, there are no guarantees; only time will tell. I am sending you home with a supply of antibiotics and steroids with explicit written instructions to follow. If he continues to improve, which we hope he does, we want to see him in five days. However, I must tell you that his seizures can recur; it may be something he will have to live with. I am also giving you an increased dose of phenobarbital to control his seizures. All we can do is hope for the best."

I can't tell you how excited I was that our Rusty was coming home, but Johnny was a little reserved. "Doctor Baum, I am delighted Rusty came out of this, but are there any signs we should look for in case he takes a turn for the worse?"

"Yes. In fact I wrote them down for you." Handing Johnny the paper, he started explaining. "You may not want to hear this, but I have to enlighten you on the worst-case scenario. Neurological signs to look for include loss of balance, lack of coordination, muscle weakness, bleeding from his nose, and blood in his urine and paralysis. Other signs may include multiple seizures and convulsions, which will lead to permanent brain damage."

"Oh my God! That would be horrible for him!" I shouted.

Dr. Alan calmly said, "Hopefully, he can beat this, and these symptoms will not happen, but keep in your mind that it is a possibility. One more thing: try to keep him calm. I know this is difficult for an Irish setter, but for now let's be extra cautious."

Both Dr. Alan and Dr. Gary were sympathetic, knowledgeable, and wonderful men who truly cared about Rusty and wanted to make him well. They told us that if we needed to reach them after hours, to call their service and they would call us back immediately, no matter what time it was.

Walking through the parking lot, as soon as Rusty saw the Bronco, he had a big smile on his face and started wagging his tail. Johnny helped him in, and we were finally taking him home.

As soon as we pulled up in front of our house, Rusty knew he was home. Opening the front door, Johnny let him in as he was eager to go inside. Rusty looked so happy. He took charge and went exploring all the rooms with his tail wagging as Kristine and I followed him.

Later that day, I sat him down, and we had one of our talks. "Listen, Rusty, now that you are home you need to stay calm. No barking like crazy, no running inside or outside. We don't want any setbacks; you can get really sick again, and we don't want that to happen. We love you very much, and you need to be a good boy."

Rusty enjoyed our talks and he gave me a big wet kiss right on my lips. Dealing with an animal and not a human, it was difficult to know if he fully understood the ramifications that any crazy actions on his part could be life threatening.

Making sure he received all his medication at the proper times, I wrapped each pill in turkey breast—one piece for him and one piece for Kristine (but only the meat for Kristine.) He just loved taking his medicine; it was a treat for him.

For the first few days, Rusty did take it slow and we were very happy. He was perfectly satisfied just playing with his toys and hanging out with us, especially with Kristine. It was great having him back home.

We followed up with Dr. Alan and Dr. Gary a few days later. After the examination, Dr. Alan said, "Rusty is improving, but he isn't out of the woods yet. Keep him on all his medications, and remember there are no guarantees. This disease was extremely severe, and it can flare up at any time, but let's remain hopeful."

For the next few weeks while Rusty was at home recuperating, he was doing better and improved each day. It seemed as if the antibiotics, steroids and phenobarbital were working. I could actually feel that my mother-in-law, Kay, was watching over Rusty to make him well again.

Life was getting back to normal. My little boy followed me around the house and was giving me his paw again with his very strong handshake, or, should I say, paw shake. Rusty started looking out the bay window, just like the good old days. I couldn't be happier.

At three o'clock every afternoon, as soon as Rusty heard the music from *Sesame Street* on the TV, he went into the family room to join Kristine. She would get off the couch and lay on top of him as they watched the show together. She had her big red furry brother back.

Rusty's appetite was back full-speed, and he was eating Milk-Bone dog biscuits five at a time. For breakfast on Sunday's, Johnny made Rusty pancakes with syrup, and for dinner I made pasta with sauce and meatballs, with lots and lots of Locatelli grated cheese for our royal redhead.

One night when Johnny came home from work, Rusty nudged him with his big red head and ran up the stairs into the bathroom. Johnny followed him as Rusty jumped right in the bathtub. Instead of Johnny washing up before dinner, it was bath time for Rusty. This time Johnny didn't complain, he was more than happy to give Rusty a bath. All the good signs we were hoping and praying for were coming true.

Both Dr. Alan and Dr. Gary encouraged short daily walks, but they said physical activity should be limited. Even at two and a half years old, Kristine held Rusty's leash when we walked him slowly up and down the block. After he went for his walk, Rusty and Kristine rolled around on the front lawn and played on the grass. *Thank God, my little boy is back!*

In my heart I knew he would recover. After all, our redhead was resilient, dynamic, and unstoppable, as well as being affectionate, caring, and loyal. Rusty was a beautiful dog with a heart of gold. Since Rusty was on the road to recovery, Johnny and I decided we would start working on having another baby, a little brother or sister for Kristine and Rusty.

Kristine walking Rusty

Ma and Rusty

Rusty's "Knot of Knowledge" bump with Mommy

My Little Girl, My Little Boy and Mommy

My Redheaded furry twin and me

Chapter 31

A Freak of Mother Nature

Who would have thought that with things going so well, danger would lurk nearby? We were trying to fight the odds, but a terrible turnaround occurred. Rusty, Kristine, and I were outside in the yard; I was pushing Kristine on the swing while Rusty was moseying around. One minute the sun was shining, and then dark clouds spanned the sky above as I heard thunder rumble in the far distance. Immediately, I told Kristine to go inside and wait by the kitchen door for me. She went in the house without any hesitation.

Knowing our Rusty, I expected that his fearlessness with storms would result in his chasing the lightning and barking at the thunder. I grabbed his leash that was hanging outside by the door. Trying to attach it to his collar was difficult since he had gotten his stamina back and fought me. As the thunder rumbled overhead, the raindrops started to fall. God knows where I got my strength from, but I was able to drag him back into the house. I knew it would be extremely dangerous for him to be outside during a thunderstorm; especially since Dr. Alan and Dr. Gary specifically said to keep him calm. I assumed that once he was inside, he would settle down and be good, but not a chance. Our thickheaded redhead was still as stubborn as could be. I brought Kristine downstairs to her grandma so she could stay with her since I had to attend to Rusty.

Lightning flashed and thunder followed. The loud explosive rumbles of the thunder turned him into a panic mode, causing him to bark uncontrollably. Charging to each window, he ran up and down the stairs and to each door, wanting to break out. He knocked over anything that was in his way: the silk ficus tree, Kristine's tricycle, and one of the lamps in the living room. I tried my hardest to get hold of him, but it was impossible. Rusty was on another one of his unstoppable missions, and that was not good.

My plan was to put him in the downstairs bathroom, and I would go in with him—since there were no windows in that room—and lay low. That way, he couldn't hear the thunder outside. I tried bribing him with treats to go into the bathroom, assuming he would take them, but to no avail. I tried to catch him, but he was too fast for me.

After a half dozen times, I finally caught him when I got hold of his collar near the downstairs bathroom. Pulling him, I tried to get him into the bathroom to safety. Shockingly, he jumped on me and pushed me out of his way. He literally knocked me down on the ceramic tile floor and stood over me growling and barking at me. The look on Rusty's face was filled with pure anger and hatred. Then he took off again, running to all the windows and doors to get out. For the first time, I was actually scared of him as he displayed another side of him with such vengeance.

Finally, the rain stopped, and all was quiet outside. That had to be one of the most intense pre-summer thunderstorms that I could remember. We even lost the electricity for about forty-five minutes. After Rusty tired himself out, he drank some water, went in the family room and fell asleep. The whole incident was very strange and emotionally overwhelming for me.

Through all his bizarre behavior, I had never been afraid of him. Something was seriously wrong; that dog wasn't my lovable Rusty. I called Crawford Animal Hospital and spoke to Dr. Alan. He told me to give Rusty another dose of phenobarbital and try to keep him calm. There was nothing we could do but let the medicine work. If we noticed any of the symptoms he told us about, we were to let him know immediately. As soon as I hung up the phone, I woke Rusty up, gave him his medicine, and then he went back to sleep while I petted him.

When Johnny came home from work, I told him about Rusty's irrational behavior during the thunderstorm. He was really concerned and watched Rusty closely. While we were eating dinner, Rusty sat in the kitchen with us, but I was still troubled about his reaction toward me earlier.

Three hours later, I brought Kristine up to bed. Of course, Rusty tagged along, as he always did. I read Kristine a bedtime story, as I did each night, while Rusty sat next to her bed. After Kristine fell asleep, Rusty and I went downstairs and joined Johnny in the family room while he was watching a movie on TV. Rusty cuddled next to me. Thankfully, the anger he had had toward me earlier had disappeared. I caressed his long red ears, and he fell asleep.

During the movie, Rusty got up, took his paw and pushed open the adjoining door leading into his grandma's apartment. About fifteen minutes later, Rusty came back into the family room, but something wasn't right, he seemed confused. Johnny and I were worried as we sat with him and petted him. A few minutes later, I went to see my mom. "Ma, how was Rusty? He didn't look good when he walked out of your place?"

"Rusty seemed sad. He walked over to me and put his head on my lap while I was sitting on the couch reading a book. He just sat there while I petted him; then suddenly he gave me a big kiss across my face."

"Okay, thanks. I'll keep an eye on him."

A little while later, Rusty slowly walked out of the family room and headed toward the split-level stairs. We followed him up the stairs, and he went into Kristine's bedroom. We stood in the doorway and watched him sitting on the floor next to Kristine's bed just staring at her. About ten minutes later, he jumped up and kissed her cheek.

After Rusty left Kristine's bedroom, he was walking down the stairs and all of a sudden he staggered on the step. We tried to get hold of him, but he missed the step and fell down on the landing between the split levels of stairs. As he collapsed, the seizures started again. Within minutes, the convulsions started, becoming frequent and violent. Body fluids started pouring out of him. Trying to hold him down, Johnny couldn't get a good grip. Rusty was rapidly hitting the walls, and he was literally bouncing on one side of one wall to the other side of the other wall. The banging was so intense that even the pictures on the wall rattled. My mom heard the banging and ran upstairs as Rusty went into another full-blown convulsion. It was frightening and heart-wrenching to watch. Together, Johnny and I tried to get control over him, but Rusty's strength was much more overpowering than both of us during the convulsions.

All of a sudden, I saw a glimpse of Rusty's face and I let out a painful scream, "Oh my God! Nooooo!"

"Honey, what?"

"Johnny, blood is coming out of Rusty's nose and his mouth. This is what they warned us about!"

"Dammit! I was hoping this wouldn't happen," Johnny responded.

Ma was crying and shouted, "Do something! Do something! He can't stay like this! You can't let him suffer!"

Once the convulsions were over, Rusty lay on the floor helplessly. I sat on the floor and held him while Johnny called Crawford Animal Hospital and left a message with their answering service. Within one minute, Dr. Alan called back. I heard Johnny telling him everything that just happened. When he hung up the phone, he was white as a sheet. I could see that he didn't want to tell me what Dr. Baum said. "Honey, it's not good. Dr. Baum said, given the circumstances, we need to bring Rusty in immediately. He can't suffer anymore; he will meet us at the animal hospital."

I just stared at Johnny. I couldn't even say one word. I felt as if all my blood was sucked out of me. I was in total disbelief. Johnny came over to me to console me, but I was completely numb.

In all probability, Rusty had a premonition. I've read that animals usually know when they are going to leave this earth. He must've sensed it when he kissed his grandma good-bye, knowing it would be the last time he would ever see her. Probably the hardest for him was saying good-bye to his baby sister. Now that I think about it, the sad expression that was on Rusty's face when he walked out of Kristine's bedroom said it all. He had to know he would never see his beloved Kristine again.

Johnny went upstairs to get a bedsheet, while I cradled my little boy in my arms, hysterical crying, not wanting to let him go. I wondered why I never got a kiss good-bye. Maybe he blamed me for what was happening to him, or maybe he was already gone.

Thank God Kristine was sleeping and didn't hear or see what was going on. For her to actually witness what Rusty was going through would have been so traumatic. Kristine loved Rusty, her protector, her best friend, her big brother. Our baby girl was going to wake up in the morning and ask where he was. This was just awful; my worst nightmare was coming true.

Johnny tried to pick Rusty up, but he was deadweight, and I wasn't much help. Johnny called our neighbor George, who lived across the street to help. Johnny and George picked Rusty up, placed him on the sheet, and carried him out of the house as I held the door open for them. They gently placed Rusty in the back area of the Bronco on top of his favorite blanket. I was climbing in the back with Rusty, but Johnny suggested, "Honey, please don't sit in the back with him; he may start convulsing again and you could get hurt."

Normally, I ignored Johnny when it came to Rusty, but he was right. All of a sudden, Rusty started convulsing again. It broke my heart sitting there watching him bouncing continuously from side to side, hitting the side panels in the Bronco, and there was nothing I could do to help him. I didn't take my eyes off of him for a second. He was losing more body fluids, and blood was coming out of his nose and his mouth again. I have never felt so helpless in all my life. After the repeated convulsions, he just lay still, not moving.

"Johnny, I can't believe this! Rusty was doing so much better. Why did that thunderstorm have to happen today? And why did I take him to that incompetent vet in the first place? This is all his fault!"

"Honey, I know. I feel terrible."

On the way to Crawford Animal Hospital, I prayed to my mother-in-law, Kay. *Mom, I hope you can hear me. I desperately need your help. Rusty is very sick and is really suffering. If there isn't a miracle tonight, Rusty is going to leave us. Please promise me that you will meet him at the gates of heaven. I know my little boy will be scared being in a strange place without us. Can you tell him how much I love him and that you will take good care of him until I meet him in heaven one day?*

Now it seemed that Rusty was in God's hands. We arrived at Crawford Animal Hospital at eleven-thirty that night, and Dr. Alan met us in the parking lot. Johnny and Dr. Alan carried Rusty and gently placed him on top of the examining table. To this day, I still remember how cold the stainless steel table was.

Dr. Alan listened to Rusty's heartbeat and touched his abdomen. Then he pulled Rusty's eyelids back and shined a bright light into his eyes. "Listen, folks, it could've been anything. The odds of him fully recovering to lead a quality life were very slim to begin with, even without the thunderstorm. I believe he was on borrowed time. Maybe the added excitement from the thunderstorm contributed just a touch, but anything could've excited him. The repeated episodes of the seizures and convulsions being so close together caused further damage. As far as I can see, Rusty's brain has minimal functioning. His heart may be beating, but he is gone. Statistics show the final stage of this disease will cause permanent brain damage, and unfortunately it did."

The finality of Dr. Alan's voice made it clear that there was nothing more he could do to save our beautiful redhead. Deep down in my heart, I knew Rusty had already left us, lying there unresponsive.

As catastrophic as the situation was, it was the only humane and right thing to do, even though it was killing me. If only I could've moved heaven and earth to save him, but I knew I couldn't. It was time; we needed to let him go. Friends of ours who had lost their dogs told me that when a dog is euthanized, it is very peaceful for the animal. I would be able to hold him in my arms, and he would drift off into a sound sleep with a peaceful expression on his face; that was what I expected.

While Rusty was lying on the examining table in an unconscious state, Dr. Alan was getting the necessary drug to end his pain and suffering, basically ending his short life.

Johnny stood at Rusty's side, while I was hugging my little boy. I whispered to him: "Rusty, my precious angel; you are not going to be in pain anymore. You are going to see Grandma Kay at the beautiful Rainbow Bridge. She is waiting for you, and she will take good care of you for me until we meet again. I want you to always remember how much I love you. I loved you from the first minute I saw you and every minute after that. You will always be my little boy. You were such a good dog, my best friend, and my redheaded furry twin. Me, Daddy, Kristine, and Grandma will miss you and love you forever and ever. I am so sorry this happened to you; please forgive me."

Johnny whispered something to Rusty as well, but all I heard him say was "Buddy Boy." I couldn't hear what else he said to him as he petted Rusty on top of his head and turned away.

Dr. Alan came toward Rusty to start the process while I was hugging my little boy. All of a sudden, Rusty went into another full-blown convulsion and got released from my arms. Dr. Alan grabbed Rusty and Johnny helped hold him down as Dr. Alan put the fine needle into Rusty's vein in his foreleg and slowly injected the euthanasia solution, putting our beautiful redhead into permanent sleep. Instead of looking at peace, passing away in my arms, he died on the cold examining table with his eyes fully open. The look on his face was far from peaceful. He had an angry, painful look on his face, and his tongue was fully hanging out of his mouth to the right side. It broke my heart to witness his brutal death. Gently, I placed my fingers over his eyes, closed them, and kissed him on his kissable knot, right on top of his big red head. Dr. Alan was kind enough to let us stay with Rusty until his warm, lifeless body started to turn cold.

As I cradled my Rusty, I thought I wouldn't have been able to handle putting our first dog down, but, surprisingly, that wasn't the case. Where I got my courage from, I have no idea. Rusty was probably watching over me, guiding me and giving me strength. First and foremost, I was Rusty's mother in every sense of the word—with all the love in my heart and soul for him. Realistically, I knew I couldn't let him suffer anymore. As his mom, I was with him every step of the way during his short life, and now during his horrific death. Of course I was devastated and heartbroken, but—this may sound strange—when Rusty took his final deep breath, I felt a wave of relief; I knew his pain and suffering was finally over.

Dr. Alan came back into the room a little while later. It was the moment we had to say our good-byes to Rusty for the last time. That's when I started crying, hugging him, not wanting to let him go. Johnny held me as I kissed Rusty over and over again, from the top of his head, on to his long red ears, down to his snoot and each paw. I told him one last time, with a huge lump in my throat, "I love you Rusty, and I always will. I will miss you forever. Rest in peace, my little boy."

Johnny tried to hide it, but I saw the devastation that was on his face when he kissed Rusty on top of his head, and ruffled his ears for the last time.

Dr. Alan was walking us out to the door leading to the parking lot. "I am very sorry. We tried everything we could possibly do to save him, but unfortunately his case was very severe. There was nothing more that could've been done."

I could tell from the expression on Dr. Baum's face that he was deeply upset. I know that he wanted a better outcome for Rusty. I didn't say anything because I would start crying again, so I just gave him a quick hug. Johnny shook his hand and thanked him for trying to save Rusty.

In silence, we held hands as we walked to the Bronco, feeling total emptiness. We just looked at each other with blank faces. We wouldn't be visiting Rusty anymore at the animal hospital, and he wouldn't be coming home with us. Our dog was always stronger than life, and now he was gone.

When we got into the car I asked Johnny, "What did you say to Rusty before he died?"

Getting slightly emotional, he said, "Jo, I don't want to talk about it. It was between my buddy and me."

Johnny never did tell me those final words he said to Rusty. I guess Johnny will take it to his grave. My assumption is that Johnny apologized to Rusty for all the times he yelled at him, threatened to get rid of him, and threatened to kill him. And most likely, he must've told him that he loved him, which I knew in my heart he always did.

I couldn't believe that our beautiful redhead was really gone; he was so young. My little boy didn't even make it to his fifth birthday, dying five weeks before.

I was overwhelmed by the enormity of his death. Rusty's passing put a haze of helplessness on me—a void that I had to accept, which wasn't going to be easy. Losing Rusty was as devastating as it gets, but to make it even worse, Rusty died on my twenty-ninth birthday at 12:05am; needless to say, it was one birthday I wouldn't be celebrating.

During a quiet ride back to Massapequa, we were in our own thoughts. A little while later, I glanced over at my husband as he turned away to hide the tears that began to spill down his face. Apparently, Johnny took Rusty's death pretty hard, too. Seeing him, I lost it and couldn't stop crying the rest of the way home.

When we arrived home, my mom was still up, sitting on the couch waiting for us. As soon as we walked in the door, she ran over to us as tears began to flood her eyes. My mom and I hugged each other and cried. In the almost five years that Rusty was a part of our family, she was with him as much as we were. After trying everything we could do for our beautiful redhead, there was nothing that the doctors or any of us could do to save him. But I do have to say, we never gave up on him no matter what challenges we faced.

Rusty was such a big part of my life, truthfully and humorously. Honestly, Rusty stole my heart the first minute I saw him. He gave me so many joyful and wonderful memories that I will cherish always. When Rusty was taken away from me, he took a piece of my heart along with him. This may sound crazy, but Rusty was truly one of the loves of my life.

Throughout all his craziness and destructiveness, Rusty turned out to be a great family pet who we enjoyed. Showing us his loyalty, his devotion, his affection, his sweetness, and his huge heart gave further meaning to our lives. We loved Rusty with all of our hearts, and we are very thankful for all the special, joyful, fun, and crazy moments we shared with him. Rusty gave us the biggest gift, his unconditional love. He provided us with plenty of entertainment and a love like no other. Rusty was surely one unique redhead. I am very lucky and proud to have been his mommy. It was truly a privilege to have had him as a member of our family.

JO ANN ROSEO

RED RUSTY ROSEO
July 15, 1980 – June 8, 1985

Life After Rusty

The following morning, we told Kristine that Rusty was very sick and the angels called him up to the Rainbow Bridge. She asked us what the Rainbow Bridge was. I explained to her that when an animal dies, that animal goes to this beautiful bridge. It is filled with rainbow colors and meadows all around it, connecting heaven and earth. The sun is always shining, and it has lots of hills and green grass for Rusty to play in. Since Rusty was so big, they needed him to take care of the other dogs, and Grandma Kay was going to be with him and take care of him for us. She cried for the longest time when we told her he wouldn't be coming back home. I said that at the Rainbow Bridge, Rusty wouldn't be sick anymore. He would be running around and playing with the other dogs and having fun. Rusty would miss us, just like we would miss him, but he would be happy at the Rainbow Bridge. We wanted Rusty to be happy and not sick anymore. She smiled through her tears, and I think it brought her comfort. We looked at pictures of Rusty in our photo albums and watched videos of him that made us laugh. Later that day, as hard as it was, I packed up all Rusty's belongings and put them in my closet.

It didn't hit me back then, but now when I think about it, a series of coincidental things happened when Rusty left us: My daughter and

I both lost our dogs at such a young age. Duchess ran away when I was two and a half years old, and Rusty passed away when Kristine was two and a half years old. Rusty was born in Lynbrook at the breeder's house, and he died in Lynbrook at Crawford Animal Hospital. Rusty was almost five years old when he died. According to the vet, the age for a dog is one dog year for the first human year of its life. After that it is seven dog years for each human year. In dog years, that put Rusty at twenty-nine years old matching my age. About a week after Rusty was taken away from us, I was watching one of those entertainment shows on TV, and they announced that the song, "Everybody Wants to Rule the World," the single by the English band Tears for Fears was the first number one hit for the band, and it made it to number one in the United States on the Billboard Hot 100 chart on June 8th, 1985, the day Rusty died. About a month later, I decided to call the breeder to tell him what happened to Rusty. I wondered if he took Rusty and his siblings to Crawford Animal Hospital when they were born since he lived in Lynbrook. During our conversation, he said he remembered us, the litter, and the puppy with the long red ears. He told me that he did take the puppies to Crawford Animal Hospital for their original checkup and first set of inoculations, and the veterinarian who took care of the puppies was none other than Dr. Alan Baum. Imagine that.

After almost three months, my grief over losing Rusty was still enormous. I had a tremendous heartache that just wouldn't go away. I missed Rusty more than words could say, as if a part of me was missing. Kristine missed Rusty and was constantly asking me if he was happy at the Rainbow Bridge. I would tell her that Grandma Kay was taking good care of him, and Rusty was having fun playing with the other dogs.

My husband felt bad seeing me crying every night when Kristine went to sleep and blaming myself for what happened to Rusty. He told me it was time to move on, and we needed to get another dog for all our sakes. At the time, I guess I wanted to bring my little boy back and thought that another male Irish setter could do it. So I agreed and told him that I only wanted a male Irish setter. He said that if that was what I wanted, it was fine with him. He suggested I get in touch with Mary, the owner of Oscar, because she might know of a rescue Irish setter who needed a home.

I called Mary the following day and told her what happened to Rusty; she was shocked and felt terrible, but said we were in luck. She knew of a six-year-old male Irish setter who needed a home. The dog's parents were older, and they were moving to a condo in Florida, so they wouldn't be able to take him. I told her that I would talk to Johnny and get back to her. When I told Johnny, he was open to meeting the dog.

Mary came over that Saturday afternoon with the dog, whose name was Charley. Mary hugged me, and right away I choked up when I saw the dog. He was big and beautiful and looked a little like Rusty.

At that point Kristine came into the kitchen with her grandma. Johnny said, "Kristine, look at Charley. Isn't he a pretty dog?" She looked at the dog and yelled, "He is not Rusty. I want my Rusty!" And she ran out of the room crying. I saw that Mary felt bad. She apologized and told us that she was happy that we wanted to get another Irish setter, but she thought that a puppy would be more suitable for our daughter. To be honest, it was killing me looking at Charley. It was harder than I thought it would be. I just wasn't ready for another Irish setter yet, let alone another male; it was too soon after losing my little boy. I felt bad for Charley and asked her where he would go. Thankfully, she said there was another family with two little boys, and he would be a good fit for them. I was relieved that he would have a good home, even if it wasn't with us.

After Mary and Charley left, we decided a puppy of another breed was the better choice. The next day I went to the library to read up on dog breeds other than Irish setters that are good with children. A woman saw me looking through the books and told me that she had two golden retrievers. I told her that we had lost our Irish setter. She offered her condolences and said that we should look into golden retrievers. She said goldens by nature are very calm, sweet, and gentle dogs—but a little smaller than Irish setters—and are also great with children. I was happy to hear that, since Rusty was so amazing with Kristine.

Searching for our next dog, Johnny looked through the classified section in *Newsday* and found one golden retriever puppy for sale. When Johnny called the breeder, he told her that we had just lost our dog and he wanted to get our daughter a puppy. She apologized and told him that she changed her mind because this puppy was the only one in the litter and she decided to keep her. Johnny understood, but you know us dog people—we all talk to each other about our dogs. She expressed interest in Rusty, and Johnny told her about his illness and his brutal death at such a young age. She felt just awful after she heard Rusty's story, so she allowed us to see the puppy. The breeder lived in Setauket, about an hour away.

When Johnny told Kristine about the puppy, she was so excited. I wasn't quite ready, but I agreed to see the puppy for Kristine's sake. My mom came with us, and when we arrived at the breeder's house, this woman introduced herself as Ann. Her puppy was really adorable, but I couldn't even hold her. I felt I was betraying my little boy. The dam was also at the house, and she was very sweet, but I didn't bother with her either.

Ann was very proud as she told us that this puppy had champion bloodlines on both sides of her parents dating back four generations.

When she showed us the picture of this puppy's sire, Champion Cloverfield Oliver Twist, I have to admit that he was stunning. In addition to this puppy's family being champion goldens, three of her ancestors on the dam's side were also hall of famers, and her great grandfather was the top golden in history at that time. Johnny didn't know from talking to Ann earlier, but this puppy came with a high price tag. (Considering she was from a family full of champions, it was a given.) Johnny and I looked at each other thinking the same thing. *What did we get ourselves into coming here? This is so out of our league.*

Johnny told Ann that we loved the puppy, but we couldn't afford her; we were still paying Rusty's medical bills which amounted to a few thousand dollars. Ann was watching Kristine playing with the puppy, and she said she couldn't take our daughter's happiness away. She asked if we could pay just for the cost of the veterinarian who delivered the puppy, and for her shots, which totaled five hundred dollars. Ann said she was touched by what we did for Rusty. She would rather see the puppy go to a loving home, to caring parents who would do everything possible to take care of her. For Ann, that was more important than any amount of money. We were overwhelmed by her offer and gladly accepted.

Ann preferred for us to pick a name for the puppy before we left so she could put it on paper. Trying to think of a name, Johnny suggested that since the puppy was blonde, we should name her Marilyn Monroe, after the blonde actress. Even though I wasn't ready to be her mommy yet, my motherly instinct came out and I told him, "No way! This sweet innocent puppy can't look like a sexy dog. All the male dogs will be after her." Ann laughed when she heard my response. I said she looked more like a Kimmy. Kristine liked the name Kimmy too, but Ann said we needed a name more official since the puppy had strong champion bloodlines. She said Sandbrook Kennels was where the dam was from, so a name with Sandbrook in it would be appropriate. So Johnny suggested for the American Kennel Club—Sandbrook's Only Kimberly, since she was the only puppy in the litter. Ann loved the name, and it sounded good to me, but we would call her Kimmy. I wrote the check to Ann, silently begging Rusty not to hate me. Ann gave us the certificate showing all the champions in Kimmy's bloodline.

When we left Ann's house, Ma held Kimmy in the car on the way home, and then Kimmy threw up all over her.

Kristine and Johnny formed an immediate attachment to the puppy, but not me. It felt weird bringing her into Rusty's home. So Johnny became Kimmy's only parent. He fed Kimmy, he walked Kimmy, he played with Kimmy, and he bathed Kimmy while I stayed away.

About two weeks later, Kristine asked me why I didn't like Kimmy. I felt terrible because she noticed, and she was absolutely right. I totally ignored this beautiful, innocent, sweet little puppy. Then something just clicked. I had so much love to give, and this little puppy needed me. I had to face the fact that my little boy was gone, and he was never coming back. However, he would live forever in my memory and in my heart, and he would want me to be happy, so I needed to move on. I picked Kimmy up and looked right into her eyes. Then she gave me a gentle little kiss. I cradled her in my arms, and that was it; I fell in love with our baby girl. She was beyond sweet and loving. She looked at me as if to say, *Finally, I have a mommy. I've been waiting for you.* From that day on, she melted my heart.

Kristine adored Kimmy and enjoyed playing with her, but she would still ask about Rusty and whether he was happy with the other dogs at the Rainbow Bridge. It brought me comfort knowing that she still wondered about Rusty and didn't forget him.

It took me quite a while, but I came to the realization that when our precious dogs pass on, we can't stay discouraged forever. We have to smile and be thankful that we had them in our lives, even if it was only for a short time. We will never forget them and no other dog will ever take their place, but it is okay to love another dog. In return, that dog will lavish us with more love than we deserve or could ever dream of.

In closing, I just want to say that dogs become a part of your family, and we take many journeys in life together. They become your best friend, as well as your child—even a brother or sister to your children. Yes, some dogs are crazy and some are not, but each one will give us more devotion and more joy than anyone could ever ask for, with lots of laughter and amazing memories to last a lifetime. There is nothing better than the unconditional love and compassion that they give to each member of the family. Unfortunately, with so much love comes the sorrow when they leave us for the Rainbow Bridge, ending in a broken heart; but to go through these journeys with your beloved pet is truly worth taking. Owning a dog is rewarding and a gift; they all will leave everlasting paw prints in our hearts forever.

About the Author

J o Ann Roseo, an avid dog lover, wrote *Life with Rusty* to share the special story of unconditional love between her and her first "child"—her red Irish setter.

Originally from Brooklyn, New York, Jo Ann currently resides in South Florida with her husband, John and their sweet and beautiful golden retriever, Sofie. The couple has raised two lovely daughters, Kristine and Jennifer, who have now started families of their own. Her biggest joy is being a grandmother, and spending quality time with her family, friends and Sofie.

Jo Ann and John have filled their hearts and their home with furry friends over the years; including an Irish setter, a chocolate lab, and two golden retrievers. They cherish the precious memories of their beloved angels who crossed over the rainbow bridge.

Made in the USA
Middletown, DE
23 April 2017